HISTORICAL SKETCHES

HYMNS,

THEIR WRITERS, AND THEIR INFLUENCE.

BY

JOSEPH BELCHER, D.D.

AUTHOR OF "WILLIAM CAREY: A BIOGRAPHY;" "GEORGE WHITEFIELD: A BIOGRAPHY;" "RELIGIOUS DENOMINATIONS OF THE UNITED STATES," ETC. ETC.

PHILADELPHIA:
LINDSAY & BLAKISTON.
NEW YORK: SHELDON & COMPANY.
1859.

STEREOTYPED BY L. JOHNSON & CO.
PHILADELPHIA.
COLLINS, PRINTER.

PREFACE.

THAT the subject of this volume is of great interest no reader will deny. That more than one writer has published important matters relating to it is well known; but assuredly comparatively little truly interesting to the mass of Christian readers has yet been collected. No one is more aware of the difficulties of the task than the author of the present small work, for which he has been collecting materials for many years. Importunity of friends may truly be pleaded in this instance; and he has at least the confidence that he has done what he could, and will rejoice if his work shall provoke a wiser man to produce a better.

To the casual reader it may appear that a small degree of labor, given now and then in moments of leisure, would soon produce a volume like that now in his hand. It would, however, convince such a one of his mistake were he to attempt the task. He would soon find that the most attractive volume must often be laid aside, that "*No*" must be given to the kindest invitation to the tempting social party, and that even the meetings of the most delightful revival of religion recorded in history must be sacrificed, to complete what years and disease tell him may not otherwise be accomplished before death summons him from earth.* To verify a fact, to confirm a date, or to answer what some might consider an unimportant query, has often demanded hours which inclination or the gratification of friendship would have otherwise claimed.

The author feels a pleasing confidence that his labors will tend to increase an interest in the great duty and privilege of *praise*, and do somewhat to advance a spirit of union with those, not a few of whom are now in a better world, who have so greatly aided our worship on earth. As such, he commends his feeble effort to the favor of his adorable Master and to the kindness of his readers.

J. B.

PHILADELPHIA, July, 1859.

---

* The Rev. Dr. Belcher seems to have anticipated a result which has since taken place. He departed this life on Sunday morning, July 10th, 1859, not many hours after his labors had ceased on this volume.

CONTENTS.

HISTORICAL SKETCHES.

AUTHORS AND ORIGIN OF HYMNS.

ILLUSTRATIONS OF THE INFLUENCE OF HYMNS ON PERSONAL AND SOCIAL HAPPINESS.

INDIVIDUAL PERSONS.

THE DOMESTIC CIRCLE.

MINISTERS AND CONGREGATIONS.

GENERAL SOCIETY.

HISTORICAL SKETCHES

OF

CHURCH MUSIC AND CHOIRS.

2*

Historical Sketches.

Before entering on the principal design of this volume, it may be proper very briefly to glance at the character of hymns, and the opinions entertained of them by Christians in successive ages.

A writer in the "*Presbyterian Quarterly Review*," not long ago, says of a good hymn, "It forms words that thrill thousands of all classes and characters, and thrill them all at once. Words that will do this must be at the same time simple and dramatic, understood in a moment, and yet carrying profound feeling,—those universal things that are 'borne inward unto souls afar.'"

As to the character and influence of hymns on the hearts of Christians, our views are so well delineated by the graphic pen of Henry Ward Beecher, that we shall borrow his language, as far more conducive to the benefit of the reader than our own:—"Hymns are the exponents of the inmost piety of the Church. They are the crystalline tears, or blossoms of joy, or holy prayers, or incarnated raptures. They are the jewels which the Church has worn,—the pearls, the diamonds, and precious stones, formed into amulets more potent against sorrow and sadness than the most famous charms of wizard or magician. And he who knows the way that hymns flowed, knows where the blood of piety ran, and can trace its veins and arteries to the very heart.

"No other composition is like an experimental hymn. It is not a mere poetic impulse. It is not a thought, a fancy, a feeling threaded upon words. It is the voice of experience speaking from the soul a few words that condense and often represent a whole life. It is the life, too, not of the natural feelings, growing wild, but of regenerated feeling, inspired by God to a heavenly destiny, and making its way through troubles and hinderances, through joys and victories, dark or light, sad or serene, yet always struggling forward. Forty years the heart may have been in battle, and one verse shall express the fruit of the whole. One great hope may come to fruit only at the end of many years, and as the ripening of many experiences. As there be flowers that drink up the dews of spring and summer, and feed upon all the rains, and only just before winter burst forth into bloom, so is it with some of the noblest blossoms of the soul. The bolt that prostrated Saul gave him the exceeding brightness of Christ; and so some hymns could never have been written, but for a heart-stroke that wellnigh crushed out the life. It is cleft in two by bereavement, and out of the rift comes forth, as by resurrection, the form and voice that shall never die out of the world. Angels sat at the grave's mouth; and so hymns are the angels that rise up out of our griefs, and darkness, and dismay.

"Thus born, a hymn is one of those silent ministers which God sends to those who are to be heirs of salvation. It enters into the tender imagination of childhood, and casts down upon the chambers of its thought a holy radiance which shall never quite depart. It goes with the Christian, singing to him all the way, as if it were the airy voice of some guardian spirit. When darkness of trouble, settling fast, is shutting out every star, a hymn bursts through and brings light like a torch. It abides by our side in sickness. It goes forth with joy to syllable that joy.

"And thus, after a time, we clothe a hymn with the memories and associations of our own life. It is garlanded with flowers which grew in our hearts. Born of the experience of one mind, it becomes the unconscious record of many minds. We sang it, perhaps, the morning that our child died. We sang this one on that Sabbath evening when, after ten years, the family were once more all together. There be hymns that were sung while the mother lay a-dying; that were sung when the child, just converted, was filling the family with the joy of Christ new-born, and laid, not now in a manger, but in a heart. And thus, sprung from a wondrous life, they lead a life yet more wonderful. When they first come to us, they are like the single strokes of a bell ringing down to us from above; but at length a single hymn becomes a whole chime of bells, mingling and discoursing to us the harmonies of a life's Christian experience."

Mr. Beecher elsewhere says, with great truth, that

"when the Church is cold and dead, these hymns which were written by God's saints in moments of rapture seem extravagant, and we walk over them on dainty footsteps of taste; but let God's Spirit come down upon our hearts, and they are as sweetness to our tongues; nay, all too poor and meagre for our emotions; for feeling is always tropical, and seeks the most intense and fervid expression."

In glancing at the history of praise and its various modes of expression, we may remark that nothing in the whole records of history can be found to compare with the splendid musical establishments of David, at once the king of Israel and the psalmist of the Lord. From the narrative given us in the twenty-third chapter of the First Book of the Chronicles, we must infer that both music and poetry were then in a highly-flourishing state. No less than four thousand singers or musicians were appointed from among the Levites, under two hundred and eighty-eight principal singers or leaders of the band, and distributed into twenty-four companies, who officiated weekly by rotation in the temple, and whose whole business it was to perform the sacred hymns One portion of them chanted or sung, and the other played on different instruments. The chief of these were Asaph, Heman, and Jeduthun, who were also composers of hymns. Milton himself must have admitted that the choir was worthy in its amplitude of those frequent songs throughout the law and the prophets which he held "incomparable," not in "their divine argument alone, but in the very critical art of composition, over all the kinds of lyric poetry."

Dr. Lyman Coleman, in his "*Apostolical and Primitive Church*," very properly tells us that the singing of songs constituted a great part of the religious worship of all ancient nations. In all their religious festivals, and in their temples, the pagan nations sung to the praise of their idol gods. The worship of the Jews, alike in the temple, their synagogues, and their private dwellings, was celebrated with sacred hymns to God. Christ himself, in his final interview with his disciples before his crucifixion, sung with them the customary paschal songs at the institution of the Supper, and by his example sanctified the use of sacred songs in the Christian Church. In the opinion of the most eminent writers, the gift of the Holy Spirit on the day of Pentecost was accompanied by poetic inspiration, to which the disciples gave utterance in spiritual songs. Paul and Silas, lacerated by the cruel scourging which they had received, and in close confinement in "the inner prison," prayed and sang praises to God at midnight. The use of "psalms, and hymns, and spiritual songs" was enjoined upon the churches at Colosse and Ephesus. Many evidences are furnished us, too, that in private, as well as in public, the first Christians were warmly attached to singing the praises of God.

Indeed, it appears that this practice of uniting to sing the high praises of Christ was one of the charges brought against the first Christians by their enemies.

Hence Pliny wrote in the commencement of the second century to Trajan, the Roman emperor, that they were accustomed to meet before day, to offer praise to Christ as a God; and Justin Martyr mentions the songs and hymns of the Ephesian Christians:—"We manifest our gratitude to him by worshipping him in spiritual songs and hymns, praising him for our birth, for our health, for the vicissitudes of the seasons, and for the hopes of immortality." Not very long after this, we have a clear intimation of the existence of a hymn-book.

The great topic of the ancient psalms and hymns was Christ, the only-begotten of the Father. The doctrine was set forth of his being the incarnate Word of God, God and man. His mediatorial character was the joy of the primitive churches, and this sacred theme inspired their earliest anthems. The manner of their singing must have been very simple, consisting of a few easy airs, which could be readily learned and by frequent repetition become familiar to all. Ambrose says that the injunction of the apostle, forbidding women to speak in public, relates not to singing, "for this is delightful in every age and suited to every sex;" and Chrysostom says, "It was the ancient custom, as it still is with us, for all to come together and unitedly to join in singing. The young and the old, rich and poor, male and female, bond and free, all join in one song. . . . All worldly distractions here cease, and the whole congregation form one general chorus."

We may add a few lines more on this interesting topic.

Several of the Fathers sought to edify their flocks by supplying them with devotional poetry; and instances are referred to by Eusebius in his "*Ecclesiastical History*" of private individuals composing hymns. Speaking of the mode of administering the Lord's Supper, Tertullian remarks, in his "*Apology*," "After the water is brought for the hands, and lights, we are invited to sing to God, according as each one can propose a subject from the Holy Scriptures or of his own composing." Hilary of Poictiers, in the fourth century, presented his church with a collection of hymns; and the Milanese Christians, about the same period, were accustomed to assemble at night, to chant those composed by Ambrose, their bishop. This practice began in Milan about the time the emperor persecuted Ambrose. The pious people watched in the church, prepared to die with the pastor. Augustine says, "There my mother sustained an eminent part in watching and praying. Then hymns and psalms, after the manner of the East, were sung, with the view of preserving the people from weariness; and thence the custom has spread through Christian churches." When Chrysostom occupied the episcopal throne of Constantinople, the Arians were accustomed to parade the streets of the city, singing hymns strongly tinctured with the peculiarities of their creed; on which the bishop, fearing the propagation of the heresy, furnished his choristers with some of his own compositions in accordance with the opinions of the orthodox.

Assuredly this holy duty of singing was not confined

to their public assemblies. Jerome says, "Go where you will, the ploughman at his plough sings his joyful hallelujahs, the busy mower regales himself with his psalms, and the vine-dresser is singing one of the songs of David." Fearless of reproach, of persecution, and of death, they continued, in the face of their enemies, to sing their sacred songs in the streets and market-places, and at the martyr's stake. Eusebius declares himself an eye-witness to the fact that, under their persecutions in Thebais, "they continued to their latest breath to sing psalms and hymns, and thanksgivings to the God of heaven." Speaking of the earliest hymns of the Latin Church, Herder asks, "Who can deny their power and influence over the soul? They go with the solitary into his cell, and attend the afflicted in distress, in want, and to the grave. While singing these, one forgets his toil, and his fainting, sorrowful spirit soars in heavenly joys to another world. Back to earth he comes to labor, to toil, to suffer in silence, and to conquer. How rich the boon, how great the power, of these hymns!"

Nor ought we to forget here the account which Augustine gives us of the power of this holy music over his heart on occasion of his baptism. He says, "Oh, how freely was I made to weep by these hymns and spiritual songs, transported by the voices of the congregation sweetly singing! The melody of their voices filled my ear, and divine truth was poured into my heart. Then burned the sacred flame of devotion in my soul, and gushing tears flowed from my eyes,—as well they might."

We may remark, here, that as early as the fourth century the appointment of *singers* as a distinct class crept into the Church, and other evils also, which soon tended to impair the purity and lessen the enjoyments of Christian worshippers.

Time has been, even in England, when singing the high praises of God was deemed a fit employment in a palace. As long ago as 1087, William the Conqueror lay on his death-bed. His closing hours formed a night of half sleep, half stupor, the struggling expiring body taking a dull, painful, unrestful rest before its last long earthly repose; but as the sun was just rising above the horizon, shedding brightness on the walls of the apartment, William was aroused by the tolling of the great cathedral bell, and inquired what the sound meant. "It is the hour of praise," was the answer of his attendants. Then were the priesthood in full choir welcoming with voices of gladness the renewed gift of another day, in the words common to all the Western liturgies, beginning,—

"Jam lucis orto Sidere,"

a translation of the whole of which will be acceptable to our readers:—

"Now that the sun is gleaming bright,
Implore we, bending low,
That He, the uncreated Light,
May guide us as we go.

"No sinful word, or deed of wrong,
Nor thoughts that idly rove,
But simple truth, be on our tongue,
And in our hearts be love.

"And while the hours in order flow,
O Christ, securely fence
Our gates beleaguered by the foe,
The gate of every sense,

"And grant that to thine honor, Lord,
Our daily toil may tend;
That we begin it at thy word,
And in thy favor end."

But the day of labor and struggle, sin and repentance, was already past; and before the close of the hymn William lifted up his hands in prayer and expired.

In one congregation alone in England is this beautiful Latin hymn now sung. When the scholars of Winchester College annually separate for the Whitsun vacation, they sing it in the original Latin. Surely it ought, at least in the translation, to be far better known; and, so thinking, we have ventured so far to depart from the general plan of our volume as to extend its knowledge as far as we can.

As we are speaking of the customs of England in reference to the old Latin hymns, we may here say that to the present day the choristers and lay clerks of Magdalene College, Oxford, annually ascend the outside of the top of the tower of the building at five o'clock in the morning of the first of May, where they sing the *Te Deum* before a vast crowd of spectators.

It has been well said that in many cases the ancient hymns were the only conservatives of gospel truth when heterodoxy grew and flourished beneath papal influence. They were themselves too pure to be defiled by Romish contaminations; and although hymn after hymn was added to swell the aggregate by those whose faith succumbed to their superstition, yet these have come down to us in all their first purity. So far from rejecting them, we ought rather to love them the more, because they flowed with clear and living stream through the barren wastes of error, until at length popery gathered up her strength in a useless effort to taint them. As the Romish Church added dogma after dogma to her creed, the lustre faded from her hymnal, until at last all that her votaries could produce were fulsome laudations of the saints and idolatrous invocations of Mary. But the two classes of hymns must ever be kept distinct: it is easy at once to perceive the difference between the utterance of a Christian soul and the panegyrics of false dogmas and imagined demigods.

We are told that Augustine was sorely perplexed by his love of music, fearing to indulge in ornamental psalmody for its own sake, yet conscious that his devotional feelings had often been powerfully excited by the influence of religious song. He says, "When I remember the tears I shed at the psalmody of the Church, in the beginning of my recovered faith, and how at this time I am moved, not with the singing, but with the things sung, when they are sung with a clear voice and modulation most suitable, I acknowledge the great use of this institution. Thus I fluctuate between peril of pleasure and approved wholesomeness,—inclined the rather, though not as pronouncing an irrevocable opinion, to approve of the use of singing in the church, that so by the delight of the ears the weaker minds may rise to the feelings of devotion."

During the disastrous period emphatically termed "the dark ages," when ignorance and superstition almost universally prevailed in the west of Europe, singing the praises of God was a part of divine worship from which the people were debarred. Not only were the words sung in a language unknown to the great body of the people, but the music was so complex that none could bear a part in it unless they had studied it scientifically.

But when the Reformation dawned, it was no difficult task to induce the people of England to prefer plain psalmody, in which they could easily join, to the intricate music which was too refined and scientific for their comprehension; and congregational singing gradually found its way into the parish churches, in pursuance of a statute of Edward VI., "to use openly any psalm or prayer taken out of the Bible, at any due time, not letting or omitting thereby the service, or any part thereof." It is certain that gradually full permission or connivance introduced metrical psalmody into the Church of England; for Strype states that in the month of September, 1559, "began the new morning prayer at St. Antholin's, London, the bell beginning to ring at five, when a psalm was sung after the Geneva fashion, *all the congregation, men, women, and boys, singing together.*"

The late Josiah Conder, in his admirable "*View of all Religions,*" testifies to the great influence of congregational singing in England at an early period of the Reformation. Bishop Jewel says, "A change now appears visible among the people, which nothing promotes more than inviting them to sing psalms. This was begun in one church in London, and did quickly spread itself, not only through the city, but in neighboring places. Sometimes at Paul's Cross there will be six thousand singing together." By the Act of Uniformity, passed in 1548, the practice of using any psalm openly "in churches, chapels, oratorios, and other places" was authorized. At length, after being popular for a while in France and Germany, among both Roman Catholics and Protestants, as psalmody came to be discountenanced by the former as an open declaration of Lutheranism, so in England psalm-singing was soon abandoned to the Puritans, and became almost a peculiarity of Nonconformity.

In the reign of Henry VIII., the Common Prayer Book, and the singing of psalms as found in the Bible, were generally used as a test for all to sing who loved the Reformation; and in the Confession of the Puritans, published in 1571, they say, "We allow the people to join in one voice in a psalm-tune, but not in tossing the psalm from one side to the other, with intermingling of organs."

We cannot forbear to remark here that some of the

best hymns were composed in "the dark ages." They were, as Professor Edwards says, "sombre and monotonous, but simple and sublime, and never to fade till that last day which they so often celebrate." As he elsewhere says, "The study of centuries only corroborates the universal voice. The reason of this is perfectly obvious. The road is not beaten. There is a dewy freshness on them, such as Adam saw in Eden. The artist can work unrestrained by artificial rules."

It is remarkable that the Baptists, after the Reformation, were very generally opposed to singing in their congregations. They had seen so many evils encouraged by those who practised it, that they persuaded themselves it was but a human ordinance. The Rev. Benjamin Keach, in 1691, published "*The Breach Repaired in God's Worship; or, Psalms and Hymns proved to be a Holy Ordinance of Jesus Christ.*" He first labored earnestly, with great prudence, to prevail on his people to sing at the close of the Lord's Supper; he then, six years afterward, persuaded them to sing on thanksgiving-days, and, at the end of fourteen years, to sing in each service at the close of the last prayer, that so those who objected to it might retire. In all this he was strenuously opposed by Mr. Isaac Marlowe, who designated the practice as "error, apostasy, human tradition, pre-limited forms, mischievous error, and carnal worship." In 1692 the General Assembly urged both parties to cease from their disputes, and their recommendation tended to peace. Still, however, there was difficulty;

and ultimately a division took place, and the seceders organized a new church in Maze Pond, Southwark, "where it was twenty years longer before singing the praises of God could be endured." At length, the congregations, being left to their own calm reflection, gradually introduced psalmody into their worship.

While popery never favored congregational singing, and among themselves Jesuits were never heard to chant the praise of Immanuel, the Reformers at once saw its influence on the great work before them. Calvin introduced into his congregation at Geneva the elegant version of the Psalms into French rhyme which had been made by Clement Marot, valet of the bedchamber to Francis I. This man, having happily become tired of the vanities of profane poetry, and anxious to raise the tone of public taste and feeling, aided by Theodore Beza and encouraged by the Professor of Hebrew in the University of Paris, published the Psalms in metre; and, as the translation did not aim at any innovation in public worship, it received the sanction of the Sorbonne. This version soon eclipsed the madrigals and sonnets of its author; and suddenly, in the festive and splendid court of Francis I., nothing was heard but the psalms of Clement Marot, the royal family and principal nobility choosing and adapting them to popular ballad-tunes.

Under the direction of Calvin, these compositions were adapted to plain and easy melodies, and became a characteristic of the newly-established worship. Germany next caught the sacred ardor, and the choral mode of service yielded to the attractive and popular character of a devotional melody in which all might join without distinction of rank or character.

Especially was the practice of congregational singing greatly revived, and became almost universal, in Germany, where, emphatically, the people are all singers. From that time to the present it has been rarely the fact that any one is found in a German church who does not sing. They abound in hymn and tune books; and even to this hour, as we learn from Dr. Lyman Coleman, an eye-witness, one-half of the time occupied in public worship is taken up in singing.

Martin Luther well understood this method of propagating truth and refuting error, and employed it with a skilful hand. His own poetical talents and love of music were very great. He learned the science with the first rudiments of his native language; and when, as a wandering minstrel, he earned his daily bread by exercising his musical powers in singing before the doors of the rich in the streets of Magdeburg and Eisenach, he was as truly preparing for the future reformer as when, a retired monk in the cloister of Erfurt, he was storing his mind with the truths of revelation, with which to refute the errors of popery. One of his earliest efforts at reform was the publication of a psalm-book, in 1524, composed and set to music chiefly by himself. One of his earliest hymns was consecrated to the memory of the martyrs of Brussels; and the whole Reformed Church felt the mighty influence of his song. A few sentences which Luther wrote when he versified some of the Psalms and appended them to a collection of hymns which he published in 1524, all of which were set to music in four parts, cannot be unacceptable. He tells us this had been done "for no other reason than because of my desire that the young, who ought to be educated in music as well as in other good arts, might have something to take the place of worldly and amorous songs, and so learn something useful and practise something virtuous, as becometh the young. I would be glad to see all arts, and especially music, employed in the service of Him who created them."

In the preparation of this music, Walther, a distinguished musician of that day, lent his assistance. He says, "I have spent many a happy hour in singing with him, and have often seen the dear man so happy and joyful in spirit while singing that he could neither tire nor be satisfied. He conversed splendidly upon music. He also composed music or tunes for the Epistles and Gospels, particularly for the words of Christ at the institution of the Supper, and sung them to me and asked my opinion of them. He kept me three weeks writing the notes for a few Gospels and Epistles, till the first German mass was sung in the parish church, and I was obliged to stay and hear it and take a copy of it to Torgua."

In the writings of this distinguished Reformer we find several good paragraphs on music and singing, with which the reader will be happy to renew his acquaintance. He says, "Music is one of the fairest and most glorious gifts of God, to which Satan is a bitter enemy; for it removes from the heart the weight of sorrows and the fascination of evil thoughts. Music is a kind and gentle sort of discipline; it refines the passions and improves the understanding. Even the dissonance of unskilful fiddlers serves to set off the charms of true melody,—as white is made more conspicuous by the opposition of black. Those who love music are gentle and honest in their temper. I always loved music, and would not, for a great matter, be without the little skill which I possess in the art.

"Music is one of the best arts: the notes give life to the text: it expels melancholy, as we see in king Saul. Kings and princes ought to maintain music, for great potentates and rulers should protect good and liberal arts and laws: though private people have desire thereunto and love it, yet their ability is not adequate. We read in the Bible that the good and godly kings maintained and paid singers. Music is the best solace for the sad and sorrowful mind: by it the heart is refreshed and settled again in peace. We must teach music in schools: a schoolmaster ought to have skill in music, or I would not regard him. Neither should we ordain young men as preachers unless they be well exercised in music. Singers are merry and free from sorrows and cares."

None of our readers will be displeased with a glance at the public singing in England in the year 1644. At that time, when the Royalists and the Roundheads were in incessant collision, both as to political and religious matters, and when no small contest was carried on between choirs and organs on the one hand and plain congregational singing on the other, Master Mace, in his "*Music's Monument*," describes, in the rapturous language we now transcribe, the singular compromise between the parties at York Minster:—"The psalm-singing was the most excellent that has been known or remembered anywhere in these latter days. Most certain I am that to myself it was the very best harmonical music that ever I heard,—yea, excelling all other, either private or public, cathedral music, and infinitely beyond all verbal expression or conceiving. Now, here you must take notice that they had there a custom in that church which I hear not of in any other cathedral, which was this: always before sermon the whole congregation sung a psalm together with the choir and the organ. You must also know that there was then there a most excellent, large, plump, lusty, full-speaking organ, which cost, as I am credibly informed, a thousand pounds. This organ, I say, when the psalm was set, before the sermon, being let out unto all its fulness of stops, together with the choir, began the psalm. Now, when the vast concord and unity of the whole congregational choir came, as I may say, thundering on, even so as to make the very ground shake under us,—ah! the unutterable ravishing soul's delight!—I was so transported and rapt up with high contemplation, that there was no room left in my body and spirit for any thing below divine and heavenly raptures. The abundance of people of all ranks, beside the soldiers, crowded the church. Oh, how unutterably ravishing, soul-delighting!"

Delightfully are we reminded, by this description, of the animated language of the holy Baxter:—"Methinks, when we are singing or speaking God's praise in the great assemblies, with joyful and fervent souls, I have the liveliest foretaste of heaven on earth. I could almost wish that our voices were loud enough to reach through all the world, and unto heaven itself; nor could I ever be offended, as many are, at the organs and other convenient music, soberly and seasonably used, which excite and help to tune my soul in so holy a work, in which no true assistance is to be despised."

We joyfully come now to our own happy land; and though it was long before our fathers made much progress in the *science* either of singing or of hymn-writing, we are glad to see them cultivating the spirit of praise. As Gould says, "Here let us pause for a moment and imagine ourselves spectators of the scene when our forefathers mounted the Plymouth Rock, and listening to the first song of praise to Almighty God proceeding from strong lungs and pure hearts. There they stood, and, with the women and children, burst forth, and with united voices rehearsed some tune and words that they perhaps had before prepared and had been anxiously waiting and longing for an appropriate time to sing. That time had come; and think you there would not have been a difference between the effect of their singing and that which we so often hear, 'where not the heart is found'?"

As we have already seen, before the Pilgrim Fathers came to this country there had been in England, especially among the Baptists, much controversy on the subject of singing, and not a few churches divided on the subject of its introduction. We believe, however, that, whatever differences existed in this country on the matters of singing by notes, "lining out the hymns," or instrumental music, all approved of singing itself, and pretty generally acted on the exhortation of William Billing:—

"Oh, praise the Lord with one consent,
And in this grand design
Let Britain and the Colonies
Unanimously join."

The Rev. Mr. Symmes, speaking of the first settlers of New England, tells us that from the first founding of the first college singing was a regular study, and adds, "There are many persons of credit now living, children and grandchildren of the first settlers, who can very well remember that their ancestors sung *by note,* and they learned so to sing of them." Dr. Cotton Mather, in his "*Church Discipline,*" tells us that, before 1720, "The former and larger prayer of the pastor being finished, a psalm usually succeeds. In some [places], the assembly being furnished with psalm-books, they sing without the stop of reading between every line. But ordinarily the psalm is read line after line by him whom the pastor desires to do that service; and the people generally sing in such grave tunes as are most usual in the churches of our nation."

After a while, as every one knows, the Colonies began to be disturbed by contention and party strife; religious errors also crept in; and the few music-books which had been imported were rapidly decreasing: so that at the commencement of the eighteenth century scarcely any of the congregations could sing more than three or four tunes. The knowledge and use of notes had become neglected, until no two persons sung them alike. Every melody was "tortured and twisted as every unskilful throat saw fit." The Rev. Mr. Walker says of their singing, that it sounded "like five hundred different tunes roared out at the same time, so hideously and disorderly as is bad beyond expression. I myself have twice in one note paused to take breath." Mr. Symmes further testifies, "It is with great difficulty that this part of worship is performed, and with great indecency in some congregations, for want of skill. It is to be feared singing must be wholly omitted in some places, for want of skill, if this art is not revived."

Reform, however, was on the way, though attended in the outset with no small confusion. September 16, 1723, the "*New England Courant*" contained this paragraph:—"Last week a council of churches was held at the south part of Braintree, to regulate the disorders occasioned by regular singing in that place,—Mr. Niles, the minister, having suspended seven or eight of the church for persisting in their singing by rule, contrary, as he apprehended, to the result of a former council; but the suspended brethren are restored to communion, their suspension declared unjust, and the congregation ordered to sing by note and by rule, alternately, for the satisfaction of both parties."

December 9, 1723.—"We have advice from the south part of Braintree, that on Sunday, the first instant, Mr. Niles, the minister of that place, performed the duties of the day at his dwelling-house, among those of the congregation who are opposers of regular singing. The regular singers met together at the meeting-house, and sent for Mr. Niles, who refused to come unless they would first promise not to sing regularly; whereupon they concluded to edify themselves by the assistance of one of the deacons, who, at their desire, prayed with them, read a sermon, etc."

About 1720, singing by note was introduced into Boston, in Dr. Coleman's meeting-house, and singing-schools were introduced, both there and in other parts of New England. The most influential of the clergy encouraged the cultivation of music; and the study of it, during the controversy, revived in the college. In 1745, the first organ was built in this country, by Edward Bromfield, Jr., of Boston; and though this instrument was greatly opposed, it soon made its way. Choirs soon followed, and the "*Records of the Church at Topsfield,*" the "*History of Ipswich,*" and other documents, show the animated character of this controversy. Two short paragraphs from the "*History of Worcester*" will give the reader a fair specimen of the proceedings of those days:—

"The final blow was struck to the old system by the resolution of the town, August 5th, 1779:—'Voted, that the singers sit in the front seats of the front gallery, and that those gentlemen who have hitherto sat in the front seats of said gallery have a right to sit in the front and second seat below, and that said singers have said seats appropriated to said use. Voted, that said singers be requested to take said seats, and carry on the singing in public worship.' The Sabbath succeeding the adoption of these votes, after the hymn had been read by the minister, the aged and venerable Deacon Chamberlain, unwilling to desert the custom of his fathers, rose and read the first line, according to the usual practice. The singers, prepared to carry the alteration into effect, proceeded without pausing at the conclusion. The white-haired officer of the church, with the full power of his voice, read on, until the louder notes of the collected body overpowered the attempt to resist the progress of improvement, and the deacon, deeply mortified at the triumph of musical reformation, took his hat and retired from the meeting-house in tears. His conduct was censured by the church, and he was for a time deprived of its communion, for absenting himself from the public services of the Sabbath."

This was by no means the only instance in which an offended deacon showed his displeasure. Another Massachusetts brother in office, determined to take revenge on a choir who had led off the singing without giving him time to read, patiently waited till they had concluded, and then, gravely putting on his spectacles, opened his book and said, "Now let the people of God sing;" and, from respect and pity for the good old man, they joined with him in his psalm. Nay, even ministers did not formerly restrain their feelings on the subject. When Dr. Joseph Bellamy once heard his choir sing in sad style, he read another psalm, and said, "You must try again; for it is impossible to preach after such singing."

Some of our young readers will be pleased to have before them a few lines more as to the manner and trouble of forming choirs, and the way of choosing a leading singer. We give, therefore, a few extracts from the "*History of Rowley*:"—

1762.—"The parish voted that those who had learned the art of singing may have liberty to sit in the front gallery. They did not take the liberty;" probably because they would not sing after the clerk's reading.

1780.—"The parish requested Jonathan Chaplin, Jr., and Lieutenant Spafford to assist Deacon Daniel Spafford in *raising the tune* in the meeting-house."

1785.—"The parish desire the singers, both male and female, to sit in the gallery, and will allow them to sing once on each Lord's day without reading by the deacon."

About 1790, the *lining out* the psalm or hymn by the deacons was wholly discontinued.

A few lines from the "*Topsfield Church Records*" will confirm the general views of the subject:—

"1764, June 5.—Voted that the pastor be desired, Sabbath preceding the next lecture, in the name of the church, to desire the congregation, after the lecture is over, to tarry and consult with the church about choosing some person or persons to set the psalm when Captain Averill is absent."

"1764, March 13.—Mr. Moses Perkins and Mr. Jacob Kimball were, by the brethren of the church, and also by the congregation, chosen to set the psalm.

"Voted that the said Perkins and Kimball sit in the elders' seat."

In the year 1756, the congregation of the first church in Kittery, Mass., who had the Rev. Benjamin Stevens for their pastor, "voted that the petitioners for a singing-pew have liberty to sit in the hind seat but one, and to move the hind seat three inches, at their own cost." This was probably an incipient step to the formation of a choir. The next year the church "voted that Tate and Brady's version of the Psalms, with the addition of Scriptural Hymns, collected from Dr. Watts, etc., be sung in this church."

It seems that human nature makes similar manifestations of pride in all ages. Dr. Sprague, in his admirable "*Annals of the American Pulpit,*" tells us that on one occasion the Rev. Samuel Moody, a well-known, eccentric minister in Maine in the first half of the last century, had a lecture in a private house, and there was no one present competent to conduct the singing except his own hired man. So Mr. Moody called on John to tune the psalm while the line was given out in detail. John obeyed; and after they had got through, Mr. Moody said to him, "John, you never shall set the psalm again; for you are ready to burst with pride."

It is pleasant to turn from these facts to observe the influence of singing in the great revival which took place in our land, under Edwards, Whitefield, and others, from 1735 and onwards. Jonathan Edwards will not be accused of rashness or of overcoloring the facts of the case; and he says, "Our public praises were then greatly enlivened. God was then served in our psalmody, in some measure, in the beauty of holiness. It has been observable that there has been scarce any part of divine worship wherein good men among us have had grace so drawn forth and their hearts so lifted up in the ways of God, as in singing his praises. Our congregation excelled all that I ever knew before in the external part of the duty,—the men generally carrying well and regularly three parts of the music, and the women a part by themselves; but now they were evidently wont to sing with unusual elevation of heart and voice, which made the duty pleasant indeed."

To an American Christian it is pleasant to know that the very first book printed here was a portion of the inspired volume "done into metre." The first press was "put up" at Cambridge, in 1639, by Stephen Day. His first book was "*The Psalms in Metre*, faithfully translated, for the use, edification, and comfort of the saints, in public and private, *especially in New England*, printed at Cambridge in 1640." The version was made by Thomas Welde, of Roxbury, Richard Mather, of Dorchester, and John Eliot, the Apostle of the Indians. Speaking of their work, they say, "We have respected rather a plain translation, than to smoothe our verses with the sweetness of any paraphrase, and so have attended to conscience rather than elegance, and fidelity rather than poetry, in translating Hebrew words into English language, and David's poetry into English metre." Blessings on the Pilgrim Fathers, that we find on their records, "Stephen Day, being the first that set up printing, is granted three hundred acres of land, where it may be convenient without prejudice to any town."

We are told that when Eliot translated the Bible into the now entirely-forgotten *Nipmuck* language, which was printed at Cambridge in 1663, the whole of the type being set up by an Indian, the Psalms were "done" into that form of verse which in our hymn-books is called "common metre;" and nothing could be more clumsy and uncouth than the structure of the rhymes. Even Sternhold and Hopkins may be read with exquisite pleasure after looking over a few stanzas like the following from the nineteenth Psalm:—

"1. Kesuk kukootumushteaumoo
God wussohsumoonk
Mamahehekesuk wumahtuhkon
Wutanakausnonk.

"2. Kohsekoeh kesukodlash
Kuttoo waantamonk
Kah hodsekoe nukonash
Keketokon wahteauonk."

A somewhat remarkable book was issued in 1718, by Dr. Cotton Mather, called "*Psalterium Americanum:* the Book of Psalms in a translation exactly conformed unto the original, but all in blank verse, fitted unto the tunes commonly used in our churches. Which pure offering is accompanied with illustrations of digging for hidden treasures in it, and rules to employ according to the glorious and various intentions of it. Whereunto are added some portions of the Sacred Scriptures, to enrich the Cantional. Boston, in N. E."

In this singular production, which is a close translation from the Hebrew, Dr. Mather has not only disregarded the modern practice of breaking the lines, whether rhymed or not, but he has "run out," to use a printer's phrase, the whole matter; so that, while each psalm looks exactly like prose, and may be read as such, it is in fact modulated so that it may be sung as lyric verse. In an "*Admonition concerning the Tunes,*" Dr. Mather states that "The director of the psalmody need only say, 'Sing with the black letter,' or, 'Sing without the black letter,' and the tune will be sufficiently directed." The following extract from the twenty-third Psalm will give the reader some idea of this extraordinary translation:—

"PSALM XXIII.

"*A Psalm of David.*

"1. My Shepherd is th' ETERNAL God, || I shall not be in [any] want:

"2. In pastures of a tender grass || He [ever] makes me to lie down: || To waters of tranquillities || He gently carries me [along].

"3. My *feeble and my wandering* soul || He [kindly] does fetch back again; || In the plain paths of righteousness || He does lead [and guide] me along: || Because of the regard he has [ever] unto His *glorious* Name." ||

We hope to be forgiven if we occupy another page or two with matter relating to books of hymns and tunes. The first book containing music printed in America, as we learn from the "*American Musical Almanac*" for 1852, was issued in 1690. It was a versification of the Psalms, with a collection of tunes, in two parts only, at the end. In 1712, another work was issued, entitled "*A very plain and easy Introduction to the Art of Singing Psalm Tunes; with the Cantas or Trebles of Twenty-Eight Psalm Tunes, contrived in such a manner as that the learner may attain the skill of singing them with the greatest ease imaginable.* By the REV. MR. JOHN TUFTS. Price, 6*d.* 5*s.* the doz." In 1761, a work called "*Urania, or a Choice Collection of Psalm Tunes, Anthems, and Hymns, by* JAMES LYONS, A.M.," price, 15*s.*, was published at Philadelphia. Tradition says that it ruined its publisher,—which we can imagine to be very probable. In 1770, Mr. William Billings published his "*New England Psalm-Singer, or American Chorister,*" containing one hundred and twenty tunes. In the introduction to this work its author boldly declared his independence of all the rules of harmony,—a declaration which he fully acted out in this and all his future works. We may add here that, in 1754, a bookseller in Philadelphia advertised, as just published, "*The Youth's Entertaining Amusement; or, a Plain Guide to Psalmody: being a choice Collection of Tunes sung in the English Protestant Congregation in Philadelphia; with Rules for Learning. By* WILLIAM DAWSON." This title, probably unintentionally, expresses with great simplicity a fact,—that young persons, and many of their friends too, often resort to the practice of psalmody—which should be a holy exercise—for mere amusement.

Let not the young author who is conscious of the possession of talent be discouraged by difficulties at the outset of his career, but go on till he achieves success. This, no doubt, would be the counsel of the eminent singer, Dr. Lowell Mason: at all events, this was his own early conduct.

In early life, while engaged in conducting the choir of a church in Savannah, Georgia, he felt the want of a collection of church-music even tolerably adapted to the wants of choirs, and was thus led to compile such a work himself, more with a view of preparing a book for his own choir than with any expectation of producing a work which should be generally used.

Having finished his manuscript, our young author obtained leave of absence from the bank in which he was then a clerk, and directed his steps northward in search of a publisher. Arriving at Philadelphia, he offered to give the copyright to any house which would publish the work and give him a few copies for his own use; but in the estimation of the booksellers and music-merchants it was too hazardous an enterprise for wise men to engage in. Failing in Philadelphia, he went to Boston, and made the same offer to the publishers of that city. But the shrewd Yankee publishers laughed at him, and intimated that their forecast and prudence were not to be so easily thrown off their balance.

Finding that every one looked at his book so coldly, our young author put his manuscript crotchets and quavers into his pocket, and was about returning to Savannah, when he accidentally met a gentleman of considerable knowledge of music, who wished to examine the volume. Having done this, he expressed his satisfaction, and asked Mason what he intended to do with it. "Take it home with me," was the reply. The gentleman proposed to show it to the Handel and Haydn Society, who at once published the book, giving its author a share in the copyright. His remarkable success as a teacher is well known.

One or two amusing matters may here be added, which may at least provoke a harmless smile.

One of our most popular monthly periodicals for 1853 tells us that, not long since, the chorister of a choir in Vermont wrote to a publisher in Boston for a copy of that popular singing-book, "*The Ancient Lyre.*" His communication ran, "Please send me the *Ancient Liar, well bound.*" The publisher replied, "My dear Sir:—I do not doubt that the *devil* has been and still is in Boston; but it will be difficult to comply with your request, for the reason that Boston influence is so strong in his favor, it will be impossible to *bind* him."

A Boston astrologer long ago predicted that an extraordinary literary work would be produced in New England about the middle of the nineteenth century. According to "*Gleason's Pictorial Drawing-Room Companion,*" the prediction was fulfilled in 1853, to the letter. A Boston publishing-house "got up" a Quaker hymn-book, having heard that no work of the kind existed. At first it appeared to be "a pretty good opening;" but one unlucky circumstance was soon discovered: *the Quakers never sing.*

The "*Bay-State Collection of Sacred Music*" includes a tune called "*California,*" with the words,—

"My soul lies cleaving to the dust."

A correspondent of the "*Newark* (N.J.) *Advertiser,*" writing from Bramfield, Connecticut, says, "By the way, a good story may be told of our chorister's attempt at improving the psalmody as well as the music of our church. He set some music of his own to the ninety-second Psalm of Watts, in which occur the lines,—

'Oh, may my heart in tune be found,
Like David's harp of solemn sound!'

"Calling on his pastor, he asked his approbation of a

new version of these lines, which would render them more readily adapted to the music he had composed. He suggested that they should read,—

'Oh, may my heart be tuned within,
Like David's sacred violin!'

"The good pastor had somewhat of an inclination to laugh in the singing-man's face; but, maintaining his gravity as he best could, he thought he could suggest a further improvement of the version, admirable as it was. The highly-delighted chorister begged him to do so; and the minister wrote before his parishioner,—

'Oh, may my heart go diddle, diddle,
Like Uncle David's sacred fiddle!'

"The poor man, after a vain attempt to justify his own parody, retired to sing the psalm as it stands."

It sometimes happens that preachers and choristers are not entirely united in their views, even in the church itself. Some years since, a Millerite preacher in Vermont declared, during the delivery of a sermon, that he did not expect to die, but anticipated being alive when Christ came, and hoped to dwell with him on this earth forever. The chorister took quite a different view of the matter, and selected, as the closing piece for the choir,—

"I would not live alway; I ask not to stay
Where storm after storm rises dark o'er the way."

A minister can reprove as readily as a chorister can. At a church in New England, a stranger was called to officiate in the absence of the pastor, and, not being familiar with some rules of the choir, so much offended them that they would not sing. After several efforts, the preacher determined not to be discomfited, and read the verse,—

> "Let those refuse to sing
> Who never knew our God;
> But children of the heavenly King
> May speak their joys abroad."

This roused the whole choir and congregation, who at once joined in with the minister, and the service passed off very pleasantly.

Not many years since, a minister in New Hampshire fell, as will sometimes happen, into a difficulty with his choir, which for some time prevented their accustomed services. At length the choir relented, and appeared, as heretofore, at the usual time of service. The minister most unexpectedly saw them in their places, and in due time, looking very significantly, rose and read the hymn,—

> "And are ye wretches yet alive,
> And do ye yet rebel?"

All parties were pleased when the affair was ended.

The Methodist body, founded by the Rev. John Wesley, have always been a singing community. The two brothers Wesley published, during their lives, not less than forty-eight books and tracts of hymns, for the use of their people. "Some of these," says John Wesley, "had such a sale as I never thought of." Nothing, indeed, has contributed more to their extension than the almost universal discharge of this important part of worship; and especially was this true before the modern introduction of choirs. As early as 1752, Mr. Wesley published a collection of tunes for the use of his followers; and in 1761 he published "*Select Hymns, with Tunes annexed, designed chiefly for the use of the People called Methodists,*"—in the preface to which he says, "I want the people called Methodists to sing true the tunes which are in common use among them. At the same time, I want them to have in one volume the best hymns we have printed, and that in a small and portable volume, and one of an easy price. I have been endeavoring for more than twenty years to procure such a book as this, but in vain. Masters of music were above following any direction but their own; and I was determined whoever compiled this should follow my direction,—not mending our tunes, but setting them down neither better nor worse than they were. At length I have prevailed."

So intent was John Wesley on this part of his work that, in travelling through England, he often stood in the pulpit familiarly directing this part of worship, calling in turn on the men and the women to take their parts in the holy song. One of the happy effects of Methodist singing, which is observed alike in the great congregation, the social prayer-meeting, and the family circle, is that we have known more than one congregation, where there has been very unacceptable preaching, kept together by animated singing.

The Rev. G. W. Hervey, in a recent interesting article in the "*Christian Review*," tells us that this eminent man was fully persuaded of the necessity of a musical revival, which should give utterance to the new experiences of his converts. Happening one day to hear a sailor singing in the street, it struck him that the melody he was pouring forth would, above all others, suit the words of some of his hymns, and greatly delight and edify the people. Knowing how to write music, he wrote down the notes on the spot, introduced them into his meetings, and always declared that it was the most solemn and appropriate of all the tunes which were sung by his followers.

Nor was the eminent George Whitefield less interested in lively, simple congregational singing. He was most decidedly averse to the cathedral-music of his day, and to "the linked sweetness long drawn out" of the parochial psalmody of England. He would not suffer a bar of it to be warbled in his houses of worship. He also thought that the lively ballad-airs of secular origin were more suitable to the joy and gladness of the new-born soul. He declared that it was shameful to praise God in the drawling strains of the Church, and downright sacrilege to allow the devil the monopoly of all the jubilant music.

Every one, too, knows that the great awakening in the days of our own Jonathan Edwards was attended by general song. He defended the practice in a masterly manner, and showed that to complain of it was to resemble the Pharisees, who were disgusted with the multitude of the disciples when with loud voices they praised God and shouted "Hosanna" as Christ entered Jerusalem.

The Rev. Charles Wesley has a beautiful hymn on "*The True Use of Music*," founded on 1 Cor. xiv. 15, "I will sing with the spirit, and I will sing with the understanding also." Well does he say of this charming science,—

"Listed into the cause of sin,
Why should a good be evil?
Music, alas! too long has been
Pressed to obey the devil."

In the hymn now before us he says,—

"Still let us on our guard be found,
And watch against the power of sound
With sacred jealousy:
Lest, haply, sense should damp our zeal,
And music's charms bewitch and steal
Our hearts away from thee."

The venerable John Wesley, who was both a poet and a warm lover of music, when asked his opinion of the propriety of the introduction of instrumental music into the worship of the Methodists, said, in his own terse manner, "I have no objection to instruments of music in our chapels, provided they are neither HEARD NOR SEEN."

The late Dr. Adam Clarke wrote, "Music, as a science, I love and admire; but instruments of music in the house of God I abominate and abhor. This is the abuse of music; and I here register my protest against all such corruptions in the worship of the Author of Christianity."

Certain it is that this "delight of the ears" has done very much, in modern times, to increase attendance on public worship. One denomination among us, at least, has done as much by its singing as by its preaching to attract vast crowds. Nor is this peculiar to Protestants. Southey tells us, in his History of Brazil, that, finding the Tupis passionately fond of music, the Jesuit suited himself to their taste, until he began to hope that the fable of Orpheus was a type of his mission, and that by songs he was to convert the Brazilian pagans. He usually took with him four or five choristers on his preaching expeditions. When they approached an inhabited place, one carried the crucifix before them, and the rest began singing the litany. The savages, like snakes, were won by the voice of the charmer, and everywhere received him joyfully.

We are tempted, in this place, to make a few remarks on the almost intolerable evil of making alterations in good old-fashioned psalms and hymns, which is generally done by persons of great affectation or great conceit, or for the sake of a closer conformity to their "new and superior music." For some of our hints we own ourselves indebted to the "*Presbyterian.*"

We have elsewhere referred to a most popular and useful hymn by Gregg. He wrote the first verse,—

"Jesus! and shall it ever be?
A mortal man ashamed of thee!

Ashamed of thee, whom angels praise,
Whose glory shines through endless days!"

See how miserably the last two lines are converted into *bathos* in a popular hymn-book:—

"Jesus! and shall it ever be?
A mortal man ashamed of thee!
Scorned be the thought by rich and poor;
Oh, may I scorn it more and more!"

Perhaps the same thinker and would-be "improver" substituted for the following line of Watts,—

"When God, the mighty Maker, died,"

the softened language,—

"When Christ, the mighty Saviour, died."

We cannot doubt that both these alterations were intended to modify the ascriptions of Deity to the Lord Jesus, and are therefore unpardonable, at least with those who love the old scriptural doctrine conveyed in language which long since became endeared to their hearts.

Here is another exquisite verse from the same author:—

"My willing soul would stay
In such a frame as this,
And sit and sing herself away
To everlasting bliss."

There is both beauty and poetry in the idea of the soul "singing herself away;" but the "improvers" make it read,—

"Till called to rise and soar away
To everlasting bliss."

Can any one give us the reason for the change of a single word in the last verse of Watts's seventeenth Psalm?—

"Then burst the chains with *sweet* surprise."

Why must it be so altered as to read—

"Then burst the chains with *glad* surprise?"—

which assuredly destroys the author's idea.

The *poet* Cowper wrote in one of his hymns,—

"What peaceful hours I once enjoyed!
How sweet their memory still!
But they have left an aching void
The world can never fill."

Could words be chosen more precise and expressive? What then must be the effect of such an "improvement" in the third line?—

"But now I *feel an aching* void,"—

as though the victim had a sudden sense of *goneness,* or an attack of the colic.

Another of Cowper's most precious hymns has suffered even more cruelly than this, the alteration being at once barbarous and unpoetical, though made to render it more readily adapted to the music:—

"Then, in a nobler, sweeter song,
I'll sing thy power to save,
When this poor lisping, stammering tongue
Lies silent in the grave."

The last two lines, slightly altered, have been placed first, and the whole verse is thus presented :—

"When this poor lisping, faltering tongue
Lies silent in the grave,
Then, in a nobler, sweeter song
I'll sing thy power to save."

We cannot be surprised that Dr. Bethune, himself a poet of no mean order, should have once indignantly said from the pulpit, "I should like to know who has had the presumption to alter Cowper's poetry."

A recent number of the "*Presbyterian Quarterly Review*," when speaking of Charles Wesley's admirable hymn,—

"Thou God of glorious majesty!"

says, with great propriety, "Our menders of sacred lyrics have violated all decency in their transformation of the original, and have really altered, not the phraseology merely, but the sense :"—

"Lo! on a narrow neck of land,
'Twixt two unbounded seas I stand,
Secure, insensible!"

The poet represents, in this triplet, a half-awakened sinner, not wholly alive to his position, just beginning to discern, but not fully to apprehend, his danger,—"*secure*, insensible," until clearer light falls from the Spirit of God upon his soul: then, indeed, he sees the yawning gulf beneath him, on either side, and cries out,—

"A point of time—a moment's space—
Removes me to that heavenly place,
Or shuts me up in hell!"

How miserably tame and meaningless, compared with the original, is the "improved" rendering!—

"*Yet how* insensible!"

If we needed additional proof that our compilers failed to appreciate the living, burning thought of the poet, we have it in the next stanza,—

"O God, my inmost soul convert,
And deeply on my *thoughtless* heart."

The poet wrote "*thoughtful* heart:" his genius had called into being a sinner who had been insensible,—who had imagined himself secure on the narrow promontory of probationary life, but whose eyes are now open to his danger. He begins to think. No longer thoughtlessly secure, he is now thought-*ful*, and beseeches God that eternal things may be impressed more deeply on his mind.

But, as though this amount of alteration were not sufficient to satisfy us, the author is made to say,—

"Give me to feel their solemn weight,
And save me ere it be too late."(!)

We suppose that if God saves at all, it will be "ere it be too late."

Who can forgive this literary theft of one of the finest and boldest lines ever penned by poet?—

"*And tremble on the brink of fate.*"

This is true poetry; and the strong expression at the end of the line, which our compilers seem to have shunned, so far from being unwarrantably bold, is appropriate and effective, and its use is sustained by numerous scriptural examples.

While we are on this subject of "emendation" of hymns, and especially of the "improved" versions of those composed by the Wesleys, we cannot forbear to quote the words of John Wesley, in which he "sharply" rebukes some of the trespassers on his domain, in language like this:—"Many gentlemen have done my brother and me, though without naming us, the honor to reprint many of our hymns. Now, they are perfectly welcome so to do, provided they print them just as they are. But I desire they would not attempt to mend them; for they really are not able. None of them is able to mend either the sense or the verse. Therefore I must beg of them one of these two favors: either to let them stand just as they are,—to take them for better or for worse,—or to add the true meaning at the bottom of the page, that we may be no longer accountable for the nonsense or for the doggerel of other men."

After all, however, alterations are sometimes needful, and occasionally are great improvements: as, for instance, John Wesley's own "improvement" of Watts' hundredth Psalm. The author wrote its first two lines,—

"Nations, attend before his throne,
With solemn fear, with sacred joy."

Wesley changed it to,—

"Before Jehovah's awful throne,
Ye nations, bow with sacred joy."

"Another distinguished hymn of Watts," says the unknown author from whom we are quoting, "was altered by the same hand, in its first stanza, and the change has become classic. No one would propose to print the following verse as Watts wrote it:—

'He dies! the heavenly Lover dies!
The tidings strike a doleful sound
On my poor heart-strings. Deep he lies
In the cold caverns of the ground.'

Wesley's transformed stanza is almost infinitely preferable:—

'He dies! the Friend of sinners dies!
Lo! Salem's daughters weep around;
A solemn darkness veils the skies,
A sudden trembling shakes the ground.'"

Nor can it be denied that our more recent editors do, occasionally, give us an emendation; but we trust that in their future acts of this character they will remember their vast responsibility, and further, that, of every hundred of the changes they make, at least ninety and nine are for the worse.

It has long been to us a matter of surprise that our congregations do not acquire a habit of *chanting*,—a practice at once both easy and delightful. To use the correct language of Dr. Whitaker, in his "*Life of St. Neot*," "The chant not merely assists the voice and gives it a larger volume of sound for an extensive church, but, what is of much more consequence, augments its devoutness by the modulation of its tones,—by the rapid flow at one time, by the solemn slowness at another,—

by the rise, the fall, and the swell, much more strongly marked than any of these can be in reading,—much more *ex*pressive of devoutness in the officiating clergyman, and much more *im*pressive of devoutness upon the attending congregation. A chanted prayer is thus the *poetry* of devotion, while a prayer read is merely the *prose* of it. So, at least, thought the wisest and the best of our ancestors,—men peculiarly qualified to judge, because their intellects were exalted and their spirits devout,—who therefore carried the chanted prayer from our churches into their closets."

May we be allowed here to touch on a subject of some delicacy? We refer to the complaint often made as to the congregational services in our churches being too long, and as to the part to be abbreviated. We are not aware of any cases in which a Christian would abridge the duty of adoration and prayer: so that the real question is, which shall be shortened, the singing or the preaching? Our answer may be given in a few words. If the hymn selected be one containing little that is devotional, and only intended to gratify the intellect, or if it be chiefly employed to call out the taste and the science of the choir and to claim the admiration of the unconverted listeners, by all means abbreviate the singing; but if the psalmody be strictly what it professes to be,—devotional and heavenly,—if many hearts of the truly devout are engaged in it, and if it produces a soul-subduing influence, raising the heart to God and heaven, by no means shorten that portion of the worship. There can be no difficulty on the part of the preacher, with proper labor and thought, condensing the matter of his sermon so as to make it five minutes shorter; and it will often prove beneficial to the preacher's intellect and heart that his performances should pass through such an ordeal. In such matters, after all, "wisdom is profitable to direct."

At the risk of being charged with prolixity in these miscellaneous introductory pages, we will refer, in closing, to a few general facts, which we hope will not be without their use to at least some of our friends.

Bishop Horne, in his admirable sermon on Church-Music, quotes from Collier, the ecclesiastical historian, as saying, "Religious harmony must be moving, but noble withal, grave, solemn, and seraphic, fit for a martyr to play and an angel to hear." Sad havoc has been committed, in modern times, by the introduction into many of our churches of vulgar and light productions, devoid of the slightest pretensions to taste, and full of the grossest offences against the laws of musical composition. Solos, and every attempt at fugue, and the like, should be most rigidly excluded. We are quite aware that a very great number of persons prefer vulgar and trashy compositions to sound classical music, and argue that because a melody happens to please *them*, it must necessarily be good. This is just as absurd as though an educated man were to maintain that some vulgar ballad, full of offences against syntax and prosody, was superior poetry. Music has its grammar as well as language.

We have noticed, of late, an increasing love of old congregational tunes; and perhaps few persons are aware of the antiquity of some of these. One called "*York*" has been ascribed to no less a personage than Milton the poet; but it was really composed by his father. The history of "*Old Hundred*" is the subject of a volume recently published by an English clergyman. Martin Luther was long considered to be its author; but it has now been discovered that it was originated in the sixteenth century, by William Franc, a German, though it has been considerably changed from the original,—in part, probably, by Luther himself.

To advance the favorable reception of the old tunes, it should be remembered that they were formerly sung much faster than we sing them, and by a far larger number of voices. Our forefathers in the Church were cheerful Christians, and a psalm of twelve verses was but short to them. Old Hundred is sung as a dirge now; but then it was a joyous canticle:—

> "All people that on earth do dwell,
> *Sing to the Lord with cheerful voice.*"

York, too, now often placed among the dull and obsolete, was originally the most lively and popular of tunes.

Whatever may be the quality of our hymns and tunes, we are assuredly far beyond all former years in the *quantity* we use. Many years ago it was announced that more than sixty thousand copies of the "*Methodist Hymn-Book*" were sold annually in London; and in the United States the number must be much larger. And, as we write, an advertisement tells us that "*Hallelujah*," a volume of devotional tunes published in London, contains compositions in one hundred and thirty-six different metres.

A few lines, written some years since by Dr. Joshua Leavitt, may be here introduced with advantage. He says, "In revivals of religion a species of music is sought entirely different from that which is ordinarily used. The state of feeling is such then that it swells beyond the shackles of musical authority, and the music is sought for and employed which is known to produce *effects*. A class of tunes which has long been under the sentence of banishment from our music-books and singing-schools is then sought for. The squeamish affectation of not using, in the service of God, music of known power to move because it has been already proved in the service of the world or of Satan is abandoned. Singing assumes a new character, and the rejoicing people of God are amazed at its powers. I wish the musicians should explain, especially those of them who love revivals. And I desire that ministers should ask how they can excuse themselves if they thus allow a powerful means of grace to be neutralized by submitting all their music to the control of a scientific theory.

"It is not unfrequently found that persons who have not what is called a musical ear are yet keenly susceptible to the practical influence of musical sounds. Those who are awakened or enlightened by the singing that takes place in a revival will not, by any means, be confined to the singers. Many Christians have seen this, and have felt the want of a reform in our musical system. A great deal of that which is found useful in revivals is passed along by tradition and learned by rote. Many congregations where revivals are known are destitute of such music; but, where they have a knowledge of it, the denunciations of the music-master and the organist are disregarded. People *will* sing music that means something and that meets their feelings more than ordinary psalm-tunes. It is astonishing to learn the rich variety of such music which is thus preserved by tradition, and preserved thus because it is excluded from books. All musical writers denounce these tunes and proscribe them from their pages, and yet they are preserved. There are tunes now sung in prayer-meetings which have, in this way, outlived whole generations of what is called scientific music. Is it not time that we should act a little from facts and experience, and leave musical theories to their proper sphere,—in the speculations of writers whose professed object is something aside from the salvation of souls?"

In entire accordance with these remarks are some thus expressed by the venerated theologian, Andrew Fuller:—"The criterion of a good tune is not its pleasing a scientific ear, but its being quickly caught by a congregation. It is, I think, by singing as it is by preaching:

a fine judge of composition will admire a sermon which yet makes no manner of impression upon the public mind, and therefore cannot be a good one. That is the best sermon which is adapted to produce the best effects; and the same may be said of a tune. If it corresponds with the feelings of a pious heart and aids him in realizing the sentiments, it will be quickly learnt, and be sung with avidity. Where this effect is not produced, were I a composer, I would throw away my performance and try again."

AUTHORS

AND

ORIGIN OF HYMNS.

AUTHORS AND ORIGIN OF HYMNS.

SARAH F. ADAMS.

THE admirable hymns published with this signature were written by a lady eminent for her musical talents. She wrote, besides hymns and criticisms, several works collected under the title of "*Adoration, Aspiration, and Belief.*" She died in 1848.

JOSEPH ADDISON.

ADDISON, who flourished in the latter part of the seventeenth and the early portion of the eighteenth centuries, commands the respect of all who value religion and morals. Though in the early part of his life he devoted himself to political affairs, he soon abandoned them, as also an earlier design of taking orders in the English Church, and gave his days and nights to literature, in which, contrary to the majority of writers, he was successful. Especially did he advance literature and fine taste by the publication of the "*Spectator,*" the happy results of which are still felt in literary circles in

England. His hymns, originally printed in the "*Spectator*," are still increasingly admired, and are extending in their usefulness. In 1716 he was married to the Countess Dowager of Warwick, whose son, it will be remembered, he sent for on his death-bed, in 1729, to see in what peace a Christian could die. It has been very truly said that he has divested vice of its meretricious ornaments, and painted religion and virtue in the modest and graceful attire which charms and elevates the heart. In addition to his hymns, he wrote a part of a version of the Psalms, which was never completed.

CHRISTOPHER ANGELUS.

THIS eminent person, who died in the seventeenth century, was the author of the beautiful hymn, recently introduced into one or two of our books,—

"Loving Shepherd, kind and true."

His origin was Greek; and, being driven from Peloponnesus by the Turks, he went to England, and studied at the Cambridge University, under the patronage of the Bishop of Norwich. He afterward studied at Baliol College, Oxford, where he proved very useful in instructing the students in Greek. His most valuable work was an account of his sufferings, printed in 1716, in Greek and English. The hymn to which we have referred is beautiful alike for its simplicity and its evangelical unction.

REV. JAMES ALLEN.

"Sinners, will you scorn the message?"

was written by James Allen, who was born in Yorkshire, England, in 1734, and died in his native village, in 1804. His father, intending him for the ministry in the Established Church, placed him under the care of a clergyman, whose immoral conduct, and that of his followers, so disgusted young Allen that he at once dissented from a Church that could tolerate such men. Converted under the ministry of Mr. Ingham, the leader of a small sect of the Methodists, Allen joined his connection, among whom he was a popular minister for nine years. He then built a house of worship for himself, in which he successfully labored till his death.

Before Mr. Allen fully entered on his ministry, he spent a few months in the University of Cambridge, where he became acquainted with a gentleman named Ashton, who settled in Westmoreland. Mr. Allen, many years afterward, was preaching near Kendal, where a mob was raised and the preacher made a prisoner. It providentially happened that Mr. Ashton was present: he rushed through the crowd, took the dissenting minister by the hand, expressed his great pleasure at seeing him, reminded him of the happy days they had spent together at college, and arm in arm walked with him to the village. The mob were vexed when they found the preacher to be a friend of their squire, and the clergyman regretted that so worthy a man had left the Established Church.

MRS. G. W. ANDERSON.

THIS estimable lady, the author of the truly beautiful hymn,—

"Our country's voice is pleading,"

is, we believe, of English birth, though she came to this country in very early life, and has for some years been the wife of Professor G. W. Anderson, for some time engaged in the University at Lewisburg, Pa. We believe that Mrs. A. has written nothing but a few hymns, with a small volume or two for children, and some articles in newspapers and magazines, which have afforded much interest and profit to children. We hope she may yet contribute largely to our hymnology.

REV. LEONARD BACON, D.D.

THE hymns of this gentleman, while they aid our devotion, also command our esteem for their sound judgment, correct imagery, and scriptural theology. He was the son of a missionary to the Indians, and was born at Detroit in 1802, entered Yale College in his sixteenth year, graduated in 1820, studied theology at Andover, and was ordained pastor of the First Congregational Church at

New Haven, in 1825, when he was twenty-three years of age. Pulpit labors and literature have well occupied his days and nights. His love of controversy is well known; but generally he has been found on the side of scriptural truth. Some years ago he travelled in Europe and Asia, and escaped death at the hands of the Koords, in Nestoria, in a very extraordinary manner, by the influence of woman,—the Agha's wife. His natural resolution and steadiness of purpose were, under God, of no small value in the dangerous circumstances in which he was placed.

REV. JOHN BAKEWELL.

In reference to the authorship of the beautiful hymn,—

"Hail! thou once despised Jesus!"

or, as in some books,—

"Paschal Lamb, by God appointed,"

there has been some difference of opinion. It has been said by some to have been written by Madan; and certainly he published it in a collection as early as 1760. But preponderating evidence will show it to have been the production of John Bakewell, of Greenwich, England, who was born in 1721. He was one of the earliest Methodist local preachers under the Wesleys, having commenced his ministry in 1749. He wrote many hymns, and in his own family circle this was regarded as one of the number. It is a fine production, and is very properly introduced into most of our collections.

Mr. Bakewell died in 1819, aged ninety-eight years, and was interred in the City-Road burying-ground, London. He had been a preacher more than seventy years.

REV. THOMAS BALDWIN, D.D.

WITH what delightful and tearful interest have we stood, at the close of a meeting of days, surrounded by a group of Christians, and sung what is called "*the union hymn,*"—

"From whence does this union arise?"

Its author was born in Bozrah, Conn., in 1753, and in very early life, though amidst many discouragements, his original thinking powers were greatly improved by reading. He married while yet young, and before he was thirty was sent as a representative to the Legislature of his native State. In 1780 he became a decided Christian, and shortly afterward was baptized. He had entertained thoughts of the law, but was gradually led into the office of the ministry, to which he was ordained in 1783. In 1790 he became the pastor of the Second Baptist Church in Boston, a position which he occupied with ever-growing success till his sudden decease when on a journey from home in 1825. He was very amiable in his spirit and deportment, and greatly beloved by a very large circle of friends.

ANNA LETITIA BARBAULD.

Of this lady, the author of several of our hymns, including,—

"When, as returns this solemn day,"

we have but little to write. She was one of the most distinguished female writers of her day within the British dominions. Theologically she belonged to the more evangelical class of English Unitarians, often in her views approaching what are considered the orthodox body of Christians. She was the daughter of the Rev. John Aikin, and at 1774, at the age of thirty-one, was married to the Rev. R. Barbauld, after which she wrote her "*Early Lessons*," "*Hymns for Children*," and many other works. She died in 1825, in her eighty-second year, her husband having died three years before her. It is said that, in her early years, Mrs. Barbauld was favored with many of the instructions of Dr. Doddridge, and that her later years were given to the instruction of young ladies.

BERNARD BARTON.

This "Quaker poet," as he is usually called, from the fact that both his parents and himself lived and died among that people, was born in London, in 1784, and spent the far larger portion of his years as clerk in a bank in Suffolk, having in very early life buried his young and only wife. His literary character has been well described by his daughter, who was also his biographer:—"He was not learned,—in language, science, or philosophy. Nor did he care for the loftiest kind of poetry, 'the heroics,' as he called it. His favorite authors were those who dealt most in humor, good sense, domestic feeling, and pastoral feeling." The hymn,—

"The waters of Bethesda's pool,"

was originally written for a friend greatly oppressed with sorrow.

We are tempted here to quote from one of Barton's own letters a scene which occurred at the funeral of a young lady which he attended in 1841. "When the usual service was ended, the clergyman stated that it was the wish of the deceased, or rather of her relatives, that a little hymn which had ever been a great favorite of hers should be sung on this occasion, and he had much pleasure in complying with the request. After a few minutes, way was made for the children of the village school, which this estimable girl had almost made and managed, to come up to the grave-side,—about twenty or twenty-five little things, with eyes and cheeks red with crying. I thought they could never have found tongues, poor things! but, once set off, they sung like a little band of cherubs. What added to the effect of it, to me, was that it was a little almost-forgotten hymn of my own, written years ago, which no one present, but myself, was at all aware of."

Mr. Barton died in 1849. One of the English periodicals has said, "Mr. Barton's style is well suited to devotional poetry. It has great sweetness and pathos, accompanied with no small degree of power, which well qualify it for the expression of the higher and purer feelings of the heart."

REV. CHRISTOPHER BATTY.

"SWEET the moments, rich in blessing,"

was written by the Rev. Christopher Batty, a minister among the Inghamites, a small sect of the early Methodists. He was a zealous, laborious, and disinterested Christian, and was so much esteemed by a family named Green, in the city of York, England, that Mr. Green told him that, as he had, under God, led his daughter to Christ, and as she had been removed from earth, he intended to leave him the whole of his property; but Mr. Batty positively refused to accept of it. While an itinerating minister, Mr. Batty, his two brothers,—who were also ministers,—and their friends were exposed to much persecution. At Gisburn, in Yorkshire, they were interrupted in their religious meeting by the curate of the parish, heading a large mob, entering the place where they were assembled for worship; but, amidst all opposition, there and elsewhere the word of the Lord had free course and was glorified. Dr. Stevens tells us that Mr. Batty often accompanied the Wesleys in their tours for preaching, and stood with them like "a good soldier of Jesus Christ."

REV. RICHARD BAXTER.

Of this eminent minister of Christ we need not say much, as the man must indeed be ignorant who knows not the author of "*The Saint's Rest*," and his other works, which could not be printed in less than sixty octavo volumes. He made no pretensions to poetical talent; but we should pity the want of taste on the part of the reader who did not highly appreciate the hymn, in the Rev. Henry Ward Beecher's "*Plymouth Collection*,"—

"Christ leads me through no darker rooms,"

and several others to be found scattered through his ponderous and invaluable volumes. He was born in 1615, was ejected from the Church of England by the Act of Uniformity, in 1662, and, after enduring great persecution, died "in great peace and joy" in 1691. When Dr. Samuel Johnson was asked by Boswell which of Baxter's works he should read, he wisely replied, "Read them all: they are all good."

Montgomery gives us a somewhat glowing description of Baxter's hymns and poetry, and tells us that he also left, fully prepared for the press, an entire poetical version of the Psalms of David, with other hymns, which were published in 1692 by his friend Matthew

Sylvester. His poetical works have been most cherished by those who have read them with most attention.

REV. BENJAMIN BEDDOME.

Most of our hymn-books contain a large number of compositions by the Rev. Benjamin Beddome, a man of considerable talents and high attainments, but who spent the far greater portion of a long life in the seclusion of a small country village. He was the son of a Baptist minister, was called by divine grace at the age of twenty, and baptized by the Rev. Samuel Wilson, of London, about two years afterward. He visited Bourton-on-the-Water in 1743, and was prevailed on to accept a call to the pastorate, three years afterward. In 1749 he suffered a very severe illness, and on his recovery wrote a hymn which he afterward replaced by one commencing,—

"If I must die, oh, let me die
Trusting in Jesus' blood,—
That blood which hath atonement made
And reconciles to God."

Not long after his recovery he was earnestly entreated to succeed Mr. Wilson, his pastor in London. So determined were this church to obtain him that, after sending call after call in vain, they deputed one of their number to urge the matter with him. This was discovered by a poor man, a member of his church, to whom the care of the gentleman's horse had been intrusted; and having, with excited feelings, brought the horse to Mr. Beddome's door, the poor man said to the Londoner, "Robbers of churches are the worst of robbers," and at once set the horse free to take his own course. Mr. Beddome's final reply was, "I would rather honor God in a station even much inferior to that in which he has placed me, than intrude myself into a higher without his direction," and remained in his pastorate at Bourton till his death.

That Mr. Beddome's attachment to Bourton was early as well as deep, may be seen from some lines he wrote about 1742, entitled "THE WISH:—

"Lord, in my soul implant thy fear:
Let faith, and hope, and love be there.
Preserve me from prevailing vice
When Satan tempts or lusts entice.
Of friendship's sweets may I partake,
Nor be forsaken, or forsake.
Let moderate plenty crown my board,
And God for all be still adored.
Let the companion of my youth
Be one of innocence and truth:
Let modest charms adorn her face,
And give her thy superior grace:
By heavenly art first make her thine,
Then make her willing to be mine.
My dwelling-place let Bourton be,
And let me live, and live to thee."

It was not, however, till 1749 that he entered the marriage-state, which was to an excellent young lady, daughter of one of his deacons, who was for thirty-four years his beloved companion.

Mr. Beddome's ministrations retained to the very last all their liveliness and attractions, improved by the increased solemnity and wisdom of age. His earnest desire that he might not be long laid aside from his beloved employment was fully gratified; for, having during his infirmities been carried to the house of God, he preached sitting, and was only confined to his house one Lord's day. Only an hour before his death he was found composing a hymn, of which he wrote,—

"God of my life and of my choice,
Shall I no longer hear thy voice?
Oh, let the Source of joy divine
With rapture fill this heart of mine.

"Thou openedst Jonah's prison-doors,—
Be pleased, O Lord, to open ours:
Then will we to the world proclaim
The various honors of thy name."

This excellent man fell asleep in Jesus, September 3, 1795, in the seventy-ninth year of his age, having labored at Bourton fifty-two years. In the year 1818 a volume of his hymns was published, with a short but beautiful preface by the late eloquent Robert Hall, who says, "The man of taste will be gratified with the beautiful and original thoughts which many of them exhibit, while the experimental Christian will often perceive the most sweet movements of his soul strikingly delineated, and sentiments portrayed which will find their echo in every heart."

REV. CHARLES BEECHER.

This gentleman is one of the thirteen children of the venerable Dr. Lyman Beecher, and is also the brother of Dr. Edward and Henry Ward Beecher, and of Mrs. Beecher Stowe. No member of that family can be without talent. We believe that Mr. Beecher ranks with the Congregationalists; but his publications would indicate that he is a very bold and independent thinker.

BERNARD.

This name is usually printed with the prefix *St.*, as having been given him by the Romish Church. He lived in the tenth century, and was the author of a Latin hymn consisting of nearly two hundred lines. Parts of it have been translated and form at least three hymns in our books. One of these begins,—

"Jesus, the very thought of thee."

The late Dr. Byrom, of Manchester, translated another portion; and it has been said that John Newton's beautiful hymn,—

"How sweet the name of Jesus sounds!"

was also founded on that of Bernard. Nor can it scarcely be doubted that, before Dr. Doddridge wrote,—

"Jesus, I love thy charming name,"

he had read the composition of Bernard.

One of the most beautiful hymns of Gerhard was clearly suggested also by Bernard's "*Hymn to Christ on the Cross*," a translation of which may be found in a recent English publication, "*The Voice of Christian Life in Song*." We refer to the hymn translated by Wesley and found in the old Methodist hymn-books as well as the one published by the Moravian Brethren:—

"O head so full of bruises."

REV. JOHN BERRIDGE.

There are few old Christians who are unacquainted with the name of the Rev. John Berridge, one of the most successful preachers connected with the revival of religion commenced by the Rev. Messrs. Whitefield and Wesley, and author of several hymns in our books intended for the service of the sanctuary. He was a man of great learning and wit, but still more eminent as an earnest and successful minister of Christ. Some of the most important events of his history may be learned from his epitaph, written, with the exception of the last date, by himself:—"Here lie the remains of John Berridge, the Vicar of Everton, and an itinerant servant of Jesus Christ, who loved his Master and his work; and, after running on his errands for many years, was caught up to wait on him above. Reader, art thou born again? No salvation without a new birth. I was born in sin February, 1716, remained ignorant of my fallen state till 1730, lived proudly on faith and works for salvation till 1754, was admitted to Everton vicarage 1755, fled to Jesus for refuge 1755, fell asleep in Jesus January 22, 1793."

When this eminent clergyman had become fully acquainted with the value of immortal souls and with the importance of salvation by the work of the Lord Jesus, he felt the vast import of his ordination-charge, "Go and seek Christ's sheep wherever thou canst find them;" and, taking a circuit of five or six counties, he preached upon an average ten or twelve sermons and frequently rode a hundred miles a week. In this course he persevered for more than twenty years. Many extraordinary anecdotes are told of his success, which was very great. A very large man once went to hear him, and placed himself immediately before the pulpit with the full design of interrupting him, and for that purpose made various strange gesticulations and used many contemptuous expressions. Not at all intimidated, the preacher addressed him personally in so powerful a manner that he fell down in the pew in a most violent perspiration. After the service had closed, he said, "I came to confuse this good man; but he has convinced me that I am indeed a lost sinner." This man lived an ornament to the gospel and died happy in Jesus. At another time, while he was standing upon a table and preaching in the open air to a great multitude, two men got under the table with the design of overturning it; but the word of God so powerfully impressed their hearts that they could not accomplish their purpose, and, after his sermon was ended, they confessed, with strong feelings of shame, what they had intended to do. Very many facts might be told of the same general character.

Other anecdotes, of an essentially different kind, are also related concerning him. Soon after he had commenced his annual visits to London, a lady travelled from that city to Everton to solicit his hand in marriage, assuring him that the Lord had revealed it to her that she was to become his wife. He was not a little surprised at her application and for such a purpose. He paused for a few moments, and then replied, "Madam, if the Lord had revealed it to you that you are to be my wife, surely he would also have revealed it to me that I was designed to be your husband; but, as no such revelation has been made to me, I cannot comply with your wishes." Of course the wealthy lady went away greatly disappointed. Berridge never married.

The following lines were written by this worthy man and posted on his clock :—

"Here my master bids me stand
And mark the time with faithful hand:
What is his will is my delight,—
To tell the hours by day and night.
Master, be wise, and learn of me
To serve thy God as I serve thee."

When age and its infirmities came on, he met them with unabated cheerfulness. He wrote, "My ears are now so dull they are not fit for conversation, and my eyes are so weak I can read but little and write less. Old Adam, who is the devil's darling, sometimes whispers in my ears, 'What will you do if you become deaf and blind?' I tell him I must think the more and pray the more, yea, and thank the Lord for eyes and ears enjoyed till I was seventy, and for the prospect of a better pair of eyes and ears when these are gone." In his seventy-sixth year he was seen to be near his end, and his curate said to him, "Jesus will soon call you up higher." His reply was, "Ay, ay, ay; higher, higher, higher!" His hymn-book "*Zion's Songs*" was published in the year 1785.

REV. G. W. BETHUNE, D.D.

A HYMN contained in the "*Parish Psalms and Hymns*," and which we think is destined to be much more widely known than it is at present, had a pleasant origin. It begins,—

"Oh, for the happy hour,"

and its subject is that of prayer for a revival of religion. Its author, the Rev. Dr. Bethune, of New York, went to his church a few minutes before the time of a devotional meeting, and while waiting for the arrival of his people, with a heart full of his subject, he took his pencil and on a loose scrap of paper poured out feelings which must meet a response in every Christian heart, and which will doubtless guide the prayers and praises of very many long after their writer has joined the worship of the Jerusalem above.

To this gentleman the Baptists are indebted for one of the very best of their denominational hymns,—

"We come to the fountain, we stand by the wave,"

which was written at the special request of the Rev. J. S. Holme, editor of the "*Baptist Hymn and Tune Book.*"

We may add here that Dr. Bethune was born in 1805, and that his ministry seems to have received its character from the dying words of his father, addressed to him and his brother-in-law, also in the ministry, "My sons, preach the gospel. Tell dying sinners of a Saviour. All the rest is but folly."

REV. THOMAS BLACKLOCK, D.D.

This remarkable man, author of the well-known and truly grand hymn,—

"Come, O my soul, in sacred lays,"

was the child of English parents, but born at Annan, in Scotland, in 1721. When only six months old, he lost his sight by smallpox, and suffered total blindness during his life of seventy years, dying in 1791. Notwithstanding this deprivation, he acquired a respectable knowledge of Greek, Latin, French, Italian, and theology, and became a considerable author. He was licensed to preach in the Church of Scotland, and created

D.D. by the University of Aberdeen in 1756. In 1762 he married a lady admirably adapted to promote his happiness. One of his friends says, "I have known him to dictate from thirty to forty verses as fast as I could write them; but, the moment he was at a loss for verse or a rhyme to his liking, he stopped altogether, and could very seldom be induced to finish what he had begun with so much ardor." The Rev. Joseph Spence, Professor of Poetry at the University of Oxford, says, "He never could dictate till he stood up; and, as his blindness made walking about without assistance inconvenient or dangerous to him, he fell insensibly into a vibratory sort of motion with his body, which increased as he warmed with his subject and was pleased with the conception of his mind." And Burke says, in his "*Sublime and Beautiful*," "Few men blessed with the most perfect sight can describe visual objects with more spirit and justness than this blind man."

REV. JAMES BODEN.

THIS excellent Congregational minister, the author of the well-known hymn,—

"Ye dying sons of men,"

was born in the city of Chester, England, in 1757, in the very house in which the eminent commentator Matthew Henry once resided. In the garden in which James

Boden first engaged in childish sports was an alcove or summer-house, in which it is said a large part of Henry's beautiful Commentary was written; and it was thought by his friends that the association had no small influence on the mind of young Boden, who at the age of sixteen professed faith in Christ. Having pursued the usual preparatory studies for the ministry at Homerton College, in 1796, after laboring elsewhere, he settled in the populous town of Sheffield, where he preached three times on every Sabbath till nearly seventy years of age. In 1839 he resigned his charge, and in 1841 was removed from earth, in his eighty-fifth year, having been sixty-nine years a member of the Church on earth.

The state of his mind in his last illness was that of sweet serenity and peace. A friend remarking that the sun shone very beautifully, he replied, with delightful emphasis,—

> "He is my Sun, though he forbear to shine:
> I dwell forever on his heart, forever he on mine."

REV. HORATIUS BONAR, D.D.

Of this gentleman, several of whose beautiful compositions are gradually coming into our books, we do not know very much. He is a native of Scotland, and was born about the year 1810. He is a prominent clergyman of the Free Church of his native land, and has already published several beautiful theological volumes, which are increasing in their usefulness and popularity. We hope that many years of success await him.

We believe that the wife of Dr. Bonar is sister to the late very excellent Mary Lundie Duncan.

REV. T. E. BOND, M.D.

THE beautiful hymn of two verses,—

"Father of spirits, hear our prayer,"

was written by Dr. Thomas E. Bond, an excellent Methodist Episcopal clergyman of our own country. The hymn is simply an extract from a long poem prepared by its author some years ago for a periodical published in Baltimore.

This worthy man, having passed the age of three-score and ten, died in March, 1856. Many of his latter years were devoted to the service of his denomination by the agency of the press, being an editor of one of their newspapers. An intimate friend says of him, "A warmer heart we never knew, nor one more finely tuned to sympathy,—more abounding in that charity which never faileth. With calm composure, when his work was done and the time of his departure was at hand, he awaited his call, and has left us the satisfactory assurance that, although we have one less with whom to take sweet counsel on earth, we have one more friend in heaven."

JOHN BOWDLER.

The hymn,—

"Children of God, who, faint and slow,"

and one or two others used in our churches, were written by a young English barrister, who published two octavo volumes in prose and verse, in 1818, and died in early life, leaving behind him a fragrant reputation. In many respects he bore a resemblance to the amiable Henry Kirke White.

JOHN BOWRING, LL.D.

This gentleman, most remarkably distinguished for the acquirement of languages, is an Englishman, born in 1792. He has been eminent as a philologist, as a political writer, for the occupancy of various political offices, and as a poet. He is a member of the Unitarian body, —though this would not be inferred from some of his hymns, especially the one,—

"In the cross of Christ I glory."

FREDERIKA BREMER.

Miss Bremer, as is well known, is a foreigner, and has never produced any work in the English language. Her productions are chiefly novels and tales,—though she has written a very readable narrative of her visit to this country. Her hymns are few in number, but pleasing in their character.

REV. JEHOIADA BREWER.

We have, in several of our books, a hymn,—

"Hail! sovereign love, which first began,"

which is a favorite in many of our prayer-meetings. It was almost the only hymn written by the late Rev. Jehoiada Brewer, who was born in Wales in 1752, and died as a Congregational minister in Birmingham in 1817. He was a profound theologian, a popular preacher, and an earnest man. He expressed an ardent wish, in his dying hours, that no memoir of him should be published: but this wish was not regarded; for in the following year the editors of a new London periodical met a general demand by printing a very able article concerning him. The original of the hymn to which we have referred contains nine verses. We remember his person and character with great interest, and can never forget the impressive manner in which he read hymns from the pulpit, or the tone and manner in which he would quote the remark of Dr. John Owen, "A man is before God what he is in the closet, *and no more!*"

REV. JOHN NEWTON BROWN, D.D.

A very few of the hymns written by this gentleman are to be found in our books. He is attached to the Baptist body, was born in New London, Conn., in 1803, and graduated at Madison University, at the age of twenty years. He has had charge of two or three churches; but ill health has long since compelled him to give up the pastorate. Dr. Brown has for many years past been devoted to Christian literature, editing, among other valuable works, "*The Encyclopedia of Religious Knowledge.*"

PHŒBE H. BROWN.

The writer of the beautiful hymn in most of our recent collections beginning,—

"I love to steal a while away,"

was a Christian female obliged to struggle hard to support a large family. She was in the habit, after the toils of the day were over, of retiring to a quiet and shady retreat,—

"Where none but God was near,"

for prayer. Her regular visits to this spot drew the attention of a neighboring lady of wealth and influence, who, in the presence of others, censured her, intimating that, instead of rambling out in the evening, she had better be at home with her children. Grieved that her hour's communion with God after the exhausting labors of the day should be construed into the neglect of her family, she sat down that evening with a babe in her arms, and wrote her "*Apology for her Midnight Rambles.*" When Dr. Nettleton was preparing his collection of hymns, a friend, looking over her manuscripts, found this gem, and obtained its insertion.

We believe that the Rev. S. R. Brown, the first American missionary to Japan, is a son of the lady of whom we have been writing. He is connected with the Dutch Reformed Church, and has already spent some years in missionary labors.

REV. SIMON BROWNE.

THE well-known hymn,—

"Come, gracious Spirit, heavenly Dove,"

was written by the Rev. Simon Browne, who was born in 1680, began to preach before he was twenty, was soon after settled over a large congregation in Portsmouth, and in 1716 removed to the Independent Church in the Old Jewry, London.

When Mr. Brown had been in London about seven years, he was attacked by a very singular malady, which never left him through life. He imagined that God, by a singular instance of his power, had, in a gradual manner, annihilated his *thinking* powers, and utterly divested him of consciousness. Nothing grieved him more than that he could not persuade others to think of him as he thought of himself. Several causes have been assigned as the origin of his disease,—one of which was, that once, when on a journey with a friend, they were attacked by a highwayman with loaded pistols. Mr. Browne, being a strong man, disarmed him, seized him by the collar, and they both fell to the ground. Mr. Browne was uppermost, and kept the man down while his friend ran for assistance. When that assistance arrived, the man was dead. From that sad hour Mr. Browne became a prey to the awful imagination which ever after haunted him. At the beginning of the disease he had frequent propensities to destroy himself; but later in life he became more calm. Even while in this state of mind he wrote an able Defence of Christianity, and several other books, yet still maintained that he had no power to *think.* He died, very greatly respected, at the close of 1732.

We may add to this sketch the fact that the Dedication to Browne's "*Defence of Christianity*" is to be found, as a most remarkable curiosity, under his name, in "*The Encyclopedia Britannica.*" In some respects his mental delusion was more extraordinary than that of Cowper; yet, singular as the fact may seem, in none of his productions can there be found any thing exceptionable; so that Toplady very properly said of him that, "Instead of having no soul, he wrote, and reasoned, and prayed as if he had *two.*"

Since writing the above, we have read Mr. Milner's

very able volume of "*The Life, Times, and Correspondence of Dr. Watts*," from which we learn that, in a paper yet existing in the handwriting of that eminent man, it is stated that, after Browne became thus lamentably diseased, he not only wrote the production to which we have already referred, in opposition to Collins and Woolston, but also published a work on the Trinity, compiled a Dictionary, and prepared the Exposition on the First Epistle to the Corinthians in the continuation of Matthew Henry's great work.

ELIZABETH BARRETT BROWNING.

THIS lady, who has several hymns in our books, deservedly occupies a high place in English poetical literature. Her first publication was issued in her maiden name of Barrett, in 1838, being "*The Seraphim, and other Poems*." Several other English works have since proceeded from her pen, as well as one or two classical translations. What Dr. G. W. Bethune says of her poetry in general appears to us to apply especially to her hymns:—"Mrs. Browning is singularly bold and adventurous. Her wing carries her, without faltering at their obscurity, into the cloud and the mist, where not seldom we fail to follow her, but are tempted, while we admire the honesty of her enthusiasm, to believe that she utters what she herself has but dimly perceived. Much of this, however, arises from her disdain of carefulness."

In early life Miss Barrett was afflicted with the rupture of a blood-vessel on the lungs, and the consequences for several years were threatening. Partially recovering her health, in 1847 she was married to Mr. Browning, and still pursues the study and translation of Greek works and the production of beautiful poetry.

JOHN H. BRYANT.

This gentleman, a native of Cummington, Mass., and brother of William C. Bryant, was born in 1807. At nineteen he wrote a poem, "*My Native Village*," which was published in the "*United States Review and Literary Gazette*," of which his brother was then one of the editors. He removed, some years since, to cultivate the soil of Illinois. His poetical productions from time to time continue to grace our periodicals. We are not aware of the existence of many of his hymns; but one or two on Liberty as a Birthright of Man are to be found in some of our books. The late Dr. Rufus W. Griswold says of him, "He is a lover of nature, and describes minutely and effectively. To him the wind and the streams are ever musical, and the forests and the prairies clothed with beauty. His versification is easy and correct; and his writings show him to be a man of refined taste and kindly feelings, and to have a mind stored with the best learning."

WILLIAM CULLEN BRYANT.

THIS gentleman has furnished several hymns to some of our books; nor can this be matter of surprise, as he is one of the most eminent of our poets, though in our judgment he does not excel in lyrical composition. He was born at Cummington, Mass., in 1797, graduated at Williams College in 1812, and engaged in the profession of the law. In 1827 he entered on his duties as editor of the New York Evening Post,—an office he has ever since filled.

Several years ago a beautiful sketch of his genius appeared in one of our periodicals; and, though we fear the *coloring* of its *religious* character is too high, we will copy a short extract:—"No other living poet has half his imagination or half his compressed energy of conception and execution. And over all and through all his poetry, its life and soul, glows and lives a spirit of meditation and reflection, the very incarnation of truth and goodness. Religion, pure and undefiled, is the element of his genius and the life of his poetry."

WILLIAM BUDDEN.

THE hymn,—

"Come, let our voices join,"

was written by Mr. William Budden, and was first published, with the signature of W. B., in the London

"*Evangelical Magazine*" for 1795, entitled "*A Hymn composed for the Use of the Congregation and Sunday-School Children belonging to the Rev. Mr. Ashburner's Meeting, Poole, Dorset.*"

REV. W. M. BUNTING.

THIS gentleman, the author of the hymn,—

"My Sabbath suns may all have set,"

and several others, is the eldest son of the late eminent Dr. Jabez Bunting, one of the most distinguished of the Wesleyan Methodist preachers in England. The son is quite as remarkable as his father for independence of mind, for a clear exhibition of scriptural truth, and for a benevolent expenditure of the ample wealth which God has placed in his hands. He is tall and thin, of delicate, almost sickly appearance, and far from having a robust constitution. He has a fine, benevolent countenance, a noble, commanding forehead, bare of hair to a considerable elevation, and is apparently quite unable to endure the fatigues of his calling. He is, moreover, a man of fine catholic spirit, and, as we know from experience, warm in his friendships. He has not written much beside hymns,—and many of these have been published anonymously; but nearly all of them are perfect gems, and are entirely free from the spirit of sectarianism.

REV. JOHN BUNYAN.

"Glorious John," it must be confessed, had few talents of an eminent hymn-writer, though we suspect he had more than he has usually received credit for. His compositions of this order, we admit, are not to be found "in the books." There is, however, a short composition in the second part of his immortal "*Progress*" which has very long been used in some of the Baptist churches in England at the admission of members, sometimes with very happy effect. If the reader has not the volume at hand, he will be pleased to see it transcribed:—

"Let the Most Blessed be my guide,
If it's his blessed will,
Up to his gate, into his fold,
Up to his holy hill.

"And let him never suffer me
To swerve or turn aside
From his free grace and holy ways,
Whate'er shall me betide.

"And let him gather those of mine
That I have left behind:
Lord, make them pray they may be thine,
With all their heart and mind."

REV. GEORGE BURDER.

The well-known hymn,—

"Lord, dismiss us with thy blessing,"

was written by the Rev. George Burder, who was born in London in 1752, and died pastor of a Congregational

Church in that city in 1832. He was apprenticed to an engraver, but, having a literary taste, he learned short-hand, and so reported the last sermons delivered in London by the Rev. George Whitefield. He was ordained at twenty-five, and was pastor successively in Lancaster, Coventry, and London. He was among the founders of the Religious Tract Society and the London Missionary Society, to the latter of which he was for many years the gratuitous secretary. He was also for many years the editor of the "*Evangelical Magazine*," as well as the pastor of a church. The hymn to which we have referred was first issued in a supplement to Dr. Watts's Psalms and Hymns, which Mr. Burder published about the commencement of this century.

BISHOP BURGESS.

This eminent scholar, the author of several of our most evangelical hymns, was born at Providence, R.I., in 1809, and graduated at Brown University; and, after being some time a tutor in that university, he went to Europe, and studied at Göttingen, Bonn, and Berlin. After holding the rectorship of Christ Church, Hartford, Conn., for thirteen years, he was in 1847 consecrated Bishop of Maine, and Rector of Gardiner, in that State. Among his principal works are "*The Book of Psalms in English Verse*," and "*Pages from the Ecclesiastical History of New England.*"

REV. RICHARD BURNHAM.

This gentleman, the author of a hymn used in many of our conference and prayer meetings,—

"Jesus, thou art the sinner's friend,"

was born in 1749, and in 1780 he became pastor of a Baptist church in London, and ultimately settled with another church, of the same denomination, in Grafton Street in that city, where, after about thirty years' labor, he died in 1810. His life was a checkered scene of popularity and trials; but his biographer tells us he "died in peace."

In the preface to his hymn-book, Mr. Burnham says to the members of his church, "Your pastor is willing to own that he is the unworthiest of the unworthy; yet, unworthy as he is, he humbly trusts, through rich grace, he has in some measure found that the dear bosom of the atoning Lamb is the abiding-place of his immortal soul."

ROBERT BURNS.

We have a very few hymns from the pen of this gifted man in some of our books; and but very few did he write suitable for the holy purpose of praising God. We have no disposition to depreciate his extraordinary talents, but he never even laid claim to a single moral qualification for a poet of God's sanctuary. We most love the hymns with the spirits of whose authors we can hold fellowship as we sing the overflowings of their souls.

Chambers, in his "*Life of Burns*," says, "It is a remarkable fact that the mass of the poetry which has given this extraordinary man his principal fame burst from him in a comparatively small space of time,—certainly not exceeding fifteen months. It began to flow of a sudden, and it ran in one impetuous, brilliant stream, till it seemed to have become, comparatively speaking, exhausted."

Alas that of this man his first biographer and most charitable friend was compelled to write, "Only a few months from his death he would proceed from a sick-room to dine at a tavern, return home about three o'clock in a very cold morning, benumbed and intoxicated, and by that process he hastened or developed the disease which laid him in his grave." He knew only the *poetry* of religion.

THOMAS CAMPBELL,

THE author of two or three hymns, including,—

"When Jordan hushed his waters still,"

was the son of a merchant in Glasgow, where he was born in 1777. In 1798 he published his "*Pleasures of Hope*," for the copyright of which he received twenty pounds; but when the work acquired popularity his publisher generously paid him fifty pounds on each edition. His "*Gertrude of Wyoming,*" "*Specimens of British Poets,*" and several prose works, followed each other in due course, and commanded high respect for their correctness and beauty. Mr. Campbell was often called on by visitors from the United States, who admired his exact and beautiful description of our own Wyoming Valley. He died at Boulogne in 1844. Mr. Campbell did not, we believe, profess evangelical religion.

REV. JOHN CAWOOD.

THIS evangelical clergyman of the Church of England was educated at St. John's Hall, in the University of Oxford, after which he became Perpetual Curate at Bewdley. Besides his hymns, he has published "*On the Dissenting Controversy,*" and three volumes of sermons, which Bickersteth describes as "forcible, impressive, and evangelical."

REV. RICHARD CECIL.

WE have in some of our books a short hymn beginning,—

"Cease here longer to detain me,"

which was written by the Rev. Richard Cecil, once curate to the Rev. John Newton, of London, and afterward the predecessor of Dr. Wilson, the late Bishop of

Calcutta, as minister of St. John's Chapel, Bedford Row, also in London. The whole hymn, extending to seven or eight verses, was written on the death of an infant at the dawn of the day, the motto being the language of the angel wrestling with Jacob, "Let me go, for the day breaketh."

Mr. Cecil was born in London in 1748, and died in 1810. He was a highly-respectable author, but shone most brightly in the pulpit. His style of preaching partook largely of originality and pious feeling. His ideas, like the rays of the sun, carried their own light with them. Images and illustrations were at his command, and rendered his discourses not only instructive but fascinating. They were living pictures.

THOMAS VON CELANO.

THE celebrated Latin hymn "*Dies Iræ*" was written in the thirteenth century by Thomas Von Celano, a Minorite. It has very often been translated into the English language, first by the old poet Crashaw soon after his secession from the Protestant Church, and since then by not less than seventy others, some of whose versions are noticed at great length by Dr. W. R. Williams in his valuable volume of "*Miscellanies.*" We are not aware, however, of any version of this hymn in our commonly-used hymn-books except the greatly-condensed one by Sir Walter Scott,—

"That day of wrath, that dreadful day," etc.,

which his son-in-law and biographer, Mr. Lockhart, says was often on his lips during his last sickness.

Tholuck, the distinguished German preacher, had once preached in the University church on the repentance and pardon of the thief on the cross; and of that occasion, in a note to his printed sermon, the preacher says, "This is the second time that this hymn of the University church-service has been sung to the very excellent tune composed by the music-director, Mr. Naue. The impression, especially that which was made by the last words as sung by the University choir alone, will be forgotten by no one." Lord Roscommon, it is said, died while repeating with great energy and devotion two lines of his own translation of this remarkable hymn,—

"My God, my Father and my Friend,
Do not forsake me in my end."

And Dr. Park, of Andover, tells us of a clergyman of our own country who could not hear it sung in his own church without tears.

Sir Walter Scott, writing to a brother poet, Crabbe, says of this majestic hymn, "To my Gothic ear, the Stabat Mater, the *Dies Iræ,* and some other of the hymns of the Catholic Church, are more solemn and affecting than the fine, classical poetry of Buchanan. The one has the gloomy dignity of the Gothic Church, and reminds us constantly of the worship to which it is dedicated; the other is more like a pagan temple, recalling to our memory the classical and fabulous deities." It is said that Dr. Samuel Johnson could never, on account of his tears, repeat this composition in the original. And we scarcely need to add that upon the *Dies Iræ* Mozart founded his celebrated Requiem,—in the composition of which his excitement became so great as to hasten his death. Many of the most eminent musical celebrities have "sought to marry its poetry to immortal melody."

It is said that the original draft of the *Dies Iræ* was found in a box belonging to Celano after his death. He died in 1253.

Since writing the preceding paragraphs, we have observed in one or two of our hymn-books a very greatly-condensed translation of the *Dies Iræ*, in four verses, by an anonymous hand. It begins,—

"On that great, that awful day."

It is beautifully and effectively executed.

REV. JOHN CENNICK.

"JESUS, thy blood and righteousness,"

has long been a favorite hymn among all classes of evangelical Christians; and probably this is one reason why its authorship has been disputed. In many of our books it is attributed to Charles Wesley. Mr. Creamer contends that it is a translation from a German hymn of twenty verses, written by Count Zinzendorf, and translated by *John* Wesley; but it has been more commonly regarded as the composition of John Cennick, by turns a follower of Wesley, then of Whitefield, and finally dying in the fellowship and ministry of the Moravians. It has been very much abridged.

This hymn was a great favorite with the late Rev. Rowland Hill; and perhaps the history of the Church presents few scenes of deeper interest than the fact that, when the corpse of that extraordinary clergyman was being lowered into its final resting-place, under his own pulpit, in the presence of assembled thousands bathed in tears, the second verse of this hymn was sung, in slow and solemn tones:—

"When from the dust of death I rise
To claim my mansion in the skies,
E'en then shall this be all my plea,—
Jesus hath lived and died for me."

Cennick wrote also the hymns,—

"Jesus, my all, to heaven is gone,"
"Children of the heavenly King,"

and several others.

REV. E. H. CHAPIN, D.D.

THIS well-known writer of several popular hymns is a celebrated Universalist clergyman. He was born in the State of New York in 1814, and, after having studied for the law, entered the ministry, and has officiated as pastor of Universalist societies at Richmond, Va., Charlestown, Mass., Boston, and New York. In addition to a collection of hymns, he has published several volumes in prose, and is well known as a distinguished and popular lecturer.

CHARLEMAGNE.

THIS great man is usually supposed to be the author of the "*Veni Creator,*" the translation of which,—

"Creator Spirit, by whose aid,"

can scarcely be unknown to the reader. The fact of Charlemagne being its author has, however, been doubted by Mohnike, who says the emperor could not have had sufficient acquaintance with the Latin tongue to write so classical a composition. But he who was the patron of Latin letters and the friend of Alcuin, and who pardoned Paulus Diaconus for his conspiracy to murder him because he would not cut off one who wrote so elegantly, may fairly be supposed capable of dictating a Latin hymn,—though he was probably indebted to some better scribe than himself to write it down.

While we thus write, it is but justice to say that Mohnike's opinion is never to be treated with lightness. He believes the hymn to have been written by Gregory the Great, Bishop of Rome, A.D. 590, who is described by Neander as the last of the classical doctors of the Church. He was a man of great piety and learning, though of course led away by some of the errors which had already flooded the Church.

REV. INGRAM COBBIN.

Our hymn-books contain a very few of the compositions of our old personal friend, to whose memory the pen of biography is largely indebted. He was born of humble and pious parentage in the city of London in 1777, and in early life was attracted by the charms both of religion and of learning. Some verses which he then composed gained the attention of the Rev. Matthew Wilks, who introduced him to the Congregational College then at Hoxton. In 1802 he was ordained to the ministry, and, though in feeble health, he laboriously and usefully exerted himself as a pastor. After some years, however, he relinquished permanently, as was supposed, the ministry, through the failure of his health; but after a time hope of usefulness in this department of holy labor returned, and he accepted a call from a church at Crediton, where he was installed, but could not deliver a single sermon after that apparently joyous event. Relinquishing his fond labors, he became the founder and for many years the secretary of the [London] Home Missionary Society; but sickness compelled him to relinquish this also in 1828. His mental energies being yet unimpaired, he devoted himself to the compilation of a number of invaluable biblical works, including his "*Domestic Bible,*" well known and esteemed among us. He died in his seventy-fourth year, in 1851.

REV. W. B. COLLYER, D.D., LL.D.

THE hymn,

"Return, O wanderer, return,"

and many others in our hymn-books, are the compositions of the Rev. W. B. Collyer, D.D., LL.D., who died in 1854, and who for more than half a century was by far the most popular Nonconformist minister in England. He was almost the only dissenting minister heard by royalty,—to whom, as to all others, he preached in the most faithful manner the doctrines of the cross, in a style combining simple elegance, fervent feeling, and an indomitable adherence to "the truth as in Jesus."

Among the many volumes which in the early and middle stages of his life proceeded from Dr. Collyer's pen, was a volume of hymns selected and arranged for public worship, containing not a few of great beauty written by himself. In addition to these, he wrote very many which were never printed. Nearly to the close of his ministry, after his Sunday morning sermons, in imitation of the excellent Dr. Doddridge, he always read a hymn written during the preceding week founded on his text, which was sung by his congregation, and by many of them copied as he read two lines at a time to enable them to sing. Not a few of these he gave at different times, from feelings of warm friendship, to the writer of this volume, which in various periodicals were given to the public. May peace rest on his happy memory!

JOSIAH CONDER.

This excellent writer of hymns and editor of the English Congregational Hymn-Book was a member of the Congregational body, and was distinguished through a long life for sound learning, fine taste, earnest piety, and untiring industry. He was born in 1790, and died in London in 1855. For many years he was the editor of the "*Eclectic Review*," and was thus associated with Robert Hall, John Foster, Ralph Wardlaw, and other distinguished men of that day. Over the grave of this worthy man we drop a grateful tear, remembering him as a good occasional preacher, a sweet poet, and a cordial friend. The Christian and literary friends of Mr. Conder have recently erected a monument to his memory, at an expense of more than five hundred dollars.

REV. THOMAS COTTERILL,

The author of the well-known missionary hymn,—

"O'er the realms of pagan darkness,"

and of one or two others used among us, was an excellent minister of the Episcopal Church, settled in Sheffield, where also resided his intimate personal friend, James Montgomery, who says of him, "Good Mr. Cotterill and I bestowed a great deal of care and labor in the compilation of '*The Sheffield Hymn-Book*,' clipping, interlining, and remodelling hymns of all sorts as we thought we could correct the sentiment or improve the expression. We so altered some of Cowper's that the poet would hardly know them." Every one knows that Montgomery lived to complain sadly of this conduct in reference to some of his own hymns, calling it "the cross by which every author of a hymn may expect to be tested, at the pleasure of any Christian brother, however incompetent."

NATHANIEL COTTON, M.D.

THIS gentleman is supposed to be the author of the truly experimental hymn,—

"Affliction is a stormy deep."

He was an English physician, born in 1707, and died in 1788. He was remarkably successful in the treatment of insanity, keeping a private asylum for such patients at St. Alban's, having, among many others, the amiable poet Cowper, who says of him, "He is truly a philosopher, according to my judgment of the character, every tittle of his knowledge in natural subjects being connected in his mind with the firm belief in an omnipotent agent." His works in prose and verse were printed in two duodecimo volumes in 1791.

WILLIAM COWPER.

THE facts of Cowper's history are too well known to render it necessary that we should here detail them. He was the son of an English clergyman, who was a chaplain to George the Second and rector of Berkhampstead, where William was born in 1731. He grew up so timid and nervous that he was never able to engage in any profession, became deranged, and was confined in an asylum for many months. He was an exquisite poet; and poetry became his almost constant occupation till his death in 1800.

The favorite residences of the poet at Olney and Weston, the houses in which his chief labors were performed, are still objects of interest, not only to Englishmen, but to Americans visiting that land. The one at Olney still stands in the same ruinous state in which he so humorously described it; and the parlor is now occupied by a girls' school. The summer-house in the garden, in which he used to sit conning his verses, also remains, the walls being covered with the names of visitors. His residence in the neighboring village of Weston has been much altered, but is still beautiful, with a profusion of roses around it.

Where is the Christian who has not read and sung with holy profit and delight Cowper's hymn,—

"God moves in a mysterious way"?

Its original title—"*Light Shining out of Darkness*"—had reference to its remarkable origin. When under the influence of the fits of mental derangement to which he was subject, he most unhappily but firmly believed that the divine will was that he should drown himself in a particular part of the river Ouse, some two or three miles from his residence at Olney. He one evening called for a post-chaise from one of the hotels in the town, and ordered the driver to take him to that spot, which he readily undertook to do, as he well knew it. On this occasion, however, several hours were consumed in seeking it, and utterly in vain. The man was at length most reluctantly compelled to admit that he had entirely lost his road. The snare was thus broken: Cowper escaped the temptation: he returned to his home, and immediately sat down and wrote a hymn which has ministered comfort to thousands, and will probably yet afford consolation to thousands of others, even for generations to come.

Mr. Montgomery says of this hymn that it "is a lyric of high tone and character, and rendered awfully interesting by the circumstances under which it was written,—in the twilight of departing reason."

Every one knows that the admirable hymn,—

"Oh for a closer walk with God,"

was also written by the amiable Cowper, when under much darkness of soul, in one of the intervals between his seasons of deep melancholy. Every Christian who has made even but little progress in the divine life can testify to the correctness of its experimental theology; and we would hope that few persons are disposed to imitate Dr. Southey, who intimates that the composition of the "*Olney Hymns*," in connection with his friend the Rev. John Newton, tended to bring back the renewal of his insanity in 1773. Nay, after blaming Newton for what he regarded as his injudicious conduct in having engaged Cowper in such a deeply-interesting employment, he quotes two verses of this hymn as a proof of his supposed danger of a return to insanity:—

"Where is the blessedness I knew
When first I saw the Lord?
Where is the soul-refreshing view
Of Jesus and his word?

"What peaceful hours I once enjoyed!
How sweet their memory still!
But they have left an aching void
The world can never fill."

Truly has the apostle said, "The natural man receiveth not the things of the Spirit of God, for they are foolishness unto him; neither can he know them, because they are [only] spiritually discerned."

The beautiful hymn of Cowper,—

"How blest thy creature is, O God!"

is said by his biographers to have been the very first he

wrote on his recovery at St. Alban's from his second attack of insanity. He entitled it the "*Happy Change;*" and no one can read it, with its origin in view, without being struck with its beauty.

But the second strain in which he poured forth the grateful feelings of his heart,—

"Far from the world, O Lord, I flee,"

is perhaps sweeter still. Indeed, as Dr. Cheever remarks, "it is beyond comparison more perfect,—it is exquisitely, sacredly, devoutly beautiful."

Dr. Cheever throws additional beauty on this composition by describing to us the location in which it was written. He had gone from St. Alban's to Huntingdon, passing his whole time on the way in silent communion with God. He says, "It is impossible to tell with how delightful a sense of his protection and fatherly care of me it pleased the Almighty to favor me during the whole of my journey." Left alone by his brother for the first time among strangers, his heart began to sink within him, and he wandered forth into the fields, melancholy and desponding, at the close of the day, but, like Isaac at eventide, found his heart so powerfully drawn to God that, having found a secluded spot beneath a bank of shrubbery and verdure, he kneeled down and poured forth his whole soul in prayer and praise. It pleased the Saviour to hear him, and to grant him at once a renewed sense of his presence, deliverance from his fears, and a sweet assurance that, wherever his lot might be cast, the God of all consolation would still be with him.

The next day was the Sabbath, and he attended church for the first time since his recovery,—that is, for nearly two years,—and found the house of God to be the very gate to heaven. He could scarcely restrain his emotions during the service, so fully did he see the beauty of the glory of the Lord. A person with whom he afterward became acquainted sat near him, devoutly engaged in worship; and Cowper loved him for the earnestness of his manner. He says, "While he was singing the psalms I looked at him; and, observing him intent upon his holy employment, I could not help saying in my heart, with much emotion, 'The Lord bless you for praising Him whom my soul loveth!'"

After church he immediately hastened to the solitary place where he had found such sacred enjoyment in prayer the day before. "How," he exclaims, "shall I express what the Lord did for me, except by saying that he made all his goodness to pass before me? I seemed to speak to him face to face, as a man converseth with his friend, except that my speech was only in tears of joy, and groanings which cannot be uttered. I could say indeed, with Jacob, not how *dreadful*, but how *lovely* is this place!—this is none other than the house of God."

There, in this sacred spot and in the deep bliss of such experience, is the very locality and atmosphere of that perfectly beautiful hymn. There was the "calm retreat," there the unwitnessed praise, there the holy communion with the Saviour by which he prepared his servant to pour forth the gratitude of a redeemed spirit in strains which will be sung by the Church on earth till the whole Church sing in heaven.

We may add here that probably the happiest period of Cowper's whole life was from 1765, the time of his first recovery from insanity, till 1773, the time of its recurrence. During this period he composed his portion of the "*Olney Hymns.*" Dr. Cheever well says, "If Cowper had never given to the Church on earth but a single score of those exquisite breathings of a pious heart and creations of his own genius, it had been a bequest worth a life of suffering to accomplish. The dates, or nearly such, of some of those pieces, were preserved, so that we are enabled to trace them to the frames and circumstances of the writer's mind and heart, and to see in them an exact reflection of his own experience."

We have, in many of our collections, hymns by Cowper beginning,—

"Oh, most delightful hour by man,"
"He lives who lives to God alone,"

and others which had their origin in a way alike complimentary to Cowper and useful to many. The power and charm of his good sense and simplicity, as well as the tenderness of his poetry, were acknowledged when John Cox, the clerk of All Saints' parish in Northampton, a few miles from Weston, came to him with a second application for some mortuary verses to be printed with his annual Christmas "bill of mortality." Cowper told him there must be plenty of poets at Northampton, and referred him particularly to his namesake, Mr. Cox, the statuary, as a successful wooer of the muse. The clerk made answer that all this was very true, and he had already borrowed help from him, adding, "But alas, sir, Mr. Cox is a gentleman of much reading, and the people of our town do not well understand him. He has written for me, but nine in ten of us were stone-blind to his meaning." Cowper felt all the force of this equivocal compliment: his mortified vanity came near refusing, if the merit of his own verses was considered by the *smallness* of his reading; but, finding that the poor clerk had walked over to Weston on purpose to implore his assistance, and was in considerable distress, he good-naturedly consented, and supplied the clerk's mortality-bill with his beautiful verses for several years.

Perhaps the beautiful composition by Cowper,—

"No longer I follow a sound,"

is to be found in more of the English hymn-books than our own. Its origin shows how the amiable poet loved, even in his hours of social amusement, to dwell on tender devotion and pathetic solemnity. His cousin, Lady Austen, was fond of playing on the harpsichord; and, to suit several of her favorite airs, he wrote Christian hymns. The air "*My fond shepherds of late*" was in our own early days a special favorite in many parties, and Cowper's lines were considered remarkably well adapted to it.

Cowper's own account, in a letter to his friend Joseph Hill, Esq., in 1789, of the origin of his beautiful Sunday-school hymn,—

"Hear, Lord, the song of praise and prayer,"

will be read with pleasure:—"My friend the vicar of the next parish [Olney] engaged me, the day before yesterday, to furnish him by next Sunday with a hymn to be sung on occasion of his preaching to the children of the Sunday-school,—of which hymn I have not yet produced a syllable."

The well-known and much-admired hymn of Cowper,—

"To Jesus, the crown of my hope,"

is not to be found in the "*Olney Hymns*," as it was not written till after the early editions of that work had been published. There can be no doubt of its being the production of his pen, or that it was the last hymn he ever wrote.

To very many of our readers it will be pleasant to read a line or two relating to Cowper from the pen of the world-renowned theologian, Andrew Fuller:—"At Olney he continued for a number of years in the enjoyment of religious pleasures to a degree seldom known; uniting in social prayer-meetings with Mr. Newton and his friends, to the wonder and admiration of all that heard him. I knew a person who heard him pray frequently at these meetings, and have heard him say, 'Of all the men that I ever heard pray, no one equalled Mr. Cowper.'"

The reader who remembers that the "*Olney Hymns*," the joint compositions of Newton and Cowper, were written for these very prayer-meetings, will see the connection of this extract with the design of our volume.

REV. A. C. COXE, D.D.

THIS gentleman, who has favored us with several original hymns, besides others translated from the German, was born in Mendham, New Jersey, 1818, and graduated at the University of New York. He has acquired great reputation for classical and poetical talents, and has already published many valuable works, especially of a poetical character. Dr. Coxe is connected with the Episcopal Church.

REV. W. CROSSWELL, D.D.

SEVERAL beautiful hymns have been given us from the pen of this excellent clergyman of the Episcopal Church. He was born in 1804, and was rector of Christ's Church, Boston, St. Peter's Church, Auburn, in the State of New York, and afterward became rector of the Church of the Advent in Boston, where he died in 1851. He was a scholar, and possessed a fine taste in literature. Among his poems are several of remarkable gracefulness and sweetness.

The death of Dr. Crosswell was solemn and affecting.

While engaged in the public Sabbath-afternoon service, at the conclusion of the last collect, instead of rising from his knees, he sank upon the floor, whence he was removed to his own house, where he soon after ceased to breathe. His memoir and remains were published, after his decease, in New York.

Among the compositions of Dr. Crosswell was the beautiful hymn,—

"Lord, lead the way the Saviour went,"

which was written for an anniversary of the Howard Benevolent Society in the city of Boston.

ROBERT CRUTTENDEN,

The author of the hymn,—

"Let others boast their ancient line,"

and several others in our older books, was a correspondent and friend of the Rev. Dr. Doddridge, the Rev. James Hervey, and Lady Huntingdon. He resided in London, and his great intelligence and generous hospitality rendered his house the frequent resort of many of the *literati* of that day. One of his grandsons was, a few years since, Archdeacon of London.

Though Mr. Cruttenden was educated for the ministry, and often in early life preached for his uncle, the Rev. Robert Bragge, of Lime St., London, he renounced that profession, conscious of his entire destitution of genuine piety. Indeed, the happy event of his conversion did not take place till his fifty-second year, under the powerful ministry of the distinguished John Cennick,—the account of which he afterward published, with a preface by Whitefield. He died in 1763, aged seventy-three. When writing to Mr. Keen, Whitefield says, "Mr. Cruttenden, I find, is gone. God be praised that he went off so comfortably! May our expiring hour be like his!"

REV. J. W. CUNNINGHAM.

THIS truly venerable clergyman of the Church of England was the author of the hymn,—

"Dear is the hallowed morn to me,"

which has elevated the devotion of thousands on the Lord's day morning. Like the rest of his hymns, it is highly evangelical. We remember, some forty years ago, when he did not cherish the scripturally affectionate feelings toward his dissenting brethren which now glow in his soul, but when controversial publications indicated his displeasure that they forsook his church and cherished "the religion of barns." Nearness to Christ has brought him nearer to his brethren; and often since that period has he co-operated in the common cause of Christ with all who love Him. For many years Mr. Cunningham was engaged as Head Master of Harrow School, in preparing young men for college; and, when he shall be called away from earth, hundreds of these shall unite in shedding a tear of grateful love over his dust, with not a few who have communed with his spirit as they have sung his hymns.

REV. S. S. CUTTING.

This gentleman, now a professor in the University of Rochester, has long been a marked man as a preacher, an author, and a journalist among the Baptists. His hymns, which are not numerous, are good, and lead us to wish that we had more of them. As Professor Cutting has not yet advanced beyond the meridian of life, we may cherish the hope of our wish being gratified.

REV. THOMAS DALE.

Our books contain a very few hymns from the pen of this clergyman of the Church of England, the son of a respectable bookseller in London, who removed with the other members of his family to this country, leaving Thomas under the care of his maternal uncles. He received a fine education in Christ's Hospital, London, and went to the University at Cambridge in 1818, taking his bachelor's degree in 1823. Here he devoted himself to general literature, and published his first poem, "*The Widow of Nain,*" in 1819. His intellect is of a high order, his theology entirely evangelical, and his pastoral assiduity beyond all praise.

The poetry of Mr. Dale is elegant. While it has no majestic flow, it resembles a beautiful rivulet in a delightful landscape: it runs smooth, is always clear, and sometimes sparkles in the sunlight. We never think of Mr. Dale or his compositions without pleasure.

REV. PRESIDENT DAVIES.

THE well-known admirable preacher, Samuel Davies, a native of Newcastle, Delaware, who succeeded President Edwards at Princeton in 1759, wrote several excellent hymns, one of which,—

"Great God of wonders, all thy ways,"

was long extensively used both in this country and in Europe. It is true that he was more remarkable as a preacher than a poet; but we cannot forbear an expression of regret that this truly evangelical hymn has given place to some very far inferior. He ended a life of great usefulness in 1761, at the early age of thirty-six years.

REV. ELIEL DAVIS.

ABOUT the year 1824 we became acquainted with this young man, the son of a gentleman who held in the church we served the office of deacon, and who was also the schoolmaster of John B. Gough, the popular lecturer on temperance. Soon after that period we commenced, for the young people of our congregation, a monthly magazine in manuscript, prepared chiefly by the young people themselves. While studying for the ministry, Eliel Davis often wrote for the "*Mutual Instructor*," and among other papers was the hymn,—

"From every earthly pleasure."

The editor of a popular London magazine paying us a visit, we showed it to him, and he was so well pleased with it that he copied it for his own periodical; and, having thus attracted the attention of hymn-collectors, a part of the composition has appeared in hymn-books both in Europe and America. Certainly neither its writer nor first editor imagined the honor to which it was destined. We are sorry to say that in early life our talented friend was suddenly called from his labors to his eternal rest,—not, however, without several years' successful labor in the ministry of Divine truth.

REV. DAVID DENHAM.

The well-known hymn called "*Sweet Home*," and beginning,—

"Mid scenes of confusion and creature complaints,"

was written by the Rev. David Denham, an English

Baptist minister, who died a very few years ago. He was originally connected with the congregation of the Rev. Dr. Hawker, and, having become a Baptist, entered the ministry, and labored in Margate, London, and Cheltenham. He edited a hymn-book bearing his own name, but wrote most of his poetry, like "Sweet Home," for some of the religious magazines of England.

REV. DAVID DICKSON.

Often has the question been asked, Who wrote the well-known quaint but beautiful hymn,—

"Jerusalem, my happy home,"

which James Montgomery has spoken of as one of the finest in our language? It is a great favorite, and deservedly so, for it is really a very beautiful composition. It probably appeared for the first time in a collection of hymns published by Montgomery himself; and, in spite of all that he says to the contrary, we have heard it strenuously though strangely maintained that he was its author. It appears, with remarkable variations, in a volume published in 1693, by Burkitt, the Expositor of the New Testament; but the fact that David Dickson, of Edinburgh, who died in 1662, had long before printed it, as containing 248 lines, makes it impossible that it should be Burkitt's, and much less Montgomery's. A manuscript of about half of it, with considerable variations, as, "*A Song made by F. B. P.,—to the Tune Diana,*" proves that it did not originate with Dickson. The fact is that, like several other admirable hymns, it may be traced to some of the Latin compositions of the middle or earlier ages,—thus showing how even the darkest times may contribute to the worship of the Church in all future ages.

It is worthy of remark, after all this, that our modern hymns, though like the old ones in spirit, feeling, and manner, have scarcely a line in common with them.

We are reminded here of the fact that in Scotland this hymn, in the version of Dickson, is known in nearly every house and sung in almost every family; nor is this without good results. A few years ago, a Presbyterian minister in New Orleans was sent for to attend the death-bed of a young man. On his arrival, he found that the dying man was a native of North Britain, as well as himself; but he endeavored to introduce religious conversation with him without success; and, the more he endeavored to accomplish his object, the more determined appeared the dying man not to converse with him. After many attempts, the clergyman, almost in despair, left the bedside, walked toward the window, and half unconsciously began to sing,—

"Jerusalem, my happy home."

This effectually attracted the attention of the dying youth, who at once called out, "My dear mother used to sing that hymn," and, bursting into tears, acknowledged his sinfulness, and inquired the way of salvation, —which it was hoped he indeed found. Some years had passed away since he heard that hymn sung; but its words recalled all the scenes and feelings of home, and produced results which, it is probable, that mother had never thought of.

BISHOP DOANE.

THIS gentleman, the Protestant Bishop of New Jersey, who has contributed,—

'Thou art the Way, to thee alone,"

and two or three other hymns for the use of Christian worshippers, was born in Trenton, New Jersey, in 1799. He graduated at Union College, Schenectady, when nineteen years old, and immediately afterward commenced the study of theology. He was consecrated Bishop of his native State in 1832, founded St. Mary's Hall in 1827, and Burlington College in 1846. He published a volume of poems entitled "*Songs by the Way,*" and many sermons and tracts. He died in 1859.

REV. PHILIP DODDRIDGE, D.D.

WHO has not been charmed with the devotional hymns of this excellent Protestant Dissenting minister, so many of which are found in our best books? Dr. Stoughton has well described them as "relics choicely transparent and truly rich." These valued productions were not published by himself, but edited, with notes explaining what were then considered "hard words," by the Rev. Job Orton, who was also one of his students and his earliest biographer. To this gentleman the amiable widow of Doddridge wrote, on May 4th, 1755, "I have the pleasure to find, so far as this book has yet been known, it has met with pretty general acceptance. Many of my best friends consider it as a valuable supplement to Dr. Watts's, and, as such, are solicitous to introduce it into their respective congregations along with his. I think I can truly say I more wish this may be generally done from the hope I have they may do something to revive religion in the world than from any personal advantage."

The preparation of his hymns furnished a fine illustration of Doddridge's versatility of powers. When he had finished the preparation of a discourse, and while his heart was still warm with the subject, it was his custom to throw the leading thoughts into a few simple stanzas. These were sung at the close of the sermon, and supplied his hearers with a compend of his instructions, which might greatly aid their memories and their devotion. Thus, a sermon on "the rest which remains for the people of God" was followed by the hymn,—

"Lord of the Sabbath, hear our vows."

In like manner a sermon on 1 Pet. ii. 7 was condensed into the poetical epitome,—

"Jesus, I love thy charming name."

The Rev. Dr. James Hamilton, in the "*North British Review*," speaking of these and his other hymns, beautifully says, "If amber is the gum of fossil trees, fetched up and floated off by the ocean, hymns like these are a spiritual amber. Most of the sermons to which they originally pertained have disappeared forever; but, at once beautiful and buoyant, these sacred strains are destined to carry the devout emotions of Doddridge to every shore where his Master is loved and where his mother-tongue is spoken."

The well-known hymn,—

"O God of Jacob, by whose hand,"

often attributed to Logan, proceeded from the pen of Doddridge years before Logan was born.

In 1836 a very interesting manuscript volume was in the hands of the Rev. W. Rooker, of Tavistock, Devonshire, England, which belonged to Dr. Doddridge. It contained one hundred hymns in the handwriting of that excellent man, numbered in Roman figures: to each was prefixed a text of Scripture, and at the close of many of them were added the dates, and sometimes the places, of their composition. A few facts from this volume may not be without interest to our readers. The greater part of these compositions were afterward printed, under the direction of the Rev. Job Orton; and to these only do the facts we now give relate.

The hymn "On the death of a minister,"—

"Now let our mourning hearts revive," etc.,

he tells us was "composed at Kettering, August 22, 1736."

"Let Zion's watchmen all awake,"

was written from home,—but the name of the place cannot be deciphered,—on the occasion of an ordination, October 21, 1736.

The hymn,—

"My God, thy service well demands,"

bearing for its title, in Orton's volume, "On recovery from sickness, during which much of the divine favor had been experienced," has, in the manuscript, this note:—"Particularly intended for the use of a friend, Miss Nancy Bliss, who had been in the extremest danger by the bursting of an artery in her stomach, November 14, 1737."

The second verse, as printed by Orton, stands,—

"Thine arms of everlasting love
Did this weak frame sustain
When life was hovering o'er the grave
And nature sunk with pain."

The closing couplet of this verse in the original is far more poetical, and has a distinct reference to the painful accident which led to its composition:—

"When life in purple torrents flowed
From every sinking vein."

"Shepherd of Israel, bend thine ear,"

was composed "at a meeting of ministers at Bedworth, during their long vacancy [recess], April 10, 1735."

"And will the great eternal God," etc.,

"On opening a new place of worship," was headed, "On the opening of a new meeting-place at Oakham, from Psalm lxxxvii. 4." No date is given.

"Great God of heaven and nature, rise," etc.,

is entitled, in the manuscript, "A hymn for the First-day, January 9, 1739–40."

A few additional lines relating to Dr. Doddridge will be pardoned. He possessed a very remarkable talent for satire, which he could condense into a short epigram. One of his pupils, a weak young man, thought he had invented a machine on which he could fly to the moon. The doctor wrote,—

"And will Volatio leave this world so soon,
To fly to his own native seat, the moon?
'Twill stand, however, in some little stead
That he sets out with such an empty head."

One of his lovely daughters—the same who said she was loved by every one, because she loved everybody—wounded her foot by running a thorn into it; whereupon her father addressed to her the lines,—

"Oft I have heard the ancient sages say
The path of virtue was a thorny way:
If so, dear Celia, we may know
Which path it is you tread, which way it is you go."

Well as it is known, we will ask permission to add his epigram on his family motto, which Dr. Samuel Johnson, who has himself been called "the old king of critics," has warmly eulogized as one of the finest in the English language:—

"Live while you live, the epicure would say,
And seize the pleasures of the present day:
Live while you live, the sacred preacher cries,
And give to God each moment as it flies.
Lord, in my life let both united be:
I live in pleasure while I live to thee."

The beautiful hymn, though less known than it should be,—

"Awake, my soul, to meet the day,"

was written by Dr. Doddridge, who rose every morning throughout the year at five o'clock. It originally consisted of seven verses, and was constantly used by him as an act of devotion, on which account he entitled it "A Morning Hymn, to be sung at awaking and rising." We are told that, as the beginning of the sixth verse—"As rising now"—was yet on his lips, he sprang out of bed. The reader will remember that to this habit of early rising we owe his admirable "Family Expositor of the New Testament."

In every view of the subject, it would be improper not to refer, in this connection, to "*Doddridge's Principles of the Christian Religion, in Plain and Easy Verse.*" Very few productions, for many years, did more to diffuse evangelical religion among the young people of England, from the palace to the cottage, than did this unpretending little work. Writing to his wife, who was then distant from him, he thus speaks:—"I have been amusing myself with making some little verses for the children.

It is a work Mr. Clark, of St. Alban's, proposed to me,—that I should draw up a little summary of religion in verse for the use of little children, pretty much in sense the same with Dr. Watts's Second Catechism, which is the best short compendium I ever saw for matter and method. I have insensibly crept on for about a third part of the whole, and hope to end in a fortnight more." In a later letter to the same lady, he says, "I am not ashamed of these little services; for I had rather feed the lambs of Christ than rule a kingdom."

Those of our readers who have read the life of this excellent man will remember the details of a remarkable dream which he had after spending an evening with Dr. Samuel Clark, conversing with him on the happiness of Christians when separated from the body. Retiring to sleep, he imagined himself leaving earth and conducted by an angelic being to a part of heaven resembling a palace, where he was favored with an interview with his glorified Lord and Master, who expressed His approval of his labors and promised the eternal reward of His favor. After this he saw in the room where he had been placed, in pictures, a representation of the principal scenes of his life. This remarkable dream gave rise to the beautiful hymn,—

"While on the verge of life I stand."

JOHN DRYDEN.

SCARCELY any hymn in our language is better known than,—

"Creator Spirit, by whose aid,"

which is a paraphrase by the poet Dryden of the Latin hymn "*Veni Creator Spiritus*" of Ambrose, Bishop of Milan in the fourth century. The Rev. J. Chandler, of Corpus Christi College, Oxford, England, who translated and published, in 1837, a collection of "*Hymns of the Primitive Church*," says that, in the primitive times, each day, or twenty-four hours, was "parcelled out" into eight services,—there being a service at the end of every three hours. At nine o'clock every morning a hymn was sung to the Holy Spirit,—that being the hour in which, on the day of Pentecost, he descended on the apostles. This seems to have been observed from very early times; so that Mr. Chandler adds, "Most likely the *Veni Creator* of St. Ambrose was merely a new hymn written by him on a subject already familiar to the Church from the apostles downward."

By a reference to the article CHARLEMAGNE, in this volume, the reader will see that other claims have been set up for the authorship of this fine hymn.

Dryden wrote also a paraphrase of "*Te Deum Laudamus*;" but it is far inferior to the one by Charles Wesley:—

"Infinite God, to thee we raise," etc.

REV. GEORGE DUFFIELD, JR.

THE "*Sabbath Hymn-Book*" contains two hymns from the pen of this gentleman which are *not* anonymous, and other books have some others which are. All of them show that he possesses several very important qualifications of a good hymn-writer. One of the two hymns to which we have referred,—

"Blessed Saviour, thee I love,"

was written at Bloomfield, New Jersey, when the church of which its author was then pastor was in the midst of a very pleasant revival; and the other,—

"Stand up! stand up for Jesus!"

was composed to be sung after a sermon delivered by its writer the Sabbath following the mournfully sudden death of the Rev. Dudley A. Tyng, who was called from earth in 1858, and whose dying counsel to his brethren in the ministry was, "Stand up for Jesus."

Mr. Duffield, a son of the Rev. Dr. Duffield, a Presbyterian clergyman of Detroit, was born at Carlisle, in Pennsylvania, in 1818, graduated at Yale College in 1837, was ordained in 1840, and removed to Philadelphia in 1852. His ministerial career has been marked by much Christian activity and success; and he has already given several proofs, besides his hymns, of his talents for authorship.

REV. TIMOTHY DWIGHT, D.D.

We never read Dr. Dwight's beautiful hymn,—

"I love thy Church, O God,"

without an earnest wish that he had written many more like it. And yet, when we remember how much labor he performed, notwithstanding the defect of his sight, we are surprised that he accomplished so much. It is well known that the excellent doctor was requested by the Congregationalist ministers of Connecticut to revise Dr. Watts's version of the Psalms, and "to versify the Psalms omitted by Watts," which had been previously done, but very imperfectly, by Joel Barlow. He accomplished his task to the satisfaction of the parties by whom he was employed, adding upward of twenty compositions to the volume; but very few of them are now used.

Few men ever employed an amanuensis to so great an extent as this worthy President of Yale College. His "*Travels*," "*System of Theology*," and probably his "*Sermons*," were all written in this way. Thus by the aid of his students—for the work was generally done by them, and *gratuitously*—his name and influence will be perpetuated through many generations.

Dr. Dwight was born in Northampton, Mass., in 1752, and died in 1817. In 1785, he published his first poem, "*The Conquest of Canaan*," in 12mo, a copy of which we saw sold in England for more than five dollars.

REV. SIDNEY DYER.

The hymn,—

"Go, preach the blest salvation,"

was the production of this zealous and useful Baptist minister, who is also the author of several volumes of religious poetry. He was formerly a missionary laborer among the Indians, and has been many years a laborious servant of Christ in the Great West. He was born in the State of New York, in the year 1814.

REV. J. W. EASTBURNE.

We have, in one or more of our hymn-books, a remarkable composition for its evangelical and poetical spirit, beginning,—

"O holy, holy, holy Lord!"

written by this excellent young man, who died in New York, the city of his birth, in the year 1819, at the age of twenty-two years. He was associated in literary engagements with Robert C. Sands.

CHARLOTTE ELLIOTT.

One of the most popular hymns we have commences,—

"Just as I am, without one plea."

It has been thought by many persons not unlikely to

know, that scarcely any other hymn in our language has been so useful alike to the unconverted and to the Christian. Its author, Miss Elliott, is a somewhat elderly lady of fortune residing at Torquay, in Devonshire, England, a neighborhood which has been favored with her beneficence for many years. Some years since, she spent many months in the vicinityof Geneva, where she formed warm friendships with Drs. Malan, Merle d'Aubigné, and other gentlemen of the same evangelical school. She is said to have published several small volumes of devotional poetry, and seldom, even now, appears at the breakfast-table without more or less of Christian poetical composition in manuscript.

REV. R. ELLIOTT.

The hymn now becoming pretty well known among us,—

"Prepare us, gracious God,"

usually ascribed to Toplady, who first published it, and that in an altered form, in 1766, was written by Elliott in 1761. Its author was born at Kingsbridge, Devonshire, was admitted to Cambridge University in 1746, for a while associated with the Methodists, and ultimately settled as a Dissenting minister in London. He wrote several theological works, including "*Sin Destroyed and the Sinner Saved; or, Justification by Imputed Righteousness a Doctrine Superior to all Others for Promoting Holiness in Life.*" He died in 1788.

JAMES EDMESTON.

THIS gentleman, who has contributed several acceptable hymns to our collections, was a layman, connected with a Congregational church in London. He published several small volumes of devotional poetry, one called "*The Cottage Minstrel,*" hymns for village prayer-meetings, and a large number of hymns in various magazines. He died, at an advanced age, a few years ago.

REV. WILLIAM ENFIELD, LL.D.

THIS gentleman, the author of,—

"Behold where, in a mortal form,"

was for many years an Arian minister, first at Liverpool and afterward in Norwich, both in England, and died in the latter city, 1797, at the age of fifty-six. For several years he was a professor of belles-lettres at the Unitarian Academy at Warrington, and was the author of several popular volumes. His life was published, in connection with three volumes of his sermons, by Dr. Aikin.

REV. JONATHAN EVANS.

THE well-known favorite hymn,—

"Hark! the voice of love and mercy,

much longer than it is now generally printed, was the composition of the Rev. Jonathan Evans, of Foleshill, England. He wrote a volume of similar compositions, the manuscript of which is said yet to be in existence. Though originally in a very different profession, and unblest by the privileges of a collegiate education, Mr. Evans was, for about thirty years, a plain, earnest, and successful preacher of the gospel, chiefly in the villages of Warwickshire and among a congregation raised by his own labors at Foleshill. He was a man of sense, piety, activity, and fortitude,—a firm and generous friend, and a kind benefactor to the poor, both by rendering medical assistance and in ministerial labors. He died in August, 1809, aged sixty years.

REV. JOHN FAWCETT, D.D.

Tradition in England gives a very pleasing account of the origin of the well-known hymn,—

"Blest be the tie that binds."

It was written by the late dignified and gentlemanly Rev. John Fawcett, D.D., who died in 1817, in the seventy-seventh year of his age, nearly sixty years of which were devoted to the Christian ministry. As early as 1782 he published a small volume of hymns for public and private worship,—a new edition of which was issued in the year of his death.

After he had been a few years in the ministry, his

family increasing far more rapidly than his income, he thought it was his duty to accept a call to settle as pastor of a Baptist church in London, to succeed the celebrated Dr. Gill, which he did. He preached his farewell sermon to his church in Yorkshire, and loaded six or seven wagons with his furniture, books, etc., to be carried to his new residence. All this time the members of his poor church were almost broken-hearted: fervently did they pray that even now he might not leave them; and, as the time for his departure arrived, men, women, and children clung around him and his family in perfect agony of soul. The last wagon was being loaded, when the good man and his wife sat down on one of the packing-cases to weep. Looking into his tearful face, while tears like rain fell down her own cheeks, his devoted wife said, "Oh, John, John, I cannot bear this! I know not how to go!" "Nor I, either," said the good man; "nor will we go. Unload the wagons and put every thing in the place where it was before." The people cried for joy. A letter was sent to the church in London to tell them that his coming to them was impossible; and the good man buckled on his armor for renewed labors on a salary of less than two hundred dollars a year.

It is said that the hymn to which we have already referred was written to commemorate his continuance with his people. It was not only useful then, but has been sung by tens of thousands since, and no doubt will be for generations yet to come.

Dr. Fawcett was the author of several other works besides his hymn-book. One of these—"*An Essay on Anger*"—was a favorite book with George III., who offered its author any benefit he could confer. The good man substantially replied that he lived among his own people,—that he enjoyed their love,—that God blessed his labors among them,—and that he needed nothing which even a king could bestow. Some time afterward, however, a young man, the son of a dear friend, was sentenced to death for the crime of forgery. Fawcett interposed in his favor, and, after much labor, obtained from his sovereign a pardon. The young man afterward became an eminent Christian, and on the Sabbaths of many years read the hymns in a church in Liverpool.

Fawcett was exceedingly fond of psalmody, and often said, "If the Lord has given to man the ability to raise such melodious sounds and voices on earth, what delightful harmony will there be in heaven!"

Let us take our last look at this excellent minister of Jesus Christ. He has ascended the pulpit at an Association in Yorkshire. A thousand eyes are fixed on him in love and admiration, and all present express their conviction, by nods and smiles, that a spiritual feast has been provided for them. As a good soldier of Christ, he has endured hardness for far more than half a century. His praise has been in all the churches; his ministry has been greatly prized through the whole of that populous district; and his usefulness has been honored at home and abroad, in the cottage and in the palace itself.

He has now come to bear his dying testimony to the doctrines of the cross, and to bid farewell to the ministers and friends with whom he has been so long associated. Many of them have a strong presentiment that they shall see his face no more, and are prepared to receive his message as from the lips of a man who has finished his course and now stands at the entrance of heaven. As he rises in the pulpit, a death-like silence overspreads the crowded congregation, and all ears are opened to catch the words of inspiration. With a tremulous voice, and with deep emotion, he reads the text, "I am this day going the way of all the earth," Josh. xxiii. 14; and, long before he finishes his discourse, the place becomes a *Bochim*,—the house of God,—the gate of heaven. The sermon, which was committed to the press by the agency of its hearers, yet exists as a monument to his love of truth, his holy affection, and his zeal for the extension of the doctrines of sovereign mercy.

JOHN FELLOWS.

Several hymns on baptism, which appear in some of our books, were written by John Fellows, a poor shoemaker of that denomination, of Birmingham, England, in the latter part of the last century. He wrote several works of a poetical character, including "*The History of the Bible.*" He was contemporary with Gill and Toplady, on whose decease he wrote elegies. The fourth edition of his hymns was published in 1777. Allibone, in his very able "*Critical Dictionary of English Literature*," improperly speaks of him as a Methodist.

ELIZA LEE FOLLEN.

We have met, in our books, with two or three very pleasing hymns from the pen of this lady, who is, we believe, connected with the Unitarian body. She has published several volumes of prose, which have been well received by the public, especially in New England, to the manners of which portion of our land she appears to be very warmly attached.

This lady, formerly Miss Cabot, a native of Boston, was married in 1828 to Professor Charles Follen, who perished in the conflagration of the steamboat Lexington, in 1840. She has since published the life of her husband.

REV. BENJAMIN FRANCIS.

The Rev. Benjamin Francis, whose hymn

"My gracious Redeemer I love"

is an ornament to many of our books, was a native of Wales, and was born in 1734. At fifteen he united with a Baptist church, and began to preach at nineteen, when he was sent to Bristol College, where he remained for three years. When he went to college he did not know enough of the English language to ask in it a blessing on his food; but in a short time he became an excellent English scholar. At twenty-four he was ordained, at Shortwood, in Gloucestershire, where he remained till his death in 1799. During his ministry the house of worship was three times enlarged, and a new edifice was erected three miles from it for evening services. One of his hymns,—

"Great King of glory, come,"

was written for the re-dedication of his church-edifice after one of its enlargements. He was strongly invited to settle with a church in London; but, though he had a large and afflicted family, and a small income, he positively refused. He is said to have enjoyed through life a very heavenly state of mind, and, though frequently in great trouble, was generally happy. As he approached the end of his life, he would often weep over the remembrance of his early friends, nearly all of whom had been removed by death. He had used to speak of heaven as the residence of the larger number of his companions. He died happy in Christ, saying, a few days before his death, "If I could mention nothing of former experiences, I can, I *can*, at this moment go to Jesus, as a poor sinner, longing for salvation in his own sovereign way."

The late eminent preacher, the Rev. Thomas Flint, was the son-in-law and successor of this excellent man.

REV. RICHARD FURMAN, D.D.

The name of this truly-excellent man is not unknown to our hymn-books, though it is readily conceded that poetry was by no means the leading characteristic of his mind. Few ministers of the Baptist body, in this or any other land, have been more distinguished for sound judgment, correct theology, eminent spirituality, or successful labor than was Dr. Furman; and whatever tends to perpetuate his memory will be valued by all who knew him. He was born in the State of New York in 1755, commenced the work of the ministry at about eighteen years of age, and settled at Charleston, S.C., in 1787, where he labored with great success till his decease in in 1825. He filled in his own denomination many of its most important offices; and the influence he exerted is still powerful for good.

REV. W. H. FURNESS, D.D.

This gentleman, author of several very fine hymns in our collections, has since 1823 been the Unitarian clergyman of Philadelphia. He graduated at Harvard College in 1820, and then pursued his theological studies till his ordination. He is the author of several religious works, is a poet of fine taste, and has published many hymns, translations, and fugitive pieces. He has lately devoted himself to the reform-movements of the day, such as anti-slavery, temperance, and, we believe, woman's rights. He is also very warmly attached to the fine arts.

Dr. Furness was born at Boston in 1802.

THOMAS H. GALLAUDET, LL.D.

We know of very few hymns written by this truly distinguished man; but if he had written no other than,—

"Jesus, in sickness and in pain,"

he would be fully entitled to a place in our volume. He was born in Philadelphia in 1807, and died at Hartford, Connecticut, in 1851. He graduated at Yale College in 1805, being then but eighteen years of age, after which he suffered for several years from ill health. In 1814 he was licensed to preach, but soon after devoted himself to the deaf and dumb institution in Hartford, in which great work he was the pioneer and most distinguished of all teachers. He was also the most eminent and popular writer of juvenile literature of his day. The continued buoyancy and vigor of his mind, and the amount of his achievements, were truly wonderful; and his memory will ever remain fragrant in the land which he served and adorned.

REV. JOHN GAMBOLD.

We have yet, in some of our books, a fine old hymn beginning,—

"Oh, tell me no more of this world's vain store."

It was written by the Rev. John Gambold, a native of Haverfordwest, who took his degree of M.A. at Oxford University in 1734. After being, on the presentation of Archbishop Secker, vicar of Stanton Harcourt, in Oxfordshire, till 1748, he joined the United Brethren, among whom he was ordained bishop in 1754. He established a congregation at Coothill, in Ireland, and died in his native town in 1771. He published several works, besides a poem on the martyrdom of Ignatius, and was universally esteemed for his extensive learning and inoffensive manners.

The hymn to which we have referred was a great favorite with the eminent Rowland Hill, who published it in his own hymn-book, and during many of the last years of his life probably repeated some of its lines thousands of times, feeling intense interest in them even when he was beyond the power of uttering a single word:—

"And when I'm to die, receive me, I'll cry,
For Jesus hath loved me, I cannot tell why;
But this I do find,—we two are so joined,
He'll not live in glory and leave me behind."

It has been well said that it is impossible to read Gambold's works without being convinced that he enjoyed much communion with God and was greatly conversant with heavenly things, and that hence he had imbibed much of the spirit and caught much of the tone of the glorified Church above. The late Judge Story, writing to the Rev. John Brazer, says, "The specimens you have presented of his writings give me a high opinion of his genius, and there are occasional flashes in his poetry of great brilliancy and power. The '*Mystery of Life*' contains some exquisite touches, and cannot but recall to every man, who has indulged in musings beyond this sublunary scene, some of those thoughts which have passed before him in an unearthly form as he has communed with his own soul."

REV. PAUL GERHARD.

THIS German divine, sometimes called *Gerhardt,* was born in 1606 and died in 1676. His hymns, or rather translations of them, are becoming increasingly popular, and very deservedly so, for we know of none more scriptural in sentiment or devotional in spirit. He was the author of the hymn first translated by the Rev. John Wesley,—

"Give to the winds thy fears,"

which in some English hymn-books has been erroneously ascribed to Martin Luther. Our more modern books are giving us others of his truly excellent productions; so that he may become in this country what he has long been in Germany,—the favorite poet among orthodox Christians.

REV. THOMAS GIBBONS, D.D.

Our books contain a hymn,—

"When Jesus dwelt in mortal clay,"

and one or two others, written by Dr. Gibbons, an Independent or Congregational minister, first in Silver Street and afterward in Haberdashers' Hall, both in the city of London. He was the intimate friend of Whitefield, who tells an amusing anecdote of his once suffering sea-sickness for an hour and thus having his sympathy for sailors greatly increased. He was also intimate with Dr. Watts, whose life he wrote. He published "*Memoirs of Eminent Women,*" "*Rhetoric,*" etc. In 1785, when sixty-five years of age, he was taken suddenly in a fit, and remained speechless for five days, at the end of which he died. He was held in very high esteem.

Dr. Cotton Mather, when speaking of Dr. Gibbons's volume "*The Christian Minister,*" says, "Here you have a thousand hints respecting the reading of the best authors, the composing of sermons, etc."

ANN GILBERT.

Two or three hymns to be found in some of our books were written by this lady, who was one of the Taylor family of Ongar, and who felt a special interest in hymns for the young, and for Sabbath-schools. She was one of the authors of "*Hymns for Infant Minds.*" Her father, as is well known, was the Rev. Isaac Taylor, an excellent Congregational minister of England, and her husband was for some years a professor of classics in a Dissenting college, and for many years a Congregational minister at Nottingham.

REV. THOMAS GISBORNE.

THIS gentleman, whose hymns, we believe, are not numerous, was born in England in 1758, and died in 1846. In 1826 he was appointed as the Prebendary of Durham, an office which he filled till his death. He published five volumes of sermons, and many other works, which were well received: some of them were highly commended by the distinguished Robert Hall.

LORD GLENELG.

THIS British nobleman was the author of the well-known hymn,—

"When gathering clouds around I view."

His original name and style was Sir Robert Grant, by which name and title he was well known as a faithful servant of his sovereign in a high office in India, where also he was a warm friend of evangelical missionaries of every name. On his return from the East he was elevated to the peerage, which he has eminently adorned.

JOHN MASON GOOD, M.D.

An elegantly-written hymn,—

"Not worlds on worlds in phalanx deep!"

and a very few others, were written by this eminent philosopher and physician, a native of Epping, in England, in 1764. In addition to several highly-important medical works, and editing, in connection with Dr. Olinthus Gregory and Newton Bosworth, Esq., a valuable Cyclopedia called "*The Pantalogia*," he published a new translation of Solomon's Song and Job, as well as other works written in Oriental languages. Dr. Good was the son of a Dissenting minister, and, in early life, advocated Unitarianism in its lowest form. In his later years he became zealously attached to evangelical truth, in the triumphs of which he died, January 2d, 1827. Mr. Allibone truly says, "There are few names that cast greater lustre upon the archives of British medical science and philological learning than that of John Mason Good."

HANNAH F. GOULD.

This lady, the author of two or three hymns in our popular collections, is an extensive miscellaneous writer of our own land. She is a native of Lancaster, Vt., but removed in early life to Newburyport, in Massachusetts. Mrs. Hale, in her "*Woman's Record,*" says, "In truth, the great power of her poetry is its *moral* application. This hallows every object she looks upon and ennobles every incident she celebrates. She takes lowly and humble themes, but she turns them to the light of heaven, and they are beautiful, and refined, and elevated."

JAMES GRANT.

THE well-known hymn,—

"O Zion! afflicted with wave upon wave,"

was written by James Grant, a magistrate at Edinburgh, in Scotland. He was highly esteemed for his piety and his love of Christians. Having an ear for music, he was much pleased with the old Scottish melodies, but disliked the words to which many of them were sung. He therefore wrote some plaintive experimental hymns adapted to them, most of which are now forgotten; but the one to which we have referred will be popular, in Europe at least, for generations to come. It was written to the air of the "*Yellow-Haired Laddie;*" but modern "improvements" have prepared other tunes for it. Mr. Grant first published his hymns in 1784, with the title, "*Original Hymns and Poems, Written by a Private Christian for his Own Use.*"

THOMAS GREENE.

This gentleman was the author of the hymn,—

"It is the Lord enthroned in light."

He resided at Ware, in Hertfordshire, England, and published a small volume of hymns in 1780. He was not a minister.

REV. JOSEPH GRIGG.

About half a century ago, we saw a small pamphlet containing nineteen hymns, written by a young man named Grigg, when he was a laboring mechanic. Among the rest were the well-known

"Jesus, and shall it ever be?"

and,

"Behold a stranger at the door."

He afterward entered the ministry, preached in Silver Street, London, married a widow lady of considerable property, and died at Walthamstow, near London, in 1768.

MADAME GUION.

An extract from a letter written in 1782 by the estimable Cowper to the Rev. William Unwin, in reference to this eminent woman, will be far more accept: the reader than any thing we could ourselves w

"Mr. Bull, a Dissenting [Congregational] minister of Newport [Pagnell,] a learned, ingenious, good-natured, pious friend of ours, who sometimes visits us, and whom we visited last week, put into my hands three volumes of French poetry, composed by Madame Guion. 'A quietist,' say you, 'and a fanatic: I will have nothing to do with her!' It is very well: you are welcome to have nothing to do with her; but, in the mean time, her verse is the only French verse I ever read that I found agreeable: there is a neatness in it equal to that which we applaud, with so much reason, in the compositions of Prior. I have translated several of them, and shall proceed in my translations till I have filled a liliputian paper-book I happen to have by me, which, when filled, I shall present to Mr. Bull. He is her passionate admirer,—rode twenty miles to see her picture in the house of a stranger, which stranger politely insisted on his acceptance of it, and it now hangs over his chimney. It is a striking portrait,—too characteristic not to be a strong resemblance, and, were it encompassed with a glory instead of being dressed in a nun's hood, might pass for the face of an angel."

Many of Madame's religious views were so erroneous as to lead one of her most devoted admirers, the distinguished John Wesley, to say, "nay, such as are dangerously false." And yet the same writer says, "I believe she was not only a good woman, but good in an eminent degree,—deeply devoted to God, and often favored with uncommon communications of his Spirit."

After being vehemently opposed by the leading men of the Romish Church, Madame Guion spent ten years in prison, during which time she composed many hymns and poems on sacred subjects, filling five octavo volumes. Speaking of her imprisonment at Vincennes, she says, "I passed my time in great peace, content to spend the rest of my life there, if such were the will of God. I sang songs of joy, which the maid who served me learned by heart as fast as I made them; and we sang together thy praises, O my God! The stones of my prison looked in my eyes like rubies. I esteemed them more than all the gaudy brilliants of a vain world."

After her long imprisonment, Madame Guion lived a retired life for more than seven years at Blois, where she died, June, 1717, in the seventieth year of her age. It has been truly said that she sang her sweetest hymns in the Bastille.

REV. WILLIAM HAMMOND.

THE well-known, animating hymns,—

"Lord, we come before thee now,"

"Would you win a soul to God?"

and

"Awake, and sing the song,"

with a few others, were written by the Rev. William Hammond, "late of St. John's College, Cambridge," by whom was published, in 1745, a volume of original "*Psalms, Hymns, and Spiritual Songs,*" in which these compositions first appeared before the world. Long as they have served the churches, we can easily believe they have comparatively but just entered on their career of usefulness.

Mr. Hammond was one of the early Calvinistic Methodist preachers. He afterward, with his friend Cennick, joined the Moravian Brethren, and was interred in their burying-ground at Chelsea, London, 1783. Besides his hymns, he wrote a volume entitled "*The Marrow of the Gospel*," and left in manuscript an autobiography written in Greek.

REV. JOSEPH HART.

Every reader will remember that many hymns in almost every book bear the name of this excellent man. He was born about the year 1712, and in early life received an excellent education, which prepared him for a classical teacher, a profession he adorned for many years, not entering on the ministry till about forty-eight years of age. He settled in 1760 as pastor of the Independent Church in Jewin Street, London, where his ministry was abundantly blessed to a very large church and congregation. Here, while suffering great afflictions, he labored till his death, May 24th, 1768, aged fifty-six years. His brother-in-law, the Rev. Mr. Hughes, addressing the church in his funeral sermon, said, "He was like the laborious ox that dies with the yoke on his neck: so died he with the yoke of Christ on his neck; neither would he suffer it to be taken off; for ye are his witnesses that he preached Christ to you with the arrows of death sticking in him." He was buried in Bunhill Fields, London, where his tombstone may yet be seen. It was said that his funeral was more largely attended than that of any other person, there being more than twenty thousand spectators present. It may be remarked here that Dr. Samuel Johnson records a characteristic fact:—"I went to church,—I gave a shilling; and, seeing a poor girl at the sacrament in a bed-gown, I gave her privately half a crown, [sixty cents,] *though* I saw Hart's hymns in her hand."

REV. THOMAS HAWEIS, LL.B., M.D.

This gentleman, born about 1732, was educated in the University of Oxford, England, but was expelled, *because* he professed to be a Calvinist, and irregularly preached to large congregations. The chapel at Broadway, Westminster, was presented to him; but the Dean of Westminster refused him a license, *because* he had been expelled from Oxford. Some time afterward, he became rector of Aldwinkle, in Northamptonshire, which post he held for fifty-six years. Lady Huntingdon appointed him one of her chaplains, and for many years he itinerated throughout her connection. For several years he resided at Bath, where he died in 1820, being then the oldest "evangelical" clergyman in the Church of England. He was the author of the well-known beautiful hymn,—

"O thou from whom all goodness flows,"

as also of the "*Life of Romaine*," a "*Church History*," and "*A View of the Present State of Evangelical Religion throughout the World*." Dr. Haweis was one of the founders of the London Missionary Society; and by his influence the missions to the South-Sea islands were first entered upon.

The excellent Rev. John Newton says of this good man, "The preaching of Dr. Haweis, which had, like the report of a cannon, sounded through the country, attracted vast congregations to Aldwinkle." Some of the most profligate persons in the neighborhood were brought to repentance and "the acknowledgment of the truth" under his heart-searching addresses. Among his converts was an old tavern-keeper, who, having been a good customer to his own beer-barrel, had carbuncled his nose into the sign of his calling. He was from nature and interest averse to evangelical truth, and could not see what all the world had to run after at Aldwinkle Church. Being fond of music, however, and hearing the singing highly praised, he contrived to go six miles, avoid a drinking-party, and squeeze himself into a pew somewhat too narrow for his portly person, where he listened with delight to the hymns, but stopped his ears to the prayers. Heated and fatigued, he closed his eyes also, till, a fly stinging his nose, he took one of his hands from the side of his head to drive away the intruder.

Just at that moment, the preacher, in a voice that sounded like thunder, read his text:—"He that hath ears to hear, let him hear!" The impression was irresistible: his hands no longer covered his ears: a new sense was awakened within: it was the beginning of days to him. No more swearing, no more drunkenness, but prayer and hearing the word of God occupied his time; and, after walking with God for eighteen years, he died rejoicing in hope and blessing God for the minister of his conversion.

BISHOP HEBER.

WHO among our readers can be ignorant of Bishop Heber's missionary hymn,—

"From Greenland's icy mountains"?

Its amiable author was born in England in 1783, and was educated at the University of Oxford, where he took his degree of M.A. in 1808, and was soon after presented to the family living at Hodnet, in Shropshire. Here he discharged his parochial duties till he was offered the bishopric of Calcutta, as successor to Bishop Middleton, to which see he went in June, 1823. In 1826 he travelled in the discharge of his duties, and, while bathing, was seized with apoplexy, and suddenly died.

The hymn which may be regarded as his best monument was written at Hodnet, to be sung in connection with a sermon which appealed to the people of his charge, in 1820, on behalf of missions. He had not the slightest idea that what was written only for a small village congregation would become popular, as it has done, in at least three-quarters of the globe.

The original manuscript of this admirable hymn is yet, with a thousand others of like character, in the possession of the Rev. Dr. Raffles, of Liverpool; and from this it is seen that the line

"The heathen in his blindness"

was first written,—

"The pagan in his blindness."

REV. GEORGE HERBERT.

Devotional feeling and good taste have transferred a very few of the fine hymns of this good old poet to our books. From the pen of a grandson of the venerated Andrew Fuller, we chiefly transcribe a very few lines of this scholar, poet, and saint, who died of consumption in the trying times of the seventeenth century.

In the year 1630, George Herbert went, according to a custom in those days, to toll the church-bell at the quiet village of Bemerton, about one mile from the city of Salisbury, on his introduction to the living. He stayed much longer than usual after the bell had ceased to toll; and one of his friends, alarmed at his absence, looked in at the window and found him prostrate at the altar in prayer. On this same night, according to his biographer, Izaak Walton, he declared that "the virtuous life of a clergyman was the most powerful eloquence to persuade all that see it to reverence and love, and at least to live like him; and this will I do, because I know we live in an age that hath more need of *good examples* than precepts."

Well indeed did Herbert work out his holy resolutions. For two or three years the village of Bemerton was blessed with a ministry so self-denying, and with an example so pure and gentle in its manifestation of the Christian graces, that the memory of it "is as ointment poured forth." Twice every day, he, with his wife and child, led the villagers to prayer, and every Sabbath afternoon questioned them on the verities of the Christian faith. There was not a cottage in the village or neighborhood, where want and sorrow had found a home, that was not cheered by the visits of this holy man. He was passionately fond of music; and even when at college this was his chief recreation. Twice every week he was accustomed to walk from Bemerton to Salisbury for the sole purpose of hearing the organ, and on his return his soul seemed thrilled with ecstasy. He once met an old man, who, with his horse, had fallen on the road and were unable to get on their feet again. Taking off his coat, Herbert set manfully to work and soon put them all right. He was, however, plastered with mud, and arrived in Salisbury with a most uncanonical appearance. On his friends noticing his plight and asking for an explanation, he told them the story, adding that the thought of what he had done would prove "music to him at midnight."

No one can regret that George Herbert was called away in the very midst of his holy life, before the time of those terrible strifes in which he would have been so ill at ease. His death was truly calm and beautiful. The Sabbath preceding it, he took his well-tuned lute and proceeded to play and sing,—

"My God, my God,
My music shall find thee,
And every string
Shall have his attribute and sing."

On the day of his death he declared, "I am sorry I have nothing to present to God but sin and misery; but the first is pardoned, and a few hours shall put a period to the second." How beautifully does old Izaak Walton say, "I wish, if God be so pleased, I may die like him"!

Perhaps no poet has ever put more strong *stuff* into a single verse, or sometimes line or half a line, than George Herbert. It is not the music of the rhythm, or the even flow of the words, that *generally* charms, but that each sentence seems like a sharp thrust, which pierces the inmost recesses of the moral and spiritual life; and very often the gleam on the weapon is most golden. Our readers may rest assured that whenever they turn to "HERBERT'S *Temple*" they will find, if not hymns for the "heart and voice," yet always hymns for the *heart*.

REV. JAMES HERVEY.

THIS eminently pious clergyman, and, for the day in which he lived, elegant writer, is not generally known as a writer of hymns; but one composition of his being inserted in several of our books claims that his name be included in our volume. We refer to the hymn beginning,—

"Since all the varying scenes of time."

Mr. Hervey was born in 1714, was educated at the University of Oxford, ordained in the Church of England, and died of consumption at forty-four, in 1758. He was a fine scholar and eminently pious and benevolent. His heart was so set on the relief of the poor that, in conformity with his wish to die "even with the world," his income, and the profits derived from his popular and useful works, were all devoted to them. He wrote several works, which long had an extensive circulation, such as "*Meditations among the Tombs*," "*Reflections in a Flower-Garden*," and a doctrinal work called "*Theron and Aspasio*." These were all published, in seven octavo volumes, in 1796.

Hervey was an ardent friend of Dr. Doddridge and a fervent admirer of George Whitefield. He was a tall and spectral-looking man, and for several years before his decease was dying daily. He had a very graceful elocution, and was listened to every Sabbath by crowded congregations.

It is pleasant occasionally to meet with a man who

can form a correct estimate of his own talents; and this was the case with Hervey. Speaking of himself to his biographer, the senior John Ryland, he said, "My friend, I have not a strong mind; I have not powers fitted for ardent researches; but I think I have a power of writing in somewhat of a striking manner, so far as to please mankind and recommend my dear Redeemer."

REV. ROWLAND HILL.

THIS distinguished minister of Christ had but a small portion of poetical talent: he was, however, fond of writing hymns. Some of our older collections contain the truly pious composition,—

"Dear Friend of friendless sinners, hear,"

which he wrote for the members of his church when on a sick-bed, and which, it is said, was profitably used by many of them in their dying hours. Multitudes have passed away from singing of "the promised rest" on earth to its enjoyment in heaven. His best biographer says, "No one acquainted with Mr. Hill can read this hymn without seeing before him the image of the writer in his happiest moments, when his mind was sweetly and graciously subdued by the power of the Divine Spirit. If I were asked for a description of Mr. Hill when 'it was well with him,' I should just read this short composition. It possesses the pathos of the excellent man when he left the footstool of mercy and immediately ascended the sacred desk."

But Mr. Hill's greatest pleasure of this kind was in connection with his large Sunday-schools. He always had an annual assemblage of the children and their teachers on Easter Monday and Tuesday, when he composed a hymn to be sung, which he printed and gratuitously distributed. These little compositions were much valued by the young people, who were addressed from the text of Scripture printed at the head of the hymn. Mr. Weight tells us, in his funeral service for the venerable man, that, on the Easter Tuesday only two days preceding his death, he deeply regretted his inability to engage in his usual services. "He stood at his drawing-room window and saw the dear little children thronging the chapel-yard, and spoke with much delight of by-gone days, when he had met them and preached to them the Lord Jesus Christ."

Mr. Hill, in 1798,—two years before the death of Cowper,—published a small volume of "*Divine Hymns for Children*," which the poet kindly revised, and concerning which a letter distinguished by his characteristic humor is still in existence.

BISHOP HORNE.

This valued prelate, who died in 1792, aged sixty-two years, wrote a very few good hymns, one of which, greatly abridged from the original, begins,—

"See the leaves around us falling."

It has, however, been properly said that the purity of his taste was somewhat warped by the age in which he lived. The bishop shines most eminently in his work on the Psalms, in writing which he took his highest pleasure, and said that, if it pleased God, he would rejoice to die in meditating on this portion of his word.

REV. JOSEPH HUMPHRIES

WAS one of the early Calvinistic Methodist preachers of the last century. He wrote the hymn,—

"Blessed are the sons of God,"

and a few others, which were published at the end of Cennick's hymns in 1743. He died in London, and was buried in the Moravian cemetery at Chelsea.

REV. G. B. IDE, D.D.

THIS popular Baptist minister, author of several hymns bearing his name, most of which are printed in "*The Baptist Harp*," a selection of hymns edited by himself, is a native of Vermont, and has labored in the ministry for many years at Albany, Boston, Philadelphia, and Springfield in Massachusetts, in which places he has been favored with much success.

REV. WILLIAM JAY.

"COME, thou soul-transforming Spirit,"

is one of about twenty similar compositions from the pen of this late eminent preacher, who was born of very humble parents in 1770, and died at Bath, in England, after a ministry in one edifice of sixty-three years, in 1854, aged eighty-four years. Few men were more distinguished for a catholic spirit and constant pulpit-labor. He never forgot, when he ascended his "throne,"—as he regarded it,—that he had men, women, and children hanging upon his lips; and, instead of discoursing *before* them, he addressed himself *to* them. Whatever might be his theme, he intermixed statements and illustrations which at once explained the subject, touched the springs of human sympathy, and conveyed important suggestions for the conduct of life.

REV. EDMUND JONES.

SEVERAL of our hymn-books contain a universal favorite, beginning, as published by its author,—

"Come, humble sinner, in whose breast."

This hymn was written, with one or two others of like character, by the Rev. Edmund Jones, a highly-popular Welsh Baptist preacher of the last century. He was eminent for his piety and a remarkably amiable temper;

and his death, though at a very advanced age, was a source of very extensive grief. We believe that the only productions of his pen, in addition to the hymns to which we have referred, were contained in a pamphlet of ninety pages, a copy of which may be found in the library of the American Baptist Publication Society in Philadelphia, the whole title of which we will transcribe:—"*Samson's Hair, an Eminent Representation of the Church of God. In two parts. To which is* [are] *added Two Sermons: First, showing the Evil Nature and Hurtful Effects of Unbelief; Second, On God's Subduing and Keeping under the Strong Corruptions of his People, and Healing Them. By Edmund Jones, Minister of the Gospel.—Trevecka: printed in the year* MDCCLXXVII."

The two sermons on Samson's hair were preceded by warm recommendations from the pens of two very respectable ministers, as well as a preface from the author, enforcing the importance of his subject. The sermons furnish fair specimens of the spiritualizing tendency of that age, and suggest the propriety of combining the piety of the past with the intellectual strength of the present.

REV. ADONIRAM JUDSON, D.D.

THOUGH we have two hymns written by this excellent Christian missionary, both of them on baptism, we can scarcely claim for him the honors of a poet. His glory was of a far higher character. He was the son of an excellent Congregational minister in Massachusetts, and graduated at Brown University, intending to pursue the profession of the law. Converted by the grace of God, he changed his design, and went to study theology at Andover. While here, the missionary spirit was excited, and several of the students offered themselves for labor in foreign lands; and the Board of Commissioners for Foreign Missions sent Judson and several others to India. On their way, Mr. Judson, Mr. Rice, and their wives became Baptists. His life was devoted to preaching in Burmah, and the translation of the Scriptures, in which he spent nearly forty years. He had in his composition all the elements of a hero; and he who would look for a rare specimen of a life consecrated to noble aims, inspired with an elevated self-devotion, and exercising an energy seldom witnessed among men, must contemplate the lion-hearted missionary of Burmah. Dr. Judson died at sea, when bound to the island of Bourbon for his health, in 1850.

REV. THOMAS KELLY.

This gentleman, one of the most prolific and popular hymn-writers of the last and present generations, was the son of Judge Kelly, of Ireland. From a very early age he had powerful impressions of eternal realities, and was regarded as a very religious young man. His father had intended him for the bar, but his own heart was fixed on the pulpit. Having, in 1793, been ordained in the Established Church, he commenced preaching in Dublin, and met with great opposition from his family for preaching the doctrine of justification by faith; so that he often said that to have gone to the stake would have been a less trial to him than to have set himself against those he dearly loved.

Crowds of persons from Sabbath to Sabbath listened to the fervent appeals which Mr. Kelly made to their consciences; but before long he was much opposed by his superiors in the Church, and compelled to leave the Establishment, though he never dissented from its doctrines. He continued to labor in Dublin for more than sixty years, during which time it was testified by many that he never seemed to waste an hour. His talents were of a high order, and his attainments very considerable. Music was with him not merely a recreation, but, like his other talents, was consecrated to the glory of God. A volume of airs which he composed to some of his hymns were remarkable for much simplicity and sweetness. As a Christian he was distinguished for his *humility*, and used to rejoice that the Israelites who stood the farthest from the brazen serpent might look at it with the same benefit as those who were near. He lived almost constantly in prayer.

While preaching to his own congregation, in October, 1854, Mr. Kelly was seized with a slight stroke of paralysis, which gradually lessened his strength till he died,

May 14, 1855, aged eighty-six years. On his death-bed he was sweetly composed; and, when the words of the Psalmist were repeated to him, "The Lord is my Shepherd; I shall not want," he replied, "The Lord is my *every thing.*"

It is said of Mr. Kelly that he allowed no opportunity for doing good to pass unimproved, but even when it would have been inexpedient to attempt more he would drop a gentle hint. He had an admirable tact in adapting his mode of address to the parties he incidentally spoke to. Lord Plunket, so well known for his *puns*, was a schoolfellow with Mr. Kelly, and their occasional recognition of each other continued through life. His lordship, once meeting Mr. Kelly, told him he thought he would live to a great age. He replied, "I am confident I shall, as I expect never to die." The nobleman said, "Oh, I see what you mean."

Mr. Kelly's hymns are well known, and so much esteemed that no reader would wish to lose them.

BISHOP KEN.

THE poet Montgomery has very properly remarked that what is usually called the long metre doxology,—

"Praise God, from whom all blessings flow," etc.,

has probably been more used than any other composition in the world, the Lord's prayer excepted. It was written by Bishop Ken, a very high Churchman—frequently accused of Romanism—of the seventeenth century. The bishop wrote three hymns of the same metre for morning, evening, and midnight, each of which was closed with the doxology. The hymns are seldom read; but the doxology, which has appeared to the most rigid critics almost perfect in its character, will probably be used till the end of time.

Bishop Ken was born in 1637 and died in 1710. About 1769 he was appointed chaplain to the Princess of Orange, and went to Holland, where she then resided. Here Ken compelled a favorite courtier to fulfil a contract of marriage with a young lady of her train whom he had seduced. His zeal in this matter gave such offence to the prince, afterward William III., that he threatened to turn him out of the service,—on which Ken begged the princess to allow him to resign; nor would he consent to return till entreated by the prince to do so.

In 1684 Ken was appointed chaplain to King Charles II., and on the removal of the court to Winchester to pass the summer, Ken's house was fixed upon as the residence of the celebrated Nell Gwynne, Charles's mistress; but the inflexible clergyman positively refused her admittance; this, instead of offending that profligate monarch, led him, soon after, to appoint him Bishop of Bath and Wells.

In 1685 James II. ascended the throne, and Ken became his chaplain also. One day the king was absent, and the enemies of the bishop complained to the king of his sermon. The prelate remarked that "if his majesty had not neglected his own duty of being present, his enemies would have missed this opportunity of accusing him." When the king ordered the well-known Declaration of Indulgence to be read, Ken and six other bishops refused to comply, and were sent to the Tower; but on trial the jury acquitted them. When James abdicated the throne and the Prince of Orange went to England as William III., Ken vacated his bishopric rather than swear allegiance to his new sovereign, as he did not believe that he could free himself from the allegiance he had sworn to James while he was yet living. He lived in comparative retirement till his death.

The volume which contained the hymns to which the doxology was appended was entitled "*A Manual of Prayer for the Use of the Scholars of Winchester College,*"—of which Whitefield speaks as having been very useful to him in the early period of his college life.

Some of our readers at least will thank us for giving at length Montgomery's remarks on "*The Doxology,*" of which he says, it "is a masterpiece at once of amplification and compression. Of *amplification,* on the burden '*Praise God,*' repeated in each line; *compression,* exhibiting God as the object of praise in every view in which we can imagine praise due to him,—for all *his* blessings, yea, for *all* blessings, none coming from any other source: praise by every creature, specifically invoked here below and in heaven '*above:*' praise to him in each of the characters wherein he has revealed himself in his word,—

'*Father, Son, and Holy Ghost.*' Yet this comprehensive verse is sufficiently simple that, by it, 'out of the mouths of babes and sucklings,' God may 'perfect praise;' and it appears so easy that one is tempted to think hundreds of the sort might be made without trouble. The reader has only to try, and he will be quickly undeceived: the longer he tries, the more difficult he will find the task to be."

It has been said that Bishop Ken was accustomed to remark that it would enhance his joy in heaven to listen to his morning and evening hymns as sung by the faithful on earth.

JOHN KENT.

The author of the hymn,—

"Where two or three together meet,

was an humble man, of very humble origin. He was born in Bideford, England, 1766, and died in 1843. He never aspired to a pulpit, and only occupied a position as a shipwright. His life was marked by much affliction, and at sixty he became blind. He published a hymn-book in 1803, in which he proved that the great mystery of redeeming love through the atoning sacrifice of the Lord Jesus was the joy of his soul. In his last hour he extended his hand, cold with death, and exclaimed, "I rejoice in hope!—I am accepted,—accepted!" gathered up his feet, and fell asleep in Jesus, at the age of seventy-seven years.

FRANCIS S. KEY.

In one or two of the Protestant Episcopal collections of hymns may be found one beginning,—

"If life's pleasures charm thee,
Give them not thy heart,
Lest the gift ensnare thee
From thy God to part.
His favor seek,
His praises speak,
Fix here thy hope's foundation;
Serve Him, and He
Will ever be
The Rock of thy salvation."

It came from the pen of the author of the well-known "*Star-Spangled Banner;*" and, if the last-named composition shows the graceful patriot, the hymn certainly displays the spirit of the Christian. This was still further manifested in a scene about the year 1835, as thus described by the clergyman officially engaged. He says, "I stood within the railing, at the side of the communion-table, and had administered the sacred elements to all, it seemed, who desired to partake of them. Just then, however, as though previously restrained by profound humility, a stranger approached the altar, knelt all alone, and so received the holy memorials of our Saviour's suffering and death. I trust the service was one of true faith, and that the result was one of great peace and comfort. That last communicant was the same person,—the distinguished poet, the accomplished lawyer and orator, the modest Christian, Francis S. Key."

REV. WILLIAM KINGSBURY.

The beautiful character of the hymns,—

"Let us awake our joys,"

and

"Great God of all thy churches, hear,"

make us deeply regret that we have no others from the pen of their excellent author. We believe we are correct in speaking of them as from the Rev. William Kingsbury, for forty-five years the pastor of the church at Southampton, to which the distinguished Dr. Watts and his honored parents had formerly belonged. Mr. Kingsbury was born in London in 1744, entered on his studies for the ministry at Homerton College before he was truly a Christian, was brought to the cross of Christ by most remarkably being led to read the works of John Bunyan, was ordained at the age of twenty-one years, and died in 1818, at the age of seventy-four, having spent the whole forty-five years of his pastoral life in one pulpit. Mr. Kingsbury had the honor of being one of the founders of the London Missionary Society in 1795, being chairman of its first meeting. His biographer tells us that "he was confined to his bed for one day only before his dissolution. He suffered no acute pain. On the Sunday before he died, when one of his sons said, 'How do you do, sir?' he replied, 'Well; for I have peace with God.' He expressed an earnest wish to obtain his dismission, and frequently was heard to say, 'When will he come?' One of his attendants, supposing him to inquire after one of his sons who was hourly expected from London, said, 'We look for him every minute.' He shook his head, saying, 'No, no: when will MY BELOVED COME?'"

His senses remained to the last moment of life. He kissed the hand of his affectionate and only remaining daughter, and made a sign that his son Walter should offer prayer. While this was being done, the happy man, his hands and eyes lifted up in the attitude of devotion, drew a long breath, and, without a groan or convulsion, expired.

REV. ANDREW KIPPIS, D.D.

THE hymn,—

"Great God, in vain man's narrow view,"

and one or two others used in our evangelical churches, were from the pen of this gentleman. He was born at Nottingham, England, in 1725, and studied for the ministry under Dr. Doddridge. In 1753 he was ordained over an Arian congregation in Westminster, which he relinquished for scholastic duties ten years after. He wrote many miscellaneous books, and the lives of Doddridge, Lardner, Pringle, and Cook, and conducted the five volumes which were published of the "*Biographia Britannica.*" Though the writer of a few respectable hymns, he was no poet.

REV. MR. KIRKHAM.

Of this gentleman we know nothing more than that he was the author of the hymn,—

'How firm a foundation, ye saints of the Lord,"

which was first printed in "*Rippon's Selection*" in 1787.

Though we have no certain evidence of the fact, we believe that Mr. Kirkham was a fellow-student with the Messrs. John and Charles Wesley, George Whitefield, and Mr. Morgan, and one of the first of "the people called Methodists."

REV. JOHN LANGFORD.

The authorship of the favorite hymn,—

"Now begin the heavenly theme,"

has been usually claimed for this writer, though we have more than once found it attributed to Madan. Langford was connected with the early Methodists, but afterward united with the Baptist Church in Eagle (now Kingsgate) Street, London, under the pastorate of Dr. Andrew Gifford. He was for many years pastor of several churches in London, and died about 1790. He preached and printed a sermon on the death of Whitefield. He was long remembered as a man of great spirituality and Christian meekness.

REV. JOHN LELAND.

Those of our readers who are acquainted with Baptist history have read of the Rev. John Leland, an eminent minister of that body, who labored successfully for many years, and died in the year 1841. On a tour among the churches of the South in 1779, he had occasion to baptize a number of disciples. It was winter, and a liquid grave had to be cut in the ice. A brother in the ministry preached for him. During the sermon, Leland wrote the first three verses of a hymn, that was afterward extended to six, still well known among some of the Baptist churches. Approaching the water at the head of a number of candidates, Leland read his hymn, beginning,—

"Christians, if your hearts are warm,
Ice and snow can do no harm:
If by Jesus you are prized,
Now arise and be baptized," etc.

He struck up a familiar tune, and, as the good old people used to say, "lined out the hymn;" and it was sung then, as it has often been since, with no small degree of earnestness.

REV. JOHN LOGAN,

The author of the hymn,—

"Where high the heavenly temple stands,"

and several others, was a native of Mid-Lothian, in Scotland, was educated at Edinburgh, became minister at South Leith in 1770, and died in 1788, aged about forty years. He was distinguished as a general writer, and was a respectable poet. He was also the author of two volumes of sermons, still held in reputation.

HENRY W. LONGFELLOW.

"*The Psalm of Life*" of this author,—

"Tell me not, in mournful numbers,"

and some other productions of his elegant pen, are to be found in several of our books, and on many accounts greatly please us,—though we think that, like the rest of his Unitarian brethren, he is sadly lacking in the noble, generous, high spirit of evangelical truth. The son of the Hon. Stephen Longfellow, of Portland, Maine, Henry was born in that city in 1807. Of very high education himself, his life in various ways has been devoted to the advancement of that great cause. His poetical works have been numerous and beautiful; and of them the editor of the "*Men of the Time*" truly says, "Longfellow's poems have, together with great picturesque and dramatic beauty, a simplicity and truth to nature which commend them alike to the rudest and to the most cultivated. The tenderness and melancholy pleasure with which, in many of his works, he dwells upon a poetical aspiration or an historical incident, have, however, proved a stumbling-block to many of his countrymen, who demand more freshness, and an onward direction of the poet's eye."

ANN LUTTON.

We confess to feeling something of a personal interest in the beautiful and popular hymn,—

"When torn is the bosom by sorrow or care."

For ten years—1832 to 1841—we had the pleasure of conducting in London a small monthly magazine called "*The Revivalist.*" In 1834, at the request of several honored friends, we began to give a number of new hymns adapted to popular—but, as they were generally employed, *useless*—airs. In this we were aided by several of our correspondents, among whom was a new one, whom to this day we have never seen,—Miss Ann Lutton, of Ireland. She wrote for us the beautiful hymn on prayer to which we have referred, adapted to the air of "*Sweet Home.*"

There is something impressive in the thought that, when we commit to paper what we may consider a mere trifle, we know not the extent of its diffusion or its effects. Who shall calculate the usefulness of the hundreds of thousands of copies of this hymn now before the public, to say nothing of millions yet to be published?

REV. HENRY FRANCIS LYTE.

We have just turned to three separate hymn-books in reference to the hymn,—

"Jesus, I my cross have taken,"

and find it attributed respectively to Montgomery, to the Hon. Miss Grant, and to her brother, Lord Glenelg. In each of these cases the reference is wrong. It was published by its author, already named, in 1833, in a volume of "*Poems, Chiefly Religious*," at much greater length than it is usually given. Its author was a young man of feeble health, but of high promise. He was born at Kelso, in Scotland, in 1793, and in 1812 entered Trinity College, Dublin. Having been ordained in the Established Church, he settled as curate in Devonshire, but was compelled to spend the larger portion of his future life in travelling for his health. He died in 1847, and was buried in the English Cemetery at Nice. He published a metrical version of the Psalms, and a number of beautiful hymns.

MRS. MACKAY.

The sweet and consolatory hymn,—

"Asleep in Jesus! blessed sleep!"

is from the pen of Mrs. Mackay, a Christian lady of Scotland, authoress of several very pleasing volumes of a religious character. It originated in a visit to a burying-ground in the west of England, an account of which the reader will be pleased to see from the authoress's own pen:—

"'SLEEPING IN JESUS.'

"This simple inscription is carved on a tombstone in the retired rural burying-ground of Pennycross Chapel, in Devonshire. Distant only a few miles from a bustling and crowded seaport town, reached through a succession of those lovely green lanes for which Devonshire is so remarkable, the quiet aspect of Pennycross comes soothingly over the mind. 'Sleeping in Jesus' seems in keeping with all around.

"Here was no elaborate ornament, no unsightly decay. The trim gravel walk led to the house of prayer, itself boasting of no architectural embellishment to distinguish it; and a few trees were planted irregularly to mark some favored spots."

REV. MARTIN MADAN.

THIS gentleman, who was born in 1726, was eminent in his day both as a preacher and a writer of hymns. Like many other Christians, his conversion took place in a remarkable manner. The preaching of the first Methodists, as is well known, excited almost universal attention. Madan was then a gay young man; and, being in company one evening, in a coffee-house, with some of his companions, he was requested to go and hear Mr. John Wesley preach, that he might exhibit his sermon and manner for their amusement. He went with that intention; but just as he entered the place Mr. Wesley read as his text the words, "Prepare to meet thy God," with a solemnity which greatly struck him and inspired a seriousness which increased as the sermon proceeded. He returned to his companions; and when they asked him, "Have you taken the old Methodist off?" his reply was, "No, gentlemen; but he has taken me off." He immediately withdrew from their society, and associated only with the followers of Christ.

Mr. Madan was a gentleman of independent fortune, and soon resolved to enter the ministry in connection with the Established Church. His brother was at that time the Bishop of Peterborough; but Madan would accept of no honors in the Church. Owing to his decided evangelical doctrines, he found some difficulty in obtaining ordination, but at length succeeded through the influence of the Countess of Huntingdon. He was soon after appointed chaplain of the Lock Hospital, near Hyde Park Corner, in London, an institution for the restoration of unhappy females; and before the erection of a church edifice he preached to its inmates from a desk in the parlor, where he was frequently assisted by Mr. Romaine and Dr. Haweis.

Mr. Madan, in the peculiar situation he occupied, saw so much of the evils of prostitution that he was unhappily led to write a volume in favor of polygamy, and from that time he lost his friends; so that we afterward hear but little of him. He died in 1790. We yet sing several of his hymns.

REV. BASIL MANLY, JR.

THIS gentleman, in connection with his excellent father, is editor of "*The Baptist Psalmody*," an admirable selection of hymns recently published by the Southern Baptist Publication Society in Charleston, S.C., and already introduced into many of the Baptist churches in that region. Some of the hymns in the volume are from the pen of the junior editor, and are distinguished for sound doctrine, earnestness, and devotion. In addition to the services which Mr. Manly has thus rendered to the churches, he has most laboriously devoted himself to the pulpit and to the cause of Christian education.

REV. JOHN MASON,

OF whose good old hymns we are yet favored with a few, including,—

"Come, dearest Lord, and feed thy sheep,"

and

"Now, from the altar of our hearts,"

was for twenty years rector of Water-Stratford, England, where he died in 1694. Not a few of the lines of

Dr. Watts were borrowed from him. He himself published a hymn-book in 1686, entitled "*Spiritual Songs.*"

The well-known verse,—

"Mercy, good Lord, mercy I ask,"

usually sung in England years ago at the execution of criminals, and equally appropriate for sinners of every class, proceeded from his pen.

REV. SAMUEL MEDLEY.

We have in most of our books two hymns beginning with,—

"Mortals, awake! with angels join,"

and

"Awake, my soul, in joyful lays,

and one or two others, written by the Rev. Samuel Medley, twenty-seven years pastor of the First Baptist Church at Liverpool, England, and during about the same period a regular annual supply at Whitefield's Tabernacle and Tottenham Court Road Chapel, in London. In early life Mr. Medley was very gay and profane. He was engaged in the British navy, where he was severely wounded in one of the several actions in which he fought. Returning to his pious grandfather's house for the sake of surgical attendance, he was brought under the preaching of the excellent Whitefield and Dr. Gifford, and was soon led to the Saviour whose name he had so often blasphemed. He died, after a very successful ministry, in 1799, aged sixty-one years. In the year following his death, a volume of original hymns from his pen was issued, very few of which are now valued. He also published two or three sermons, and several humorous papers. He was eccentric in his manners, but had a pious soul and a noble heart.

A deceased critic once remarked to us that were the hymn we have first referred to deprived of its title, "*The Incarnation of Christ*," a stranger might be ready to inquire, "To what subject does it relate?"

REV. HENRY H. MILMAN.

THAT the Dean of St. Paul's, London, is a poet, none of his readers will doubt. A clergyman of the English Established Church, a dramatist, historian, Professor of Poetry in the University of Oxford, and holding several other important preferments, his reputation is high, and in some departments will no doubt be enduring. What a writer in the "*Quarterly Review*" says of one of his works will probably apply to all:—"Every page exhibits some beautiful expression, some pathetic turn, some original thought, or some striking image." We confess, however, that his hymns want more simplicity, more of penitence and faith, and more of devotion, to accord with our taste. We respect the venerable gentleman, born in London in 1791, and should be happy to see, before he is called from earth, a few hymns from his pen which would go down to posterity with those of Watts and Doddridge, Cowper and Montgomery.

JOHN MILTON.

Were there more love of real poetry in the churches of Christ than we have at present, we should hear more of Milton's hymns sung. We are truly glad to meet with his

"They pass refreshed the thirsty vale,"

and hope that those who fashionably praise his "*Paradise Lost*" will study and sing his hymns, which we are gratified to know are remembered in our land, though they are forgotten in his own. But be it remembered that the said "*Paradise Lost*" usually accompanied the Bible into the log houses of the early settlements of our country, and these commonly had, too, the minor poetry of the same author.

It has been said that, from the seventeenth year of Milton's age to the thirty-fourth, Milton's chief exercises were in poetry, that during the next twenty years he wrote scarcely any thing in verse except a few sonnets, but that in old age he renewed his allegiance to the muse, writing his great works "*Paradise Lost*," "*Paradise Regained*," and "*Samson Agonistes*" after he was old and blind, and that he intended these productions to be more especially his bequests to the literature of England.

We shall gratify our readers by adding a short paragraph as to "his manner of life," which has been thus given us:—"He rises early; has a chapter in the Hebrew Bible read to him; then meditates till seven; till twelve he listens to reading, in which he employs his daughters; then takes exercise, and sometimes swings in his little garden. After a frugal dinner, he enjoys some musical recreation; at six he welcomes friends; takes supper at eight; and then, having smoked a pipe and drank a glass of water, he retires to repose. That repose is sometimes broken by poetic musings, and he rouses up his daughter that he may dictate to her some lines before they are lost."

JAMES MONTGOMERY.

Scarcely any man who has but recently left our world has done more for the psalmody of the Church than this excellent layman. He was born in 1771, and was the son of an excellent Moravian minister, in whose communion he died, though for some years he held fellowship with the Wesleyan Methodists. The facts of his long and useful life are too well known to make it necessary that we should repeat them here. More than half a century of his years were spent in Sheffield, England, where he devoted his labors to the Christian press, by which he made a mark on the age that can never be erased. No man ever secured greater influence on society, or employed it more entirely for the honor of Christ. He died in 1854.

By a singular mistake of one of his friends, Mr. Montgomery's death was reported in this country a year or two before it really took place, and several of our periodicals paid cordial tributes to his memory. When these papers fell under his eye, he smiled at the blunder, but wept tears of grateful joy that brethren at so great a distance should pay him what he considered tokens of regard beyond all he had deserved.

We think we shall be more than forgiven if we add a few lines descriptive of a scene which took place at the Wesleyan Methodist Conference at Sheffield about two years before Mr. Montgomery's death. The Rev. Dr. Hannah, the president of the Conference, introduced the venerable poet in full session of the body, and, after alluding to the services which he had rendered to the cause of religious truth and moral purity, and to the delight which his poetry had ministered to so many, said, "We feel under great obligation to yourself and to the religious body to which you belong, and beg to assure you of the kindest affection of the Conference."

The aged poet's reply was beautifully characteristic:—"My Christian friends, father, and brethren in the Lord, I dare not waste one moment of your time, and I have very little to say; but that little will be of the greatest import. It is this:—'The Lord bless you and keep you! The Lord make his face to shine upon you, and be gracious unto you! The Lord lift up his countenance upon you, and give you peace!' in the name of Jesus. Amen."

A series of short but interesting speeches followed in the same spirit. What a contrast between the latter years of Montgomery and those of Byron and Moore!

A brief narrative connected with one class of Montgomery's hymns may be added to this article with advantage. It has long been customary in Sheffield, the town of Montgomery's residence, on every Whit-Monday, for the different Sunday-schools to meet at eight o'clock in the morning at their respective churches, and thence proceed, under the escort of their teachers, to some public square, there to exchange fraternal greetings, and engage in a united service, previously arranged, of which singing the hymns previously written and set to music for the occasion forms a considerable part. Our poet for very many years was a regular contributor to these jubilant occasions, and for him was always reserved the first hymn on the list. We are not aware that any collection of them has been made; but such a volume would be a truly noble one.

On the occasion of the Sunday-school jubilee, September 14, 1831, there must have been collected in one place, in the poet's town, not less than twenty thousand Sabbath-scholars; and throughout the kingdom, in like proportion, the various Sunday-schools met in their own towns and villages, to celebrate that joyful day. What a chaplet of undying green did those congregated hosts of "little children" wreathe for the brow of Montgomery, as with free and gladsome voice they sung one of his jubilee hymns!—

"The flowers of fifty summers gone,
  The leaves that then were green,
Have nothing left to look upon,
  To tell that they have been."

It has been said that Mr. Montgomery's last composition was a hymn for a Sunday-school Union, the last verse of which is both characteristic and truly sublime,—

"Learn we now that wondrous strain,
  In our schools, our homes, our hearts,
'Worthy is the Lamb once slain!'
  In all languages, all parts;
Then the countless chorus swell,
  Round his throne, with glad accord,
Never more to say 'Farewell!'
  But, 'Forever with the Lord!'"

The beautiful hymn,—

"Spirit, leave thy house of clay,"

was written by Montgomery during his political persecution in York Castle. It originally contained seven eight-line verses, and was occasioned by the death of one of his fellow-prisoners, Joseph Browne, a Quaker, who, with seven others of the same religious community, had suffered the loss of all his worldly goods for conscience' sake.

As one object of our volume is to give facts as to the habits of our hymn-writers, it will give no offence to our readers to refer to one or two mentioned by Mr. Everett, one of the intimate friends of Montgomery. Mr. Everett one day remarked to his companion that the beautiful village of Matlock would be a fine situation for the permanent residence of a poet, as the beauty of the scenery, according to the current opinion, would induce sublime thoughts. He partly objected to the notion, observing that he should have to lament for his own situation if it were so. "From the room in which I sit to write," said Montgomery, "and where some of my happiest pieces have been produced,—those, I mean, which are most popular,—all the prospect I have is a confined yard, where there are some miserable old walls, and the back of houses, which present to the eye neither beauty, variety, nor any thing else calculated to inspire a single thought except concerning the rough surface of the bricks, the corners of which have either been chopped off by violence or fretted away by the weather. No: as a general rule, whatever of poetry is to be derived from scenery must be secured before we sit down to compose: the impressions must be made already, and the mind must be abstracted from surrounding objects. It will not do to be expatiating abroad in observations when we should be at home in concentration of thought."

We may add here that the beautiful hymn,—

"Servant of God, well done!"

which in the original extended to forty-eight lines, was written by Montgomery on the occasion of the decease of the Rev. Thomas Taylor, a venerable and beloved Christian minister, an adherent of the Messrs. Wesley.

He labored under many trials and discouragements, but ultimately met with great success at Glasgow. He had to perform all the singing at public worship himself, but first spent nearly the whole of what he had in hiring a man, at eight cents a service, to be his precentor, after the Kirk custom, and to "lead the psalms." Necessity compelled him to dismiss both his precentor and the Scotch psalms, and to use the Methodist melodies, "the people," he says, "liking them right well." For fifty-five years he labored with the Wesleyans, though he was offered a very handsome salary to settle with a new church in Glasgow. He was nearly eighty years old when he died, honored and beloved as a noble veteran by all who knew him. In a sermon a short time before his decease he raised his venerable form in the pulpit and said, with great emphasis, "I should like to die like an old soldier, sword in hand." He was soon after found dead in his chamber.

The beautiful hymn by this writer,—

"Go to the grave in all thy glorious prime,"

was written to commemorate the decease of the Rev. John Owen, one of the first secretaries of the British and Foreign Bible Society, a gentleman distinguished for learning and holy eloquence. The hymn originally consisted of six verses.

THOMAS MOORE.

We never think of the author of the composition,—

> "Come, ye disconsolate, where'er ye languish,"

or half a dozen other hymns from the pen of Moore which are to be found in our books, without thinking also of the exclamation, "Is Saul also among the prophets?" Would to God Thomas Moore had been a Christian! for no man of his day possessed in a higher degree the qualities which constitute the lyric poet,—qualities which captivate the ear as well as the mind by the harmony of sound married with immortal verse. As a writer of songs, no man of his day equalled Mr. Moore. Alas that thousands are now mourning over the delusions thrown by his early productions over the ways of sin,—delusions which have fascinated multitudes to their eternal ruin! In the review of Moore and his influence over the public mind, we have again and again exclaimed, "Oh, the solemn responsibilities of authorship!"

Moore was of humble origin: he was born in Dublin, Ireland, in the year 1790, was educated at Trinity College, in that city, and then went to London to study law; but, mingling with the great and fascinating there, he gave himself to poetry and singing, married an actress, devoted his days and nights to vanity, and lived a man of the world. He died in 1852. His memoirs and letters were edited by Lord John Russell.

REV. THOMAS MORELL.

From the pen of this able and amiable minister of Jesus Christ we have several valuable hymns, including,—

"Go, and the Saviour's grace proclaim!"

Their writer was an English Congregational minister, dying, before old age overtook him, but a few years ago. For many years he discharged the duties of a successful pastorate, after which he became the President of Coward College, once under the control of the excellent Dr. Doddridge, but which has since merged in the new college of St. John's Wood, London.

REV. WM. A. MUHLENBERG, D.D.

The well-known hymn generally beginning in our books,—

"I would not live alway,—I ask not to stay,"

has a history worth telling. In the year 1824 appeared, in the "*Episcopal Recorder*," of Philadelphia, an admirable composition of forty-eight lines, of which the hymn now so commonly used forms a part. It was written by the Rev. Dr. Muhlenberg, without the most remote idea of any portion of it being used in the devotions of public worship. A committee of the General Convention of the Episcopal Church was appointed to prepare a new hymn-book; and the Right Rev. Bishop

Onderdonk, the rector of St. Ann's Church, Brooklyn, offered the verses, selected from the whole article, as a part of the book. The said hymn was at first rejected by the committee, of which the unknown author was a member; and, when a satirical criticism was offered upon it, he earnestly voted against its adoption. Dr. Onderdonk importunately urged its admission; and after a while the secret oozed out that Dr. Muhlenberg, one of their own number, was its author. Many years afterward, when he was the editor of the "*Evangelical Catholic*," Dr. M. explained the whole matter.

REV. JOHN NEEDHAM.

Of this gentleman, the author of the hymn,—

"Holy and reverend is the name,"

and several others, we have been able to obtain but very little information. He was for some years pastor of the Baptist church at Hitchin, Hertfordshire, England, whence he removed to become co-pastor with the Rev. John Beddome, of Bristol, about the year 1747. Five years afterward he transferred his labors to another church in that city, where he died about 1768, in which year the volume of his hymns was printed.

REV. JAMES NEWTON.

This author of a well-known hymn on baptism was for twenty years during the last century classical professor in the Baptist College at Bristol, England, and a colleague in the ministry with the Rev. John Tommas of the same city. The duties of both these stations he filled with high reputation to himself and distinguished advantage to others. He died in 1790, in the fifty-seventh year of his age. Mr. Newton left in manuscript a volume of original hymns, which the writer of this work deposited in the library of the institution now called the Regent's Park College, in London.

REV. JOHN NEWTON.

Of this excellent preacher and experimental hymn-writer, whose history is so well known, our readers will not expect us to speak in detail. All of them know that, though the son of a pious mother, he ran in his early life "to great excess of riot;" went to sea, engaged in the slave-trade, and, but that God placed restraints upon him, he must again and again have died. "Preserved in Christ Jesus," he was "called" by the grace of God, "counted faithful, and put into the ministry," first at Warwick, whence he removed to Olney, where he became associated with the amiable Cowper in writing and publishing the volume of "*Olney Hymns*," and ultimately to the rectory of St. Mary Woolnoth, and St. Mary Wool-Church Haw, in the English metropolis, where we will, as somewhat aided by a writer in the "*North British Review*," briefly sketch his sayings and doings.

Sixty years ago he might have been seen in the pulpit of St. Mary Woolnoth, within a stone's throw of the mansion-house of the lord mayor, surrounded by a congregation both numerous and wealthy. His sermon is to a great degree trite and commonplace, and you begin to wonder why he attracts so much attention, when he most unexpectedly utters some bright fancy or expresses some earnest feeling, while a somewhat stiff animation overruns his seamy countenance, and you wonder that a man of seventy-three can show you such kind and beaming eyes. The ardent affection with which he is earnestly looked at by his hearers proves to you that the preacher himself is invested with interest as well as his sermon.

If you will go to tea at his house, No. 8 in Coleman Street Buildings, some two or three hundred yards from his church, on next Friday evening, in a dusky parlor with some twenty of his choicest friends, the mystery will be, at least in part, explained. He has doffed the cassock, and in a sailor's blue jacket, on a three-legged stool, the preacher sits at ease at his own little table. The frugal meal is finished, the ever-present pipe is smoked, and the Bible is placed where the tea-tray stood some half an hour ago. The guests draw nearer to their venerable friend, and the feast of wisdom and the flow of soul begin. He inquires if any one has a question to ask; for these re-unions are for business as well as for friendship. Two or three are come fully prepared for this call. A retired old lady asks "how far a Christian may lawfully conform to the world." And the old sailor says many good things to guide her scrupulous conscience,—unless, indeed, she made the inquiry for the sake of the young gentleman with the blue coat and frilled wristbands across the table. "When a Christian goes into the world because he sees it is his *call*, yet while he feels it also his *cross*, it will not hurt him." Then, guiding his discourse toward some of his city friends, he says, "A Christian in the world is like a man transacting business in the rain: he will not suddenly leave his client because it rains, but the moment the business is done he is gone,—as it is said in the Acts, 'Being let go, they went to their own company.'" This brings up Hannah More and her book on "*The Manners of the Great*;" and the minister expresses his high opinion of her. Some of the party do not know who she is; and he tells them that she is a gifted lady who used to be the intimate friend of Johnson, Horace Walpole, and Sir Joshua Reynolds, the idol of the West-End grandees, and a writer of plays for Drury-Lane Theatre. He repeats his admiration and his hope for the accomplished authoress.

Having answered the inquiries which have been made,

Newton opens his Bible, and, after singing one of the "*Olney Hymns*," he reads the eighteenth chapter of the Acts. "You see that Apollos met with two candid people in the Church: they neither ran away because he was *legal*, nor were carried away because he was *eloquent*." And, after a short but fervent prayer,—catholic, comprehensive, and experimental, and turning into devotion the substance of their colloquy,—it is as late as nine o'clock, and the little party begins to separate. In leave-taking, the host has a kind word for every one, and has a great deal to say to one who is but a visitor. "I was a wild beast on the coast of Africa; but the Lord caught me and tamed me, and now you come to see me as people go to look at the lions in the Tower." And never was transformation more complete. Except the blue jacket at the fireside, and a few sea-faring habits,—except the lion's hide, nothing survived of the African lion. The Puritans would have said that the lion was slain and that honey was found in its carcass.

All about Newton's writings is truly delightful and perfectly natural. His hymns are sweet; but his "*Letters*" make him eminent. Our theology supplies nothing like them. They are all "CARDIPHONIA,—*the utterance of the heart*." Except his own friend Cowper, who was not a professed divine, no letters of that stiff century read so free, and none have so well preserved their writer's heart.

Newton was born in 1725, and died in 1807.

We have already referred to the "*Olney Hymns*;" and

it is a fact worthy of remark that these compositions were a few years ago translated into the Sherbro language by a colored man named Caulker, and are now sung in the very regions whose inhabitants Newton once assisted to carry men and women from liberty to slavery.

HON. AND REV. BAPTIST NOEL.

THIS gentleman, who has contributed to our hymn-books several beautiful compositions, including,—

"If human kindness meets return,"

is a branch of a noble family in England and a brother of the Earl of Gainsborough. Mr. Noel was born at Leithmont, near Leith, in the year 1799, and, after attaining a high reputation in various departments of learning, was ordained in the Church of England, and was appointed by her majesty Queen Victoria one of her chaplains. A few years ago, changing his opinion as to the propriety of a union between Church and State, and embracing the views of truth generally held by the Baptists, Mr. Noel left the Episcopal Church and united with that body, among whom he labors with much success, near his old church edifice, in the English metropolis, enjoying the full confidence and love of his church and congregation.

ANDREWS NORTON.

This gentleman, the author of several beautiful hymns, including,—

"My God, I thank thee! may no thought,"

was an eminent scholar and professor connected with the Unitarians. He was born at Hingham, Mass., in 1786, and graduated at Harvard College when but eighteen years of age. He never settled as a pastor, but occupied several important professorships, including that of Sacred Literature at Harvard. He died in 1853, aged sixty-seven years.

JOHN F. OBERLIN.

We are sorry for the man who is ignorant of the beautiful hymn,—

"O Lord, thy heavenly grace impart,"

or of its lovely author, the Rev. John F. Oberlin, the eminently distinguished pastor of Waldbach, in the Ban de la Roche. He was born at Strasbourg in 1740, of truly remarkable parents, who were soon rewarded by the extraordinary indications of piety and talents given in his earliest years. Especially was his mother distinguished for her Christian excellencies. She was in the habit of assembling her children together every evening, and of reading aloud from some instructive book, while they sat around the table copying pictures which their father had drawn for them; and scarcely a night passed but, when on the point of separating, there was a general request for "one beautiful hymn from dear mamma,"—with which she always complied. The hymn was followed by a prayer; and thus their infant steps were conducted to Him who has said, "Suffer little children to come unto me."

In very early life John Frederick became a Christian. He says, "During my infancy and youth God often vouchsafed to touch my heart and to draw me to himself. He bore with me in my repeated backslidings, with a kindness and indulgence hardly to be expressed." He entered the ministry, and in due time settled in one of the most difficult parishes in the world, where he accomplished what may be almost regarded as miracles of usefulness. Gladly would we dwell on scenes which can scarcely be thought of without rapture. His self-denial, his labors, his piety, and his success were alike admirable and animating.

This extraordinary man, who died in 1826, in the eighty-sixth year of his age, does not appear to have been remarkable for poetical talents. The hymn to a translation of which we have referred is the one best known,—which it well deserves to be. For it we are indebted to the Diary of the excellent Dr. Steinkopff, who heard it sung under the direction of its author on a very interesting occasion.

REV. SAMSON OCCUM.

Our readers have all heard of Samson Occum, a remarkable Indian preacher in this country, who died in 1792. He was converted about 1740, under the labors of Whitefield, Gilbert Tennent, and their companions. In 1766 he visited England, in company with the Rev. Mr. Whitaker, to advocate the cause of Dr. Wheeler's Indian school, which was afterward merged in Dartmouth College. He there preached from three to four hundred sermons; and, as no North American Indian had ever been seen in an English pulpit before, his ministry was popular, and his pecuniary success so great, that he returned to this country with more than forty-five thousand dollars.

Occum was one of the many writers who produced *one* good hymn: it begins,—

"Awaked by Sinai's awful sound," etc.

It originally contained seven verses; a portion of the whole is to be found in many of our books, and is still eminently useful. In 1809 it became generally known in England, and in 1814 was translated into Welsh by the late Rev. Thomas Thomas, of Peckham, London. In the Welsh revivals of religion it is still very commonly sung; and no doubt can be entertained of its having led many hundred sinners to the cross of Christ.

REV. THOMAS OLIVERS.

Almost every one knows the beautiful hymn,—

"The God of Abraham praise," etc.,

which was some years ago pronounced, in "*Blackwood's Magazine*," "one of the noblest odes in the English language." We suspect, however, that the eulogist did not know that its author was originally a shoemaker and one of the earliest Methodist preachers. This admirable hymn, the whole of which has been seldom printed, was written to a celebrated air sung by Leoni in the Jews' Synagogue. This hymn and tune reached the thirtieth edition as early as 1779. He also wrote the hymn beginning,—

"Lo, he comes, with clouds descending," etc.,

and prepared the music to which it was long sung, and which also reached its twentieth edition in the year just named. The Rev. John Wesley printed both hymns and tune in his "*Sacred Harmony*." Olivers was born in Wales in 1725, and died suddenly in London in 1799.

Mr. Olivers was distinguished in early life for great immorality of conduct. His attention to religion was arrested by the preaching of George Whitefield, and his subsequent life was marked by a very energetic and successful ministry. The Rev. John Fletcher said of him, "This author was, twenty-five years ago, a mechanic, and, like Peter, a fisherman, and Saul, or Paul, a tent-maker, has had the honor of being promoted to the dignity of a preacher of the gospel; and his talents as a writer, a logician, a poet, and a composer of sacred music are known to those who have looked into his publications." The Conference, also, after his death, said, "In his younger days he was a zealous, able, and useful travelling preacher. His talents were very considerable."

John Wesley, speaking of his compeers, thus refers to Olivers:—

"I've *Thomas Olivers* the cobbler,
(No stall in England holds a nobler,)
A wight of talent universal,
Whereof I'll give a brief rehearsal:
He with one brandish of his quill
Will knock down Toplady and Hill."

The celebrated Mrs. Carter heard Olivers's hymn,—

"Lo, he comes, with clouds descending,"

sung at St. Paul's Cathedral in London, as an advent-anthem, in 1753, and gives it at full length in her Letters.

KRISHNA PAL.

On one of the closing days of the last century, was baptized in the river Ganges, before the gate of the missionary premises at Serampore, Krishna Pal, the first Hindoo who trampled on the caste for Christ's sake and joined the standard of the cross. This man—then at the prime of life, being thirty-five years of age—became an eminent Christian, engaged in the ministry, which he pursued for many years, baptized many hundreds of converted idolaters, and then died triumphant in the Lord Jesus. Joyfully did he bear testimony that the service of Christ "was the work of love," and that in it "he got nothing but joy and comfort." He wrote two or three hymns, one of which continues to be sung in India in the Bengalee language, in which it was composed; and a part of it, translated into English, is printed in most of our books:—

"O thou, my soul, forget no more."

We think no one can read this hymn, remembering its author as a converted idolater and that he died carrying out its almost prediction, without having his interest in the composition greatly increased:—

"Ah, no! till life itself depart,
His name shall cheer and warm my heart;
And, lisping this, from earth I'll rise,
And join the chorus of the skies."

MRS. PALMER.

The hymn,—

"To thee, thou high and lofty One,"

was written by Mrs. Palmer, and sung at the dedication of the Methodist church in Mulberry Street, New York.

REV. RAY PALMER, D.D.

THOUGH we believe Dr. Palmer, an eminent Congregational minister of this country, has written many hymns, he has published very few. We have one, however, which can never be worn out, beginning,—

"My faith looks up to Thee."

This hymn, we are told, had in connection with its first publication an interesting incident. Dr. Lowell Mason, a musical composer, who was a personal friend of Dr. P., one day asked him to furnish him with a hymn which he might set to music. The excellent doctor told him he thought he had in his vest-pocket a worn-out, coarse piece of paper, on which, some weeks before, he had written a few lines which might suit his purpose, and, after some little trouble, found the almost illegible manuscript, the words and music of which were shortly after published, and which now minister to the edification of very many devout worshippers.

REV. A. P. PEABODY, D.D.

THE well-known funeral hymn,—

"Behold the western evening light,"

and several others, were written by Dr. Peabody, a learned Unitarian preacher, and professor in the Cambridge University. He has also published a great variety of sermons and other works, and produces one or more articles for almost every number of "*The North American Review.*" Dr. P. was born at Beverly, Mass., in 1811, graduated at Harvard College in 1826, and was ordained at Portsmouth, N.H., in 1833.

REV. SAMUEL PEARCE.

Perhaps the later editions of "*Rippon's Selection of Hymns*" may be the latest volume of hymns which contains two sweet compositions,—

"In the floods of tribulation,"

and

"The fabric of nature is fair."

The last was written when its author was confined by sickness to his chamber, where he died of consumption, a few weeks after writing it, in 1799, aged thirty-seven years. It contains fifteen verses, every one of them breathing the feelings of his "seraphic" soul. We make no small sacrifice in omitting the whole hymn. The reader will thank us for the closing lines :—

"There myriads and myriads shall meet,
In our Saviour's high praises to join ;
While transported we fall at his feet
And extol his redemption divine.

"Enough, then : my heart shall no more
Of its present bereavements complain ;
Since ere long I to heaven shall soar
And ceaseless enjoyments obtain."

Often have we looked on the beautiful autograph of this hymn with the pleasing thought that the hand which so beautifully wrote it, though now dust, shall, nevertheless, eternally be employed in its Saviour's service.

REV. EDWARD PERRONET.

FOR many years past most of our hymn-books have attributed the hymn,—

"All hail the power of Jesus' name!"

to the pen of Duncan, who, however, has no other claim to it than what may arise from some of the alterations which have been made in it. It first appeared, without a signature, in the "*Gospel Magazine*," issued in London in 1780, and in 1785 was published by Perronet himself in a volume of "*Occasional Verses, Moral and Sacred*," of which, though issued anonymously, a copy yet in existence was given by Perronet to a friend as his own, certified by his autograph. In 1787 Dr. Rippon published the first edition of his selection of hymns, in which it also appeared anonymously. It is only comparatively of late that it has been claimed for Duncan.

Edward Perronet was the son of an excellent clergyman of the Established Church of England, and the brother of Charles Perronet, who, as well as himself, was for a short time associated in the ministry with the excellent Messrs. Wesley. Edward, however, becoming Calvinistic in his theological views, was employed by the well-known Countess of Huntingdon, and labored at Canterbury, Norwich, and other places, with considerable success. Though the son of one of its clergymen, he is said to have been very decidedly opposed to the Church of England and to have sometimes employed his pen in satirizing it. He was the author of an anonymous poem called "*The Mitre*," which is generally supposed to have been one of the keenest satires on the national Establishment ever written. It was printed; but the publication of it was suppressed, by the influence and request, it is said, of John Wesley. His opposition to the Episcopal Church so grieved Lady Huntingdon that he left her connection and preached to a small congregation of Dissenters till his death.

About the year 1808 the hymn "All hail," etc., was printed at Canterbury, on a card, for the use of a Sunday-school, to which is appended the following notice of the author:—"The Rev. Edward Perronet died at Canterbury, January 2, 1792. His dying words were, 'Glory to God in the height of his divinity! Glory to God in the depth of his humanity! Glory to God in his all-sufficiency! and into his hands I commend my spirit.'"

The well-known tune which has been for more than half a century identified with the hymn of which we are writing was composed by a Mr. Shrubsole, an intimate personal friend of Perronet, who was organist at Spa-Fields Chapel, London, from 1784 till his death in 1806.

We are tempted, before dismissing this article, so far to depart from the plan of our work as to transcribe from Perronet's volume of 1785 the original and unaltered favorite hymn, leaving the reader to form his own opinion as to the character of the alterations since made:—

"All hail the power of Jesus' name!
Let angels prostrate fall;
Bring forth the royal diadem,
To crown him Lord of all!

"Let high-born seraphs tune the lyre,
And, as they tune it, fall
Before his face who tunes their choir,
And crown him Lord of all!

"Crown him, ye morning stars of light,
Who fixed this floating ball;
Now hail the Strength of Israel's might,
And crown him Lord of all!

"Crown him, ye martyrs of your God,
Who from his altar call;
Extol the stem of Jesse's rod,
And crown him Lord of all!

"Ye seed of Israel's chosen race,
Ye ransomed of the fall,
Hail him who saves you by his grace,
And crown him Lord of all!

"Hail him, ye heirs of David's line,
Whom David Lord did call,
The God incarnate, man divine;
And crown him Lord of all!

"Sinners, whose love can ne'er forget
The wormwood and the gall,
Go, spread your trophies at his feet,
And crown him Lord of all!

"Let every tribe and every tongue
That bound creation's call
Now shout, in universal song,
THE CROWNÉD LORD OF ALL."

An anecdote connected with this hymn cannot be unacceptable. The late William Dawson, a very plain man, but a highly popular local preacher among the Wesleyan Methodists of England, was, some years since, preaching in London on the offices of Christ. After presenting him as the great Teacher and Priest, who made himself an offering for sin, the preacher introduced him as the King of saints. Having shown that he was king in his own right, he proceeded to the coronation. Borrowing his ideas from scenes familiar to his audience, he marshalled the immense procession moving toward the grand temple to place the insignia of royalty upon the King of the universe.

So vividly did the preacher describe the scene, that his hearers almost thought they were gazing upon that long line of patriarchs and kings, prophets and apostles, martyrs and confessors, of every age and clime, until at length the great temple was filled, and the solemn and imposing ceremony of coronation was about to take place. The audience by this time were wrought up to the highest pitch of excitement; and, while momentarily expecting to hear the anthem peal out from the vast assemblage, the preacher commenced singing,—

"All hail the power of Jesus' name!
Let angels prostrate fall," etc.

The effect was electrical. The audience started to their feet and sang the hymn with such spirit and feeling as perhaps it was never sung before or since. Right loyally did that great congregation pay homage to the Saviour as their Sovereign that Sabbath morning.

We add here another anecdote; and, though it does not directly bear on Perronet's hymn, it does on his character, as on that of the eminent preacher to whom it likewise relates.

Mr. Wesley had long been desirous of hearing Edward Perronet preach; and Mr. Perronet, aware of it, was as resolutely determined he should not, and therefore studied to avoid every occasion that would lead to it. Mr. Wesley was preaching in London one evening, and, seeing Mr. Perronet in the chapel, published, without asking his consent, that he would preach there the next morning at five o'clock. Mr. Perronet had too much respect for the congregation to disturb their peace by a public remonstrance, and too much regard for Mr. Wesley entirely to resist his bidding. The night passed over. Mr. Perronet ascended the pulpit under the impression that Mr. Wesley would be secreted in some corner of the chapel, if he did not show himself publicly, and, after singing and prayer, informed the congregation that he appeared before them contrary to his own wish; that he had never been once asked, much less his consent gained, to preach; that he had done violence to his feelings to show his respect for Mr. Wesley; and, now that he had been compelled to occupy the place in which he stood, weak and inadequate as he was for the work assigned him, he would pledge himself to furnish them with the best sermon that ever had been delivered. Opening the Bible, he proceeded to read our Lord's Sermon on the Mount, which he concluded without a single word of his own by way of note or comment. He closed the service with singing and prayer. No imitator has been able to produce equal effect.

Another fact *does* bear on the hymn. In 1795 the late Rev. Dr. Bogue preached one of the first sermons before the London Missionary Society. One of Rowland Hill's biographers tells us, "Mr. Bogue, in the course of his sermon, said, 'We are called this evening to the funeral of Bigotry; and I hope it will be buried so deep as never to rise again.' The whole vast body of people manifested their concurrence, and could scarcely refrain from one general shout of joy. Such a scene perhaps was never beheld in our world, and afforded a glorious earnest of that nobler assembly where we shall meet all the redeemed, and before the throne of the Lamb shall sing, as in the last hymn of the service,—

'Crown him, crown him, crown him Lord of all!'"

Mr. Jones adds, "There is reason to fear that there has been a resurrection of this enemy of the Church; but till the close of life Mr. Hill often repeated the remark of a favorite author:—'Mr. Bigotry fell down and broke his leg. Would that he had broken his neck!'"

ALEXANDER POPE.

This singular and erratic genius, who was born in London in 1688 and died in 1744, was the author of a well-known ode, formerly exceedingly popular with our village choirs, and still retained in some of our books:—

"Vital spark of heavenly flame."

It was written at the request of Steele, to whom Pope says, "You have it, as Cowley calls it, just warm from the brain. It came to me the first moment I waked this morning: yet you'll see it was not absolutely inspiration, but that I had in my head, not only the verses of Hadrian, but the fine fragment of Sappho." Warton says he had in his head also the verses of Thomas Flatman, an obscure rhymer of Charles the Second's day:—

"When on my sick-bed I languish,
Full of sorrow, full of anguish,
Fainting, gasping, trembling, crying,
Panting, groaning, spiritless, dying,
Methinks I hear some gentle spirit say,
'Be not fearful, come away,'"—

which certainly bear a strong resemblance to some of the lines of Pope.

The excellent John Wesley, in giving an account of a visit he made to Bolton, in Lancashire, in the summer of 1787, tells us that, in the evening of a Sabbath on which he had addressed eight hundred Sabbath-school children, he desired forty or fifty of them to sing Pope's ode,—

"Vital spark of heavenly flame;"

and he adds, "Although some of them were silent, not being able to sing for tears, yet the harmony was such as I believe could not be equalled in the King's Chapel."

REV. THOMAS RAFFLES, D.D., LL.D.

PERHAPS no man in England who has never been in the United States has been so frequently seen by Americans in the pulpit as Dr. Raffles. He is a native of London, born about 1788, and was first-cousin to the late Sir Stamford Raffles, Governor of Ceylon. Converted in early life, he became a student for the ministry at Homerton College, and was ordained pastor of the Congregational Church at Hammersmith, near London, in 1809. We have already spoken of Dr. Collyer; and a short passage contained in the charge given by him to Dr. Raffles at his ordination, when Dr. C. was himself but twenty-seven years of age, will show the intimacy between these two eminent men when yet in their youth:—"The circumstances under which I am addressing you, my brother and friend, are not without interest. We have long known and loved each other; we have shared our pleasures and anxieties mutually and for some years; we have formed as clear conceptions and obtained as perfect a knowledge of each other's character as it is possible to possess in the present state. In whatever points this charge may be deficient, I am sure it will not be in affection."

In August, 1811, an event occurred at Liverpool which spread consternation through what has been called the religious world. The Rev. Thomas Spencer,—who, long before he had reached the age of twenty years, had attained popularity as a preacher to which none at so early an age had ever risen, excepting perhaps the late Rev. William Jay, of Bath,—while a new large church edifice was being built for him in Liverpool, was drowned while bathing in the river Mersey; and the pulpit he would have occupied a mysterious Providence thus reserved for Dr. Raffles; and, as the pastor of this church, now worshipping in a still larger edifice, he has ever since most efficiently labored.

Dr. Raffles out of the pulpit is one of the most affable, unaffected, and delightful of companions: good nature sparkles in his clear, large blue eye, plays about his mouth, and is imprinted in every line of his countenance. But in the pulpit, solemnity banishes every other feeling, and he is evidently impressed with a consciousness of his momentous mission as the servant of God. When he enters the sacred desk, he evidently leaves behind him all that is earthly, and stands only as the minister of mercy between a holy God and sinful man.

No man can hear Dr. Raffles even *read* a hymn without seeing and feeling him to be a poet; and the few hymns of his which we have in our books will most certainly confirm the impression. As, for instance, the one,—

"Blest hour, when mortal man retires,"

attracts us sweetly from earth and brings us into delightful communion with Deity. In using his hymns, there is nothing to lessen our confidence in the piety and eminent usefulness of their author, but every thing to increase the Christian love and sympathy we must desire to cherish.

For a long series of years Dr. Raffles has prepared and circulated among his people, on every 1st of January, a pastoral hymn adapted to that special season, which, regularly as it is published, appears in the columns of the "*New York Observer.*" Cordially do we unite in saying, with the editors of that paper, in giving the hymn "*No Night in Heaven,*" (Rev. xxii. 5,) "*For the Early Prayer-Meeting, New Year's morning,* 1858," "We trust the venerable and accomplished pastor may be spared to furnish many another spiritual song for his hearers and our readers."

REV. ANDREW REED, D.D.

Several popular and excellent hymns are to be found in our books from the pen of this now venerable Congregational clergyman, who for a very long series of years has been eminently successful in London. In 1834–35, Dr. Reed, in company with the late Rev. Dr.

Matheson, visited this country as a deputation to its churches from the Congregational Union of England and Wales: they were received with much cordiality, and their ministerial labors were highly acceptable. Dr. Reed has published a number of useful works, including "*The Hymn-Book*," consisting of original and selected compositions, used by many of the churches of his order in Great Britain.

REV. ROBERT ROBINSON.

Robert Robinson, the author of two hymns in our collections,—

"Come, thou Fount of every blessing,"

and

"Mighty God, while angels bless thee,"

was in his day a very extraordinary man. While a very poor lad, and an apprentice to a barber in Norwich, England, he was brought under deep religious feeling by the preaching of the distinguished George Whitefield, and soon after began to preach at the Tabernacle in Whitefield's connection in that city. At twenty-five he was called to the pastorate of the Baptist Church at Cambridge, where—and indeed wherever he was known—he attained great popularity. He was eccentric both in his religious views and his social habits. A few words in reference to each of the hymns we have spoken of may not be without their use.

20

The former one,—

"Come, thou Fount of every blessing,"

was written in early life, and was first published, in a somewhat different form from what we have it at present, in the collections of Mr. Whitefield and the Rev. Dr. C. Evans. From a descendant of one of the parties referred to in the narrative, we received, some twenty years since, the affecting statement we now make. In the latter part of his life, when Mr. Robinson seemed to have lost much of his devotional feeling, and when he indulged in habits of levity, he was travelling in a stage-coach with a lady, who soon perceived that he was well acquainted with religion. She had just before been reading the hymn of which we are writing, and asked his opinion of it,—as she might properly do, since neither of them knew who the other was. He waived the subject, and turned her attention to some other topic; but, after a short period, she contrived to return to it, and described the benefits she had often derived from the hymn, and her strong admiration of its sentiments. She observed that the gentleman was strongly agitated, but, as he was dressed in colored clothes, did not suspect the cause. This garb Robinson was compelled to assume in travelling, as wherever he was known he was pressed to stay to preach. At length, entirely overcome by the power of his feelings, he burst into tears, and said, "Madam, I am the poor, unhappy man who composed that hymn many years ago; and I would give a thousand worlds, if I had them, to enjoy the feelings I then had." An anecdote similar to this was often told by the late Rev. Thomas Morgan, of Birmingham, of almost the same language being used by Mr. Robinson to one of the most eminent ministers of his own denomination.

The other hymn to which we have referred,—

"Mighty God, while angels bless thee,"

the second line of which was written by Mr. Robinson

"May *an infant* lisp thy name,"

was composed for the use of the late excellent Benjamin Williams, Esq., for many years senior deacon of the First Baptist Church at Reading, England,—a man of great influence and usefulness. When a little boy, Benjamin sat on Robinson's knee while he wrote this hymn, who, after having read it to him, placed it in his hand. Well do we remember the deep feeling with which the venerable man described to us the scene as we sat with him at his own fireside.

REV. JOHN RYLAND, D.D.

VERY few Baptists, probably, can be found who have not heard the name of Ryland, borne by two eminent ministers of that body in England. The younger one, Dr. John Ryland, is the hymn-writer of whom we now speak. He was born in 1753, and even in childhood began to write hymns, some of which were printed in the old magazines of that day, with the signature of J. R., Junr. Before he had attained the age of five years, he was able to read the Twenty-Third Psalm in Hebrew, and at nine years could read the entire New Testament in Greek. At fourteen he was baptized by his father, and at eighteen preached his first sermon. After assisting his father for several years, he became his successor in 1786. In 1792, Brown University, in Rhode Island, conferred on him the degree of D.D.; and in the year following he became the President of the Baptist College in Bristol,—a position he occupied, in connection with the pastorate of a large church, till his decease, in 1825. He was one of the founders of the English Baptist Missionary Society, and after the death of the Rev. Andrew Fuller, in 1815, was elected one of its secretaries,—an office he filled for two or three years. He was regarded by the excellent Dr. John Pye Smith as the most eminent theologian of his day, as he certainly was among the most distinguished Hebrew scholars. Robert Hall preached his funeral sermon, and became his successor as the pastor of Broadmead Church in Bristol.

Most of our hymn-books contain the hymn,—

"In all my Lord's appointed ways;"

but probably it is not generally known that it is really but the smaller portion of a hymn written in the latter part of the last century by Dr. Ryland, then of Northampton,—the whole of which has never, we believe, been printed, except in Dr. Rippon's Selection of Hymns for

Baptist churches, formerly extensively used in this country. Its origin was rather singular. Several stage-coaches daily passed through the town; and, as the good pastor lived at no great distance from the inn where they exchanged horses, he generally contrived to meet every evangelical minister who travelled through the town, and not unfrequently almost compelled them to stay a day on the road, that they might give his people a sermon in the evening. On one occasion he had thus treated a brother in the ministry, who most reluctantly yielded and appeared in the pulpit with the text, "Hinder me not," (Gen. xxiv. 56.) Dr. Ryland, as is still customary in England, sat in the desk below the pulpit to read the hymns; and, as his brother proceeded, every "head of discourse" was "turned into poetry," which at the end of the sermon was duly read and a portion of it sung. It begins, in the original hymn,—

"When Abraham's servant, to procure
A wife for Isaac, went."

The whole consisted of nine verses, of which the last four only are now used.

Many of our collections, especially those intended for young people, contain a hymn beginning,—

"Lord, teach a little child to pray;
Thy grace betimes impart;"

which had an interesting origin. The late Rev. and excellent Andrew Fuller, of Kettering, England, lost a daughter in 1786, who died very young, but not without first giving good evidence of possessing experimental piety. While she lay sick,—which she did for some months,—Dr. Ryland, of Bristol, at the request of her father, wrote this little hymn for her special use. Speaking of her and the hymn, Mr. Fuller says, "She had some verses composed for her by our dear friend Mr. Ryland. These, when we rode out for the air, she often requested me to say over to her. She several times requested me to pray with her. I asked her again if she tried to pray herself: I found by her answer that she did, and was accustomed to pray over the hymn composed for her."

After the death of little Sarah, Mr. Fuller printed a large number of copies of the hymn on small slips of paper, and distributed them among the shop-keepers of the town, requesting them to wrap up the thread used by very many children in that neighborhood for making the lace then only wrought on pillows; so that when a little girl purchased a pennyworth or two of thread she obtained also a hymn. By this means thousands were circulated over the land, and soon got into several books, by which we trust its usefulness will long be perpetuated.

HON. AND REV. WALTER SHIRLEY.

SOME of our collections contain hymns beginning,—

"From heaven the loud, the angelic song began,"

"Hark! in the wilderness a cry,"

"Flow fast my tears, thy cause is great,"

"Sweet as the shepherd's tuneful reed,"

"Source of light and power divine,"

and a few others which were written in the last century by the Honorable and Reverend Walter Shirley, the friend of Whitefield and Wesley and the personal friend but doctrinal opponent of the well-known Rev. John Fletcher: he was also a relative and valued friend of the excellent Countess of Huntingdon, the pulpits of whose chapels he frequently supplied. He was eminently successful as an Episcopal minister at Loughrea, in Ireland, to the inhabitants of which place he dedicated a volume of excellent sermons. Mr. Shirley composed some very animated lines on the departure in 1772, two years after the death of Whitefield, of several missionaries from Lady Huntingdon's college to this country. He died in his sixty-first year, in 1786, of a very painful disease; but such was the extent of his holy zeal that, though for some time before his death he was unable to lie down in bed, he sat in his chair and frequently preached to great numbers, who crowded the drawing-rooms, the lobbies, and the staircase as far as his voice could be heard; and the testimony of God to his ministry was truly remarkable.

LYDIA HUNTLEY SIGOURNEY.

Where is the modern American hymn-book which does not rejoice in some of the compositions of Mrs. Sigourney? and whose hymns are more beautiful, more evangelical, or more generally acceptable? She was a native of Norwich, Connecticut, and at three years of age might be seen reading her Bible. Her early genius was happily fostered, and at the age of eight years she knew how to express her thoughts in writing with ease and beauty.

In 1819 Miss Huntley was married to Charles Sigourney, Esq., of Hartford, from whom a year or two since she was separated by the hand of death; but she is still blest with an amiable daughter. Her life has been distinguished by almost incessant activity in the duties of female education, and in writing an ample variety of volumes and essays both in prose and verse, all of which are beautiful and useful; nor will she, as we believe, regret on a dying pillow the production of any one of them. Many years ago we published in England a selection of her poetry, collected by ourselves, under the title of "*Lays from the West;*" and most of her productions since that time have been republished in that land. It has been well said that "her position as first in purity and talent among the lady writers of America has never been disputed by a person worthy the name of critic."

REV. S. F. SMITH, D.D.

This excellent Baptist minister of New England is well known as a gentleman of literary taste, and the author of many highly acceptable hymns, including,—

"Softly fades the twilight ray,"

and

"Yes, my native land, I love thee."

He was also one of the editors of the hymn-book used by his own denomination, called "*The Psalmist.*" He needs no further praise, nor need his character be more fully described.

ANNE STEELE.

This lady, usually in England called *Mrs.* Steele, having become advanced in years, unmarried, was the writer of many of our favorite hymns. She was the eldest daughter of the Rev. William Steele, pastor of the Baptist church at Broughton, in Hampshire, England, and was born in 1716. Very little is known of her, even though Dr. Caleb Evans, of Bristol, published a memoir of one whom he highly esteemed, living, and whose three volumes of poetry, under the name of "*Theodosia*," he greatly assisted to publish. At fourteen she was baptized and united with the church under the pastorate of her father, sustaining that connection till her death in 1778, in the sixty-second year of her age. Even in early life she was exceedingly fond of poetry, but was always unwilling that what she wrote should be made public; and, though she at length yielded to the importunities of her friends, she always withheld her name. In early life, she consented to give her hand to a worthy young man named Elscourt, and the day for the wedding was fixed; but a few hours before the intended event he went into the river to bathe, incautiously passed beyond his depth, and was drowned. Never again did her heart warm with human love.

The remaining part of Miss Steele's life was spent in retirement, manifesting, as Dr. Evans says, "unaffected humility, warm benevolence, sincere friendship, and genuine devotion." Her capacious mind was clothed with a weak and languid body; and the death of her father, to whom she was most ardently attached, gave such a shock to her frame that, though she survived him for some years, she never recovered from it. Though from the period of her father's decease she was confined to her chamber, she looked with sweet resignation to the time of her removal from earth; and, when it happily arrived, she was, amidst great pain, full of peace and joy. She took the most affectionate leave of her friends who stood weeping around her, uttered the triumphant words, "I know that my Redeemer liveth," closed her eyes, and fell asleep in Jesus. A very appropriate inscription, written by one of her nieces, was inscribed on her tombstone:—

"Silent the lyre, and dumb the tuneful tongue,
That sung on earth her great Redeemer's praise;
But now in heaven she joins the angelic song
In more exalted, more harmonious lays."

Mrs. Steele's hymns, as the reader well knows, are highly esteemed in all our churches: they are the breathings of a living soul, and have alike drawn forth the sympathizing tear, the rapturous song, and the prevailing prayer. Long will she continue to sing on earth and to educate saints for heaven.

REV. SAMUEL STENNETT, D.D.

THE family of the Stennetts furnished successive ministers to the Baptist denomination for more than a century, when the name became entirely extinct. The most eminent of the family was Samuel, the son of Joseph Stennett, pastor of the Baptist church at Exeter, England. Samuel was born in 1727 and died in 1795. His father moved to Little Wild Street, London, in 1737, and in early life his son became first his assistant and afterward his successor. He was an eminent scholar, and was honored with a degree of D.D. by the King's College at Aberdeen, and was a personal friend of his sovereign, George III., for whom it was said he read books, criticisms on which the king used to retail as his own. His literary style had all the elegant simplicity of Addison combined with more strength than that eminent writer. So particular was Dr. Stennett in his extempore delivery, that he often made long pauses in the pulpit to select the best word he could find to express his ideas. He was offered high preferment in the Church of England, but his answer was, "I dwell among mine own people," and he resolutely declined. His hymns are extensively known and are highly valued.

As Dr. Stennett approached old age, the death of his wife greatly afflicted him, but was sanctified so as to raise him above "this present evil world," and he gave full evidence that he had no desire to remain longer on earth. When almost confined to his bed, he prayed earnestly in his family "that God would give him an easy passage out of life;" "and God granted him that which he requested." Some vinegar combined with other ingredients being given him as a gargle for his throat, he said, with great emotion, "'And in *his* thirst they gave him vinegar to drink.' Oh, when I reflect upon the sufferings of Christ, I am ready to ask, What have I been thinking of all my life? What *he* did and suffered are *now* my only support." Referring to the tenets of Unitarianism, he said, "What should I do now if I had only such opinions to support me?"

REV. AMOS SUTTON, D.D.

The well-known hymn,—

"Hail, sweetest, dearest tie that binds!"

was written by the truly excellent and learned Dr. Sutton, who died after many years of successful missionary labor at Orissa, India. He was of very humble origin, and in early life was distinguished for ignorance and profanity. Changed by the grace of God, he attached himself to a General Baptist Church in London, and, after due preparation, engaged in missionary labors. He more than once visited this country, and deeply interested the Free-Will Baptists in the cause to which he had devoted his life. For his second wife he married an American lady. However beautiful the hymn to which we have alluded, its full excellence could only be realized by those who heard it read and sung by its author, who not unfrequently closed the public meetings he attended by leading in its use. At one of these meetings, at the close of an ordination in which we were engaged with him, in 1834, in the English metropolis, we heard it for the first time; nor do we expect, if by sovereign mercy we reach the heavenly world, to lose the still cherished feelings which it then excited.

STERNHOLD AND HOPKINS.

These gentlemen, with H. Wisdome and others, who assisted them in what is called "*The Version of the Psalms*," claim a niche in our volume, were it only, as old Thomas Fuller says, that they were "men whose piety was better than their poetry, and they had drank more of Jordan than of Helicon." Of the design of their work he says, "It was to make them more portable in people's memories, verses being twice as light as the selfsame bulk in prose;" and he adds that although "many have since refined these translations, yet their labors therein were never generally received in the Church, principally because un-book-learned people have *conned* by heart many psalms of the one translation, which would be wholly disinherited of their patrimony if a new edition were set forth."

Sternhold was indeed a singular man. He was groom of the bedchamber to Henry VIII. and to Edward VI., and impropriator of the buildings and lands of the priory of Bodmin, as well as versifier of the book of Psalms. Bishops Beveridge and Horsley strenuously defended the faithfulness of the old version as a just, accurate, and dignified rendering of the Psalms; while Collier calls this "*old version*" a popular innovation during the first years of the Reformation.

It is said of the celebrated Scaliger that he was so

delighted with the famous stanza of Sternhold and Hopkins in the eighteenth Psalm,—

> "On cherub and on cherubim
> Full royally he rode,
> And on the wings of mighty winds
> Came flying all abroad,"

that he used to profess that he had rather be the author of it than to have governed the kingdom of Aragon.

The well-known psalm,—

> "All people that on earth do dwell,"

was the old favorite version of the one-hundredth Psalm, and was the first English composition to which the tune of the "*Old Hundredth*" was applied by our English forefathers. It has, therefore, great historical value and a special adaptation to one of the noblest tunes in the "service of song."

"It is amusing," as the Rev. Henry Fish has remarked, "to look back and contemplate the strong feeling which existed at one period among a certain class of clergymen, and some of those enlightened ones, against any innovations upon Sternhold and Hopkins." Even the celebrated Romaine, on one occasion at least, argued as if the words of Sternhold and Hopkins, which were sung in the churches, were the words of the Holy Ghost.

REV. JOSEPH SWAINE.

"Come, ye souls by sin afflicted,"

and several other sweetly melting hymns by this writer to be found in our collections, were derived from a small volume which he himself published. Mr. Swaine was of the humblest origin, and was born at Birmingham, England, in 1761. In early life he devoted himself to sinful gayety; but, becoming partially enlightened as to the truths of the gospel, and while struggling for clearer views of Christianity, he began to write hymns. He was one day overheard by a neighbor singing one of them, who, hearing it was his own, invited him to go to a house of worship with him; and he said to his friend, "I am sure what the preacher said is true; for he has described my feelings better than I can myself." In 1791 he began to preach at Walworth, London, and organized a Baptist church, where he labored with great success for five years, the house within that period being three times enlarged. But at the age of thirty-five he was removed by death, leaving behind him a reputation still fragrant and precious.

Mr. Swaine always regarded the seraphic Samuel Pearce, of Birmingham, as his spiritual father; and to him he inscribed a long poem, in which he gave a highly-interesting narrative of his conversion.

WILLIAM B. TAPPAN.

Though this gentleman, who suddenly died in New England in 1849, was not possessed of the very highest order of talent,—nor did he ever do justice to himself, for want of care and pains,—he wrote several hymns for which he will long be remembered. If his heart had not been a well-spring of poetry, he could not have written,—

> "'Tis midnight,—and on Olive's brow
> The star is dimmed that lately shone,"

or,

> "Holy be this as was the place
> To him of Padan-aram known;"

nor can Christians cease to love him when, assembled to pray for the coming of Christ's kingdom, they raise the triumphant anthem,—

> "Wake, isles of the South! your redemption is near,"

or when, in the midst of storms and trials, they seize the lay of comfort and hope,—

> "There is an hour of hallowed peace,"

or rise exultingly toward that world

> "Where purity with love appears,
> And bliss without alloy,
> And they who oft have sown in tears
> Shall reap again in joy."

Mr. Tappan was especially interested in the cause of

Sunday-schools, and not unfrequently acceptably occupied the pulpits of his brethren,—which he did on almost the last day of his life.

TATE AND BRADY.

We have classed these authors together because they were associated in the publication, in the early part of the eighteenth century, of the "*New Version of the Psalms*" for use in the Church of England,—now, however, rapidly disappearing from our midst. A few—and but few—of them are truly valuable, and will continue to be used for years to come. Nahum Tate was born in Dublin in the year 1652 and died in 1715; and Nicholas Brady, a clergyman of the Church of England, who published many sermons, was born at Brandon, in Ireland, in 1659, and died in 1726. It has been remarked as a curious circumstance that both of the writers of the new version of the Psalms intended for the special use of Englishmen were natives of the Emerald Isle.

It is somewhat singular that neither the Old Version nor the New ever possessed the direct authority of Convocation, though the former so laid hold of the popular mind that not even the translation of King James I. could disturb it. The New Version only rests upon an allowance "by the Court at Kensington," in 1696, "for such congregations as shall think fit to receive it."

G. TERSTEEGAN.

TRANSLATIONS of several of the hymns of this excellent German appear in our books. Perhaps the best-known of them is the one,—

"Thou hidden love of God, whose height,"

and another,—

"Though all the world my choice deride."

He lived, in the beginning of the eighteenth century, a life of deep, still communion with God, choosing the occupation of a ribbon-weaver because of its tranquillity; and from his humble home he shed a blessed influence over large numbers who sought his counsel. His light seems to have shone and to have been diffused not so much by direct effort as because he himself dwelt so much in the light. His piety was the fountain of his poetry; and the beauty of his heavenly thoughts glows through the rudeness of the earthen vessel which holds them. He died at Müilheim, on the Rühr, in the year 1769, at the age of seventy-six.

REV. AUGUSTUS M. TOPLADY.

This eminent man was the son of a military officer, who died soon after his birth. When about the age of sixteen, he was brought to the knowledge of Christ by the preaching of a layman in a barn in Ireland. Toplady was even then a scholar, and the preacher could scarcely spell his own name. In 1762 he was ordained in the ministry of the Church of England, and was at length settled at Broad Hembury, in Devonshire, where, and in London, he remained till his death in 1778, occasioned by consumption. The well-known beautiful hymn,—

"Rock of ages, cleft for me,"

together with several others, proceeded from his pen, and will long minister to the edification of the Church of Christ. As a preacher, he united many qualifications which captivated his hearers. He was remarkably dignified and serious, yet pleasing, in his appearance, had a melodious voice, graceful action, and much fluency of speech. Nor did he fail to impress the hearts of many, whose tears frequently flowed with his own. His unflinching fidelity may be seen from the fact that, when once solicited to preach for a public charity, he saw present a noble lord accustomed to the sports of the field, and introduced a paragraph from a newspaper in which he was described as beating his opponent by "jostling" his horse into a ditch, and publicly cautioned his lordship lest he should be "jostled" into hell. Seeing some of his congregation smile, he solemnly exclaimed, "It is no laughing-matter, gentlemen, to be jostled into hell!"

The death of Toplady was indeed that of the Christian. A short time before his decease, at his own request, his physician felt his pulse, and was asked what he thought of it. His reply was that "the heart and arteries beat weaker and weaker;" the reply of the dying saint, as the sweetest of smiles sat on his countenance, was, "Why, that is a good sign that my death is fast approaching; and, blessed be God, I can add that my heart beats every day stronger and stronger for glory." Still nearer to his end he said, "Oh, my dear sir, it is impossible to describe how good God is to me! Since I have been sitting in this chair this afternoon—glory be to his name!—I have enjoyed such a season, such sweet communion with God, and such delightful manifestations of his presence and love to my soul, that it is impossible for any language to express them. I have had peace and joy unutterable; and I fear not that God's consolations and support will continue." But, immediately recollecting himself, he continued, "What have I said? God may, to-be-sure, as a Sovereign, hide his face and his smiles from me. However, I believe he will not; and if he should, yet still will I trust in him. I know I am safe; for his love and his covenant are everlasting." Within an hour of his death he said, "It will not be long before God takes me; for no mortal man can live"—bursting, while he said it, into tears of joy—"after the glories which God has manifested to my soul."

Before we lay down our pen, we are disposed to refer to a fact related by Dr. Pomeroy, in connection with a visit he made a few years ago to an Armenian church at Constantinople. He says that he was greatly pleased with their singing, though he could not understand the words. They all sung the same part, and while singing the hymn their eyes were closed, and, as they sung, the tears trickled down many cheeks. On inquiry what the hymn was, one of the missionaries told him it was,—

"Rock of ages, cleft for me."

The good doctor observes, with somewhat of deserved severity, that "most members of our American churches take precious good care that the singing shall have no such effect on them."

MISS TUCK.

A BEAUTIFUL hymn on heaven, beginning,—

"There is a region lovelier far,"

and one or two others of a similarly sweet spirit, adorn some of our books. They were written by a Baptist lady at Frome, Somersetshire, England, whose pen has long furnished articles for some of the English magazines.

REV. DANIEL TURNER.

Most of our hymn-books contain a hymn beginning,—

"Beyond the glittering, starry sky;"

and we have seen some three or four names attached to it as its author. The hymn, which may be seen at full length in the "*Baptist Memorial*" for 1849, and which contains twenty-eight verses, was the joint production of two English Baptist ministers of the last century. This question is forever set at rest in a note addressed by the Rev. Daniel Turner, of Abingdon, to the Rev. Dr. Rippon, of London, who published it in the "*Baptist Register*," of which he was the editor. The note, dated February 22, 1791, ran thus:—"As to your inquiry concerning the hymn, '*Jesus seen of Angels*,' it is true, as you were told by our good brother Medley, that one part of it was made by my dear friend the Rev. James Fanch, of Rumsey, and the other part by me."

Mr. Turner wrote also the hymn,—

"Jesus, full of all compassion,"

and one or two others in common use.

He was born in 1710 and died in 1798. He was originally a schoolmaster, but in 1748 became pastor of the Baptist Church at Abingdon, Berkshire, England,—an office he filled for fifty years. He published a work on the subject of full Christian communion among the churches of his own denomination, and an excellent volume entitled "*A Compendium of Social Religion.*"

REV. BENJAMIN WALLIN.

This gentleman, the author of the hymn,—

"Hail, mighty Jesus! how divine
Is thy victorious sword!"

was the son of the Rev. Edward Wallin, pastor of the Baptist Church, Maze Pond, London, where he was born in 1711. Though educated by his father, Benjamin says, "Under his judicious and affectionate instructions, both as a parent and a minister, I continued a long time a melancholy instance of the insufficiency of the best of means without a special blessing; but, I trust, before his removal it pleased God, who is rich in mercy, to open the eyes of my understanding and to change what was before only the form to the power of godliness." He was educated under the Rev. John Needham and the Rev. Dr. Stennett; but, having no thoughts of the ministry, he entered into business; and several attempts were made to induce him to preach before he consented. Three times did the church at Maze Pond invite his services in this way, and he replied, "When I consider the design of such a call to be employed more or less in preaching the gospel, the very thought strikes me with terror. It is a work of an awful nature." In July, 1740, he consented to preach for the first time; and in October, 1741, he was ordained as successor to his father. He occupied this position more than forty years, dying in February, 1782.

REV. W. WARD.

The well-known missionary hymn,—

"Great God, the nations of the earth,"

was written by the Rev. William Ward on his voyage to Bengal, in company with the late Rev. Dr. Marshman, to join the immortal Carey in the great work of evangelizing the heathen, in which labor they all spent their lives, with results that will extend throughout eternity.

The manner in which Dr. Ward—for such he really became, though his modesty led him to disown the title—became connected with the mission should not be forgotten. A short time before Carey went to India, he was walking in one of the streets of Hull, and was introduced to a youth who had just made a profession of religion and was then working with a printer in that town. "We shall, by-and-by," said Carey, "want some one to print our translations of the Scriptures: hold yourself in readiness by the time you are needed." The circumstance deeply affected Ward's mind; and a few years afterward he went out to do that very work, as well as to be a pastor and an itinerant.

Mr. Ward was born at Derby, in England, in 1769, and died in India in 1821. He paid two short visits to this country, where, as in his voyage to England, he did much to extend the spirit of missions, and collected considerable sums to advance the college at Serampore, which had been originated by himself and his brethren.

REV. RALPH WARDLAW, D.D.,

The author of several beautiful hymns, including the sacramental one,—

"Remember thee! Remember Christ!"

was one of the earliest Congregational ministers in Scotland, where he very successfully labored in the ministry for fifty years. He was born in 1779, sent to the University of Glasgow before he was twelve years of age, and ordained in that city in 1803. He published, besides his hymn-book, a very large number of admirable works, and left others in manuscript. He died in 1853, aged seventy-four years. Few men of his day rendered more service to Christ and his Church.

REV. HENRY WARE, D.D.

This gentleman, whose talents and learning were very eminent, was a member of a family devoted to the ministry among the Unitarians, while both his father and himself were professors in Harvard University. He was born in Massachusetts in 1794, graduated at Harvard in 1812, and ordained in Boston in 1817. He was eminently devoted to his duties, and, as the result of excessive labors, suffered greatly for several years in health. He died in 1843. His hymns, few in number, are lovely in their spirit, but seem to us defective as to the great doctrines of evangelical religion.

H. S. WASHBURN.

This gentleman, the author of several hymns, including a patriotic one in several of our books,—

"Let every heart rejoice and sing,"

is a Christian merchant, connected with a Baptist church in New England. He has rendered important literary and other services to the cause of our common Christianity, the happy results of which we hope he may long live to witness.

REV. ISAAC WATTS, D.D.

It has been well remarked, by the anonymous author of "*The Voice of Christian Life in Song*," that with the eighteenth century the history of English hymn-books begins. The two earliest names on the long list of that century link the story of the faith in England, in an interesting way, with that of the persecuted Protestants on the Continent. Dr. Watts, born in 1674, was descended, through his mother, from a Huguenot family driven from France by the persecutions in the early part of Queen Elizabeth's reign. And Dr. Doddridge doubtless, in his childhood, when his mother had finished the Bible-lesson from the pictured Dutch tiles, would often ask for the story of her father Dr. John Baumann's flight from Bohemia, with his little store of money bound up in his girdle, and Luther's German Bible, for all his heritage. Traditions of other ancestral wrongs and faithfulness deepened the early piety of the two great Nonconformist hymn-writers,—the pathetic stories of those patient sufferings for conscience' sake which, next to the martyrdoms of Mary's time, form the most thrilling chapter in the history of English Protestantism,—stories not then condensed into national history, but which the sufferers yet lived to tell; for Dr. Watts's mother also had her tales of her son's own infancy, when his father lay in prison for his convictions and she had sat on the stones of his prison-door with her first-born in her arms.

It has been well said that Isaac Watts was born a poet. His father was a deacon of the Independent or Congregational Church at Southampton, where Isaac was born in 1674. His ancestors had been musical: his father was not only a man of taste and intelligence, but was given to "versing;" and his mother used to offer in their boarding-school prizes of farthings for the best poetical effusions. When Isaac was some seven years old, his mother's copper medal was gained by a somewhat saucy couplet produced by her son:—

> "I write not for your farthing, but to try
> How I your farthing-writers can outvie."

Three years did Watts pursue his studies for the Dissenting ministry, under the superintendence of the Rev. Mr. Rowe, at Newington, now absorbed in London, and at little more than eighteen returned to his father's house to devote himself to more private reading and study in preparation for the sacred office. With the church in which his father held office he worshipped. At that period there were congregations which eschewed all psalmody, and in whose worship there was to be heard as little of the voice of melody as in a meeting-house of "Friends." But this was not the case in the congregation of the Rev. Nathaniel Robinson. They sang; and some have said it was from Sternhold and Hopkins, or from Barton's books; but, unless our memory greatly deceives us, we saw some half-century ago a volume of hymns published by one Brown, then sung at Southampton. Some of these were mere doggerel; but, if we remember rightly, some of Watts's own book only presented a revised form of what were written by his predecessor. At all events, Isaac, at about eighteen, greatly complained of the entire want of taste in the hymns generally used, and in return was challenged to produce something better. Conscious of his powers, he undertook to do so, and very shortly afterward the service of the day was closed by the beautiful composition which begins his first book:—

"Behold the glories of the Lamb."

This attempt was an innovation, and the poet was a prophet of their own country; but to the devotional instincts of the worshippers so welcome was this "new song" that they entreated the author to repeat the service, till, the series extending Sunday after Sunday, a sufficient number had been contributed to form the basis of a book. Such was the commencement of a work which has aided millions in their devotions, and which will, probably, be useful to the Church of Christ till the end of time.

This volume, however, was not published till the year 1707, when he issued the "*Hymns and Spiritual Songs.*" For the copyright, Mr. Lawrence, the publisher, gave him ten pounds; and in less than ten years six editions had been sold. Twelve years afterward he published what he regarded his greatest work, "*The Psalms of David imitated in the Language of the New Testament.*" In reference to this latter work, the American reader will assuredly examine with interest a letter written by its author to the Rev. Dr. Cotton Mather. Its date was London, March 17, 1717–18.

"*To my honored and dear friend,*

Dr. Cotton Mather of New England.

"REV. AND DEAR SIR:—I may persuade myself of a hearty acceptance of this little present I make you.

They are the fruits of some easy hours this last year, wherein I have not sought poetical flourish, but simplicity of style and verse for the use of vulgar [common] Christians.

"'Tis not a translation of David that I pretend, but an imitation of him so nearly in Christian hymns that the Jewish psalmist may plainly appear yet leave Judaism behind. My little essay that attends this manuscript will render some of my reasons for this way of introducing the ancient Psalms in the worship of the New Testament.

"The notes I have frequently inserted at the end are chiefly to render the world a reason for the particular liberties I assumed in each Psalm.

"If I may be so happy as to have your free censure and judgment of 'em, it will help me in correcting others by them. I entreat you, sir, that none of them may steal out into public. If God allow me one year more, even under my present weakness, I hope he will enable me to finish my design. To him be all the glory. Amen. Your most affectionate lover and obliged friend,

"I. WATTS."

Mr. Montgomery—and few men were more capable of forming a correct judgment—says that "Dr. Watts may almost be called the inventor of hymns in our language; for he so far departed from all precedent that few of his compositions resemble those of his forerunners; while he so far established a precedent to all his successors, that none have departed from it, otherwise than as according to the peculiar turn of mind in the writer and the style of expressing Christian truths employed by the denomination to which he belonged."

Equally true and beautiful are the same author's remarks on Watts's "*Divine Songs for Children.*" He says, "These form so small a portion of his multiform labors, that were they expunged the eye could scarcely perceive the bulk of one of the volumes diminished. Yet who can calculate the innocent pleasure and the abiding profit which those few leaves have afforded to myriads of minds through the lapse of a century? And, much more, who can estimate the treasure of instruction and delight which would thereby be lost to millions hereafter through ages untold?"

It has been well said, by another writer, "It may appear at the last day that this little work was the most useful of all his publications. He has done very much by it to Christianize more than one-quarter of the world."

We think it is Cecil who says that nothing about Dr. Watts surprised him so much as that he should have descended from writing his "Logic" to compose his beautiful "*Divine Songs for Children.*" To this we are disposed to reply that his severer exercises of mind most admirably prepared him for the clear and simple compositions in which he afterward engaged. These beautiful "*Songs*" carry about them evident indications of fine mental training and sweet condescension of spirit and manners, which will be admired in many of these compositions till the end of time.

We may mention here a tradition still prevalent in the county of Essex. Castle Hedingham, in that county, was situated not very far from London, where the doctor then resided. At the castle, from which the village took its name, lived an excellent family, named Ashhurst, who were frequently visited by Dr. Watts and other London ministers. In the beautiful and secluded grounds of that lovely spot, tradition tells us, the pious poet composed many of his "*Divine Songs.*" We can easily believe the statement, as also that the delightful scenery suggested some of the finest thoughts.

The remark often made that the interest we take in a hymn is greatly augmented when we know its history, has seldom been more strikingly illustrated than in the composition of Watts beginning,—

"How vain are all things here below!"

It is well known that the worthy doctor lived and died a bachelor. The cause of this seems to have been that in early life he met with a severe disappointment. Attracted alike by the personal, the intellectual, and the spiritual loveliness of Miss Elizabeth Singer, afterward the well-known Mrs. Rowe, Isaac Watts tendered to her his heart and his hand, and was unhappily repulsed,—the lady telling him that, though she loved the jewel, she could not admire the casket which contained it. Thus was poor Watts treated, as were others, by this excellent but surely somewhat capricious lady, whom

Mrs. Barbauld in some degree taunted when she said to her, in the language of high compliment,—

"Thynne, Cartaret, Blackmore, Orrery approved,
And Prior praised, and noble Hertford loved:
Seraphic Ken and *tuneful* Watts were thine,
And Virtue's noblest champions filled the line."

Though disappointed and grieved, the pious poet submitted to what he considered an arrangement of Divine Providence, and then wrote the hymn to which we have referred, the beauty of which both the Christian and the poet will admire. Happy the man who could at such a time pray,

"Dear Saviour, let thy beauties be
My soul's eternal food,
And grace command my heart away
From all created good!"

It was some time since observed, by a writer in the "*Presbyterian Quarterly Review*," that in the hymn of Watts beginning, "There is a land of pure delight," "every image is scriptural, every suggestion appropriate, every association holy;" and he adds, "we doubt whether any uninspired production has oftener softened the heart or moistened the eyelids."

We learn from an American writer, who obtained his information on the spot, that its author wrote this hymn at Southampton, his native town, while sitting at the window of a parlor which overlooked the river Itchen, and in full view of the Isle of Wight, "the swelling flood" celebrated in it, "beyond" which is seen "the land of pure delight,"

"Where everlasting spring abides
And never-withering flowers."

So, at least, it might seem. It is indeed a fair and beautiful type of that paradise of which the poet sung. It rises from the margin of the flood and swells into boundless prospect, all mantled in the richest verdure of summer, checkered with forest-growth, and fruitful fields under the highest cultivation, and gardens, and villas, and every adornment which the hand of man, in a series of ages, could create on such susceptible grounds. As the poet looked upon the waters then before him, he thought of the final passage of the Christian:—

"Death, like a narrow sea, divides
This heavenly land from ours."

The hymn written by Dr. Watts,—

"Am I a soldier of the cross?"

was first published by its author at the end of his thirty-first sermon, entitled "*Holy Fortitude, or Remedies against Fear;*" the text, 1 Cor. xvi. 13:—"Stand fast in the faith; quit you like men; be strong." The hymn itself is a fine apostrophe for the use of the Christian soldier, who is represented in a review of his character and duties, and with an earnest desire to engage in the conflict in which he is sure of victory by faith in Him who has already conquered all his foes. It breathes the true spirit of a soldier of the cross of Christ. He would wear no laurel that he does not gain under the banner of the Great Captain of his salvation. He disdains to be

"carried to the skies
On flowery beds of ease,
While others fought to win the prize
And sailed through bloody seas,"

and boldly asks for the foes he has to face. After expressing his resolve to fight his way to heaven, and anticipating the bliss he shall enjoy, he ascribes all the glory to Him who hath purchased it with his blood. Let every Christian soldier enter the warfare and continue in it with the spirit of this hymn.

We have elsewhere spoken of the cordial friendship which existed between Dr. Doddridge and Dr. Watts; and certainly the reader will be gratified by a short extract from a letter of the former excellent man to the latter, relative to that exquisitely beautiful hymn,—

"Give me the wings of faith, to rise."

Dr. Doddridge thus affectionately speaks to his friend:—"On Wednesday last I was preaching in a barn to a pretty large assembly of plain country-people in a village a few miles off. After a sermon from Heb. vi. 12, we sung one of your hymns, (which, if I remember right, was the one hundred and fortieth of the second book;) and in that part of the worship I had the satisfaction to observe tears in the eyes of several of the auditory; and, after the service was over, some of them told me that they were not able to sing, so deeply were their minds affected with it; and the clerk, in particular, told me he could hardly utter the words of it. These were most of them poor people, who work for their living."

While writing this article, we learn from the English newspapers that in the new park just formed in Southampton, the town in which Dr. Watts was born, arrangements are in progress for the erection of a statue to his memory, to be paid for by penny subscriptions of Sunday-school children.

We know not that we can better close this article than by a short extract from Mrs. S. C. Hall's "*Residence of Dr. Isaac Watts*," now, alas! "among the things that were." She says, "We followed our conductor to the top of the house, where, in a turret upon the roof, many of Dr. Watts's literary and religious works were composed. We sat upon the seamed bench, rough and worn, the very bench upon which he sat by daylight and moonlight,—poet, logician, and Christian teacher. We were in some degree elevated above the dense and heavy fog, for the heavens were clear and blue; but all beneath us was shrouded in a sea of mist, that would sometimes clear away and then press its yellow folds more closely round every object of interest. This was very provoking, as we desired to see what *he* had seen; but we remembered how out of this good man's naturally irritable temperament he had become gentle, modest, and patient. We could almost fancy the measured tones of his sweet, eloquent voice reproving our unthankfulness for what we had already enjoyed. . . . The chamber upon whose walls hung the parting breath of this benevolent man might well be an object of the deepest interest to all who follow, however humbly, the faith of Jesus. We were told of a little child who, knowing every hymn he had written, was taken into his room, having some vague but happy idea that she should meet him there. Learning, as she eagerly looked round, that the author of '*Watts's Hymns*' was dead, she burst into bitter tears, which did not cease while she remained in the house."

Perhaps, however, the most striking commendation of these compositions was from the pen of the energetic and accomplished William Wilberforce. With special reference to the beautiful "*Summer Evening*" of its author,—

"How fine has the day been! how bright was the sun!"

he says, "It is not for children in years alone, but for the children of God and the heirs of glory. And when we compare it, either in point of good sense or imagination, or its sterling value in sustaining hope, with the considerations and objects which feed the fancy or exercise the understanding or affections of the most celebrated men who have engaged the attention or called forth the eulogiums of the literati of the last century, we are irresistibly forced to exclaim, 'Oh, happy hymnist! Oh, unhappy bards!'"

Before we close this article, we may refer to two or three compliments paid to the poetical writings of Watts, very different in character, but equally illustrative of their influence. A copy of his Psalms and Hymns was taken into Central Africa by Mr. Anderson, the brother-in-law and fellow traveller of the celebrated but unfortunate Mungo Park, which the Landors, many years afterward, found hung up in the residence of a chieftain as a *fetishe*, to be worshipped as sacred.

Another is presented in a letter from the Rev. Dr. Colman, of Boston, under date of August 20, 1739:— "This last year, at my motion, two of our booksellers reprinted your 'Songs for Children,'—an edition of two or three thousand, I think; and your Hymns are just now out of the press, and your Treatise of Prayer in it. I know not whether you reckon our editions here any thing; but we do."

We may add yet another fact of interest,—that the Hymns of Dr. Watts were first published in this country, by Dr. Franklin, in 1741, and his Psalms the same year in Boston; but neither the Psalms nor the Hymns were generally used in worship by our fathers till after the Revolution.

Our readers will be gratified if we give the opinion written by our countryman William Wirt, Attorney-General of the United States. "I bought the other day," he says, in a letter to his wife, "a copy of Watts's Psalms and Hymns. Do you know that I never think of this man without such emotions as no other human being ever inspires me with? There is a loftiness in his devotion, and an indifference, approaching to contempt, for the praise or censure of the beings of this nether world, which is heroic and sublime. It is so awfully great that even old, surly, growling Johnson, with all his High-Church pride and arrogance, felt its influence, and scarcely dared to whisper a criticism in his life of Dr. Watts,—which is a curiosity in this particular. What a soul of celestial fire, and, at the same time, of dissolving tenderness, was that! How truly did he devote all the faculties of that soul to the contemplation of the glory of God and of the Saviour! He was, indeed, 'ever journeying home to God,' and seems to have stopped half-way between earth and heaven to compose this excellent book. His was a rapt soul; and I never feel my own worthlessness so forcibly as when I read his compositions and compare my spirit with his."

It has sometimes occurred to us that the cultivation of the art of poetry has a very happy influence on the temper. So it seems to have been with Dr. Watts; for we are told that he was of so extremely mild a disposition that, when a friend once blamed him for not having severely reprimanded a man who had done him a serious injury, he replied, "I wish, my dear sir, you would do it for me."

THE WESLEYS.

In the early years of the eighteenth century, while Dr. Doddridge, during his solitary childhood, was learning from his mother's lips, in their house in London, how the God who led Israel through the wilderness rescued his exiled grandfather from Bohemia,—while the first edition of Dr. Watts's hymn-book was being eagerly bought up in a single year,—John and Charles Wesley were spending their childhood in the country parsonage at Epworth, in Lincolnshire, John having been born in 1703, and Charles in 1709. The old Puritan blood ran in their veins: their father's grandfather and father had both been ejected from the Established Church in 1662, and the younger of these had often been in prison for his Nonconformity. Their mother's father, the Rev. Dr. Annesley, was also one of the early Nonconformists,—a man of whom his daughter said that for forty years his deep sense of peace with God through Christ had never been broken, and who died whispering, "When I awake up in thy likeness, I shall be satisfied,—*satisfied*."

None of our readers need to be told that amidst persecution and contumely John and Charles Wesley preached the gospel of Christ throughout their long lives: the hearts of thousands were awakened, and the morning hymn of rejoicing multitudes went up to that Sun of Righteousness which had arisen with healing in his wings. In one place, where an enraged crowd had rushed into the house where John Wesley was resting, he addressed them with such affectionate faithfulness, appealing to the "thirst" which lay deep in their hearts below their opposition, that the disorderly mob became a peaceable congregation and tears of penitence streamed down the faces of the ringleaders. At another time the magistrate who came to prevent Charles Wesley from preaching was himself arrested by the preacher's words, listened to the end, and went away with a softened and humbled heart. In almost every place where they were thus assailed, societies of true converts sprang up out of the very ranks of the persecutors. It was out of lives such as these that the Wesleyan hymns were distilled. As the reader has already seen, one hymn was composed after a wonderful escape from an infuriated mob, another after deliverance from a storm at sea, and all in the intervals of a life of almost incessant toil. The pressure of trial and the power of faith drew many a vigorous hymn from John Wesley; but it was Charles Wesley who—in his prime, on his preaching-tours, by the roadside, amidst hostile mobs or devout congregations, and in his old age, in his quiet journeyings from friend to friend—poured forth the great mass of the Wesleyan hymns. Those hymns are now sung in collieries and copper-mines, in our dense forests and on the battle-fields of other lands, in the cradle and on the death-bed. How many has their heavenly music strengthened in the hour of sorrow, and given courage to strong men and patience to suffering women! They have been a liturgy engraved on the hearts of thousands of the poor, and have aided in bearing the name of Jesus far and wide, writing it deep on countless hearts. Truly has it been said that the service he rendered to Methodism—and, we will add, to evangelical religion—by his hymns did as much as John Wesley's rules to bind together the rough material of early Methodism. They express even now every Sabbath the religious emotions of tens of thousands of worshippers; and during their whole history they have comforted the souls and fluttered on the dying lips of myriads now before the throne.

There is something so remarkably interesting in Mr. Moore's description of Charles Wesley when nearly eighty years old, that we are sure our readers will thank us for transcribing it:—"He rode every day—clothed for winter even in summer—a little horse, gray with age. When he mounted, if a subject struck him, he proceeded to expand and put it in order. He would write a hymn, thus given him, on a card kept for that purpose, with his pencil, in short-hand. Not unfrequently he has come to the house in the City Road, and, having left the pony in the garden in front, he would enter, crying out, 'Pen and ink! pen and ink!' These being supplied, he wrote the hymn he had been composing. When this was done, he would look round on those present and salute them with much kindness, and thus put all in mind of eternity. He was fond on these occasions of the lines,—

> 'There all the ship's company meet
>   Who sailed with the Saviour beneath;
> With shouting each other they greet,
>   And triumph o'er sorrow and death.
> The voyage of life's at an end,
>   The mortal affliction is past;
> The age that in heaven they spend
>   For ever and ever shall last.' "

The hymn,—

> "Come, Desire of nations, come,"

was written by the Rev. Charles Wesley, and formed part of a tract consisting of nineteen "*Hymns Occasioned by the Earthquake, March* 8, 1750." This tract was intended to give a right direction to the extraordinary consternation and excitement which prevailed in London and its neighborhood, occasioned by shocks which moved the earth, about London and Westminster, westward, then to the east, and then westward again, attended with a rumbling noise like that of thunder. Many houses were shaken and several chimneys thrown down; but it was believed that no lives were lost. Thousands left their houses and encamped for some days in the fields. A soldier added to the alarm by pretending that he had a "revelation" that on a certain midnight a great part of London would be swallowed up. Not a few really supposed that the day of judgment was about to commence; many churches were thrown open, and Romaine and others preached to the crowds there, while Whitefield and Wesley preached in Hyde Park and elsewhere, at midnight, to many thousands. Forms of prayer were appointed "by authority" to be read in the churches, prayers were composed for the use of families, sermons and letters were printed on the subject, and the results of the whole matter were very great. Nor was the tract to which we have referred without its use. Its publication was a happy thought. In addition to the hymn we have mentioned as thus called forth, was also another which yet lives among us,—

"How weak the thoughts and vain," etc.

In 1780, the Rev. Charles Wesley published, in pamphlet form, "*Hymns Written in the Times of the Tumults, June,* 1780." These awful mob riots, so celebrated in the annals of England, took place in London as the result of the imprudent anti-popish violence of an infatuated peer, Lord George Gordon, a man clearly insane, who collected many thousands of persons to destroy the chapels and the persons of the Roman Catholics. The cowardly fears of the London magistrates and the malice of the mob were severely lashed in a satirical poem from the pen of Charles Wesley, in which he speaks thus of the charge that the Methodists had aided the Roman Catholics:—

"Old Wesley, too, to papists kind,
Who wrote against them for a blind,
Himself a papist still in heart,
He and his followers shall smart;
Not one of his fraternity
We here beneath our standard see."

In 1782, Charles Wesley also issued a tract of forty-seven pages, entitled "*Hymns for the Nation,*" having a special reference to the fact that England was at war with her "rebellious" transatlantic colonies. One verse from these hymns, which still remains in most of the Methodist hymn-books, will be read by our friends with a smile:—

"Saviour, whom our hearts adore,
To bless our earth again,
Now assume thy *royal* power
And o'er the nations reign."

The exquisitely-beautiful hymn,—

"Come, Father, Son, and Holy Ghost,
To whom we for our children cry,"

was written by Charles Wesley, and sung "at the opening of a school at Kingswood" for preachers' sons. Mr. Creamer says, "It has been brought as a charge, in effect, against Mr. John Wesley, that he preferred genuine piety, even when associated with ignorance, to irreligion, though adorned with learning and the adventitious importance which wealth alone too often confers. To assert this, however, is only saying that he had, in spirit, sat at the Saviour's feet, heard his word, and learned of him. But he saw no necessity for either; and therefore he prayed himself, and, by putting the words into his hymn-book, instructed his societies and followers to pray,—

'Unite the pair so long disjoined,—
Knowledge and vital piety:
Learning and holiness combined,
And truth and love, let all men see
In those whom up to thee we give,—
Thine, wholly thine, to die and live.' "

We are glad of an opportunity of saying somewhat of the truly-grand hymn written by Charles Wesley,—

"Thou God of glorious majesty."

It contains, as our readers all know, a truly-sublime verse:—

"Lo! on a narrow neck of land,
'Twixt two unbounded seas I stand,
Secure, insensible!
A point of time—a moment's space—
Removes me to that heavenly place
Or shuts me up in hell!"

This fine composition was written on the promontory

known in England as "Land's End," on the coast of Cornwall. It is really "a narrow neck of land" jutting out into the Atlantic. To pass over this neck for the purpose of reaching the outmost point of English land is somewhat dangerous. With scarcely foot-room beneath you, you have on either side a precipice, with the sea washing its base; and, whether you turn to the right hand or the left, your eye meets a vast expanse of ocean.

Mr. Montgomery, in his "*Christian Psalmist*," says of this hymn, "It is a sublime contemplation,—solemn, collected, unimpassioned thought, but thought occupied with that which is of everlasting import to a dying man standing on the lapse of a moment between two eternities."

We shall add to these remarks an extract from Dr. Adam Clarke, under date of October 11, 1819:—"I write this on the last projecting point of rock of the Land's End, upward of two hundred feet perpendicular above the sea, which is raging and roaring tremendously, threatening destruction to myself and the narrow point of rock on which I am sitting. On my right hand is the Bristol Channel, and before me the vast Atlantic Ocean. There is not one inch of land from the place on which my feet rest to the American continent. This is the place where Charles Wesley composed those fine lines,—

'Lo! on a narrow neck of land,
'Twixt two unbounded seas I stand.'

Charles Wesley's hymn,—

"Stand, the omnipotent decree,"

was written and published in 1756, with special reference to the earthquake which destroyed the city of Lisbon in that year. Montgomery says, "The hymn on the day of judgment,—'Stand, the omnipotent decree,'—begins with a note, abrupt and awakening, like the sound of the last trumpet. This is altogether one of the most daring and victorious flights of our author."

"Give me the enlarged desire"

was written by Charles Wesley, and was a favorite hymn with the seraphic John Fletcher of Madely, of whom Southey speaks as "a man of rare talents and rarer virtue. No age or country has ever produced a man of more fervent piety or more perfect charity; no church has ever possessed a more apostolic minister." Mr. Fletcher was, as is well known, at one time the President, and Mr. Benson, his intimate friend, the Head-Master, of Lady Huntingdon's college at Trevecca for the education of young ministers. Speaking of Mr. Fletcher's devotional habits, Mr. Benson says, "My heart kindles while I write. Here it was that I saw,—shall I say an angel in human flesh? I should not far exceed the truth if I said so. . . . After speaking a while in the school-room, he used frequently to say, 'As many of you as are athirst for this fulness of the Spirit, follow me into my room.' On this, many of us have instantly followed him, and there continued for two or three hours, wrestling like Jacob for the blessing, praying one after another till we could bear to kneel no longer. This was not done once or twice, but many times. And I have sometimes seen him on these occasions, once in particular, so filled with the love of God that he could contain no more, but cried out, 'O my God, withhold thy hand, or the vessel will burst.' But he afterward told me he was afraid he had grieved the Spirit of God, and that he ought rather to have prayed that the Lord would have enlarged the vessel, or have suffered it to break, that the soul might have had no further bar or interruption to the enjoyment of the Supreme God. For, as Mr. Wesley has observed, the proper prayer on such an occasion would have been,—

> Give me the enlarged desire,
> And open, Lord, my soul,
> Thy own fulness to require
> And comprehend the whole:
> Stretch my faith's capacity
> Wider and yet wider still;
> Then with all that is in thee
> My ravished spirit fill.' "

The well-known hymns,—

> "Woe to the men on earth who dwell,"

and

> "By faith we find the place above,"

were written by Charles Wesley, and were first printed by him in a tract about 1756. They were parts of a long hymn he wrote on the then recent destruction of Lisbon; and, read with this fact in view, their interest is greatly increased. He wrote about that period many hymns much adapted, alike by their sentiments and beauty, to impress the public mind from the passing events of that important period.

The very excellent and graphic hymn,—

'Glory to God, whose sovereign grace,"

was written by Charles Wesley "for the Kingswood colliers;" but we are sorry to see that Wesley's last two verses have been omitted from our modern books:—

"Suffice that for the season past
Hell's horrid language filled our tongues,
We all thy words behind us cast,
And lewdly sang the drunkard's songs.

But—oh, the power of grace divine!—
In hymns we now our voices raise,
Loudly in strange hosannas join,
And blasphemies are turned to praise."

These verses, as well as such words as "senseless stories," "reprobates," and "outcasts," will be better understood when it is remembered that the tract of country called Kingswood, consisting of from three to four thousand acres, formerly a royal chase, and lying near Bristol, England, supplies to that city the greater part of its fuel. It was in the days of the Wesleys and Whitefield inhabited by a far more brutal and lawless race than any of their fathers, in the persons of the colliers, differing as much from the people of the surrounding country in dialect as in appearance. Of these people many of the Christians of Bristol said to George

Whitefield, when he was preparing to embark for Georgia to preach to the Indians, "What need of going abroad for this? Have we not Indians enough at home? If you have a mind to convert Indians, *there are colliers enough in Kingswood.*" Here, under an old sycamore-tree on Hanham Mount, that great man preached his first sermon in the open air to about a hundred colliers. This number rapidly increased, till they sometimes amounted to nearly twenty thousand persons. He says, "The first discovery of their being affected was in the white gutters made by their tears, which plentifully fell down their black cheeks, as they came up out of their coal-pits. Hundreds and hundreds of them were soon brought under deep convictions, which happily ended in sound and thorough conversion."

Compelled to embark for America, Whitefield prevailed on John Wesley to succeed him in this interesting charge; and we scarcely need to remark that Kingswood has ever since been regarded as a sacred spot in ecclesiastical history. Here houses of prayer for Wesleyan Methodists and Independents were soon erected, and in them thousands have been converted to God. Here was placed the first school for the sons of Methodist preachers; and on Hanham Mount, besides the voice of Whitefield, have been heard those of the Wesleys, Coke, and Mather; and here Pawson and Benson and Bradburn accomplished some of the mightiest effects which followed their powerful preaching.

It has been supposed that the two hymns of Charles Wesley,—

"Oft have we passed the guilty night,"

and

"Hearken to the solemn voice,"

were the first two hymns composed by this author for watch-night services. Dr. Southey terms these watch-nights "another of Wesley's objectionable institutions;" and yet they had a very lovely origin. They began among the converted colliers of Kingswood, who, having in the days of their folly given their Saturday nights to drinking in the ale-house, after their hearts had been changed gave these same hours to worship God in the school-house, continuing their hymns and prayers late into the Sabbath morning. These services contributed greatly to their spiritual advantage; and John Wesley determined to introduce them into all his societies. In 1742—the date of the first publication of these two hymns—he appointed a monthly watch-night during the full moon: this service is still continued at the close of every year, and has in later years been imitated by many congregations of other denominations

"Worship, and thanks, and blessing,"

was a "blast," as Mr. Creamer says, written by Charles Wesley "after deliverance in a tumult," and was often *sounded* on similar occasions. We have no certain information as to its precise date. One account of "a mob at Devizes," written by the author, as occurring in 1747, and copied from Jackson's Life of Charles Wesley, closes in so interesting a manner that the reader will be glad to refresh his memory with it:—

"After riding two or three hundred yards, I looked back and saw Mr. Merton on the ground, in the midst of the mob, and two bull-dogs upon him. One was first let loose, which leaped at the horse's nose; but the horse with his foot beat him down. The other fastened on his nose and hung there, till Mr. Merton, with the butt-end of his whip, felled him to the ground. Then the first dog, recovering, flew at the horse's breast and fastened there. The beast reared up, and Mr. Merton slid gently off. The dog kept his hold till the flesh tore off. Then some of the men took off the dogs; others cried, 'Let them alone.' But neither beast nor man had any further commission to hurt. I stopped the horse and delivered him to my friend. He remounted with great composure, and we rode on leisurely, as before, till out of sight. Then we mended our pace, and in an hour came to Seend, having rode three miles about, and by seven to Wraxall. The news of our danger was got there before us; but we brought the welcome tidings of our deliverance. Now we saw the hand of Providence in suffering them to turn out our horses; that is, to send them to us against [by the time] we wanted them. Again, how plainly were we overruled to send our horses down the town,—which blinded the rioters without our designing it, and drew off their engines and them, leaving us a free passage at the other end of the town! We joined in hearty praises to our Deliverer, singing the hymn,—

'Worship, and thanks, and blessing.'"

Men who could thus suffer and sing would, under similar circumstances, be as ready as Daniel to be cast into the lions' den, or to enter, like the three Hebrew children, the fiery furnace, even though it were heated seven times hotter than usual.

The hymn,—

"Oh for a thousand tongues, to sing,"

is said to have been written by Charles Wesley on the first anniversary of the conversion of himself and his brother John. It originally contained eighteen verses, and was entitled "*For the Anniversary of One's Conversion.*" It was first published in the year 1739.

The hymn,—

"Come, O thou all-victorious Lord,"

was also written by Charles Wesley "before preaching at Portland," a peninsular parish of England, opposite Weymouth, in the county of Dorset. It is remarkable for its stone-quarries, from which an abundant supply is sent to different parts of England and elsewhere and where very many of its inhabitants are engaged in this kind of labor. These facts probably suggested two lines in the first verse:—

"Strike with the *hammer* of thy word,
And break these hearts of *stone.*"

The well-known animated and emphatic hymn,—

"See how great a flame aspires,"

was composed by Charles Wesley "after preaching to the Newcastle colliers" on the joyful occasion of its author's ministerial success, and that of his fellow-laborers, among that rough and hardy people. Mr. Jackson, Mr. Wesley's biographer, says, "Perhaps the imagery was suggested by the large fires, which illuminate the whole part of that country in the darkest nights."

. The hymn,—

"Jesus, from thy heavenly place,"

was written by Charles, and in the English Methodist hymn-book has the line,—

"Our *king's* peculiar treasure prove."

Dr. Floy, in the "*Methodist Episcopal Quarterly Review*" for 1844, says, "Father Hitt, to suit it to republican America, altered the word; and we now pray that 'piety sincere' may prove the peculiar treasure of our *land*, and that it may be inspired with humble love.'"

The hymn written by Charles Wesley,—

"Long have I seemed to serve thee, Lord,"

was written under peculiar circumstances. In the year 1740, considerable disputes originated in some of the Methodist societies and rent some of them in pieces. They were occasioned by a man named Molther, who had been a Moravian, and who introduced what was called the doctrine of *stillness*, denying that divine grace or the influence of the Holy Spirit is transmitted in the use of means, especially through the ordinance of the

Lord's Supper. Mr. Jackson, the biographer of Wesley, well says, "This fine hymn guards against extremes, both on the right hand and on the left, and embodies those just views on the subject which the brothers steadily maintained to the end of their lives. Charles Wesley used to call on the right-minded people in his congregation at the Foundery, London, to unite with him in singing it; and it is difficult to conceive how any enlightened Christian could refuse to join in the holy exercise. Its effect at the time must have been very powerful." The whole hymn contained twenty-three verses.

Every one knows that the beautiful hymn,—

"Come, let us join our friends above,"

was written by Charles Wesley. Some years after his death, and not long before his own decease, the Rev. John Wesley, being in London, officiated in his own chapel in City Road. After the morning prayers had been read, he ascended the pulpit; but, instead of immediately announcing the hymn to be sung, to the great surprise of the congregation, he stood silent, with his eyes closed for, it has been said, at least ten minutes, wrapt in intense thought. Having done this, with a feeling which at once told where his spirit had been communing, he solemnly read this hymn. We can easily imagine the effect this produced on the minds of those persons who well knew both the men.

We may add here that the Rev. Thomas Spencer, a

very popular Congregationalist minister, who died, while bathing, in his twenty-first year, at Liverpool, England, in 1811, had this hymn almost constantly on his mind for several weeks before his lamentable decease. He was often heard privately to sing it, and more than once conversed on its subject with his friends,—little thinking, however, how soon he should join his friends who had "crossed the flood."

In speaking of the hymn,—

"God is in this and every place,"

Mr. Creamer, in his "*Methodist Hymnology*," says on the lines,—

"And have I measured half my days,
And half my journey run?"

"It is a coincidence worthy of notice in this connection, that when Mr. Charles Wesley composed this hymn he was about forty years old: he died aged eighty; hence he had just, in his own beautiful language,—

'measured half *his* days,
And half *his* journey run.'"

Charles Wesley's hymn,—

"The great archangel's trump shall sound,"

was written "after a deliverance from death by the fall of a horse." It originally consisted of twelve verses: two of those now omitted referred thus to the accident:—

"How blessed whom Jesus calls his own!
How quiet and secure from harms!

The adversary cast us down,—
The Saviour caught us in his arms.

"'Twas Jesus checked his straitened chain
And curbed the malice of our foe:
Allowed to touch our flesh with pain,
No further could the murderer go."

The beautiful funeral hymn,—

"Shrinking from the cold hand of death,"

was from the pen of Charles Wesley, of whose personal habits in old age we have already spoken; and connected with the third verse of this hymn Mr. Moore records a pleasing anecdote of *John* Wesley:—"When his increasing infirmities were perhaps more apparent to others than himself, he would omit none of his religious duties or labors. Herein he would listen to no advice. His almost continual prayer was, 'Lord, let me not live to be useless!' At every place, after giving to the society what he desired them to consider as his last advice,—'To love as brethren, fear God, and honor the king,'—he invariably concluded with the verse,—

'Oh that without a lingering groan
I may the welcome word receive,
My body with my charge lay down,
And cease at once to work and live!'"

Another of Charles Wesley's funeral hymns begins,—

"Again we lift our voice."

It was composed "On the death of Samuel Hitchens," one of Mr. Wesley's first preachers, who died in the year 1747, after itinerating two years. From the fifth verse we learn that he was very young:—

> "Thou, in thy *youthful* prime,
> Hast leaped the bounds of time;
> Suddenly from earth released,
> Lo! we now rejoice for thee,
> Taken to an early rest,
> Caught into eternity."

The beautiful hymn by Charles Wesley,—

> "Infinite God! to thee we raise,"

is an elegant paraphrase of the "*Te Deum Laudamus.*" Mr. Benjamin Love, in his "*Records of Wesleyan Life,*" says, "It is questionable whether there is any production merely human worthy of being considered a rival to the *Te Deum;* and that person must be dead indeed to every spiritual feeling and emotion who can utter with his lips its touching sentences and remain in heart unaffected and unimpressed. Who can repeat the solemn truth, 'We believe that thou shalt come to be our Judge,' and not be unmoved?" Or who can sing, in the strain of the Methodist poet,—

> "And thou, with judgment clad, shalt come,
> To seal our everlasting doom,"

without a fervent prayer to find mercy in that day?

> "Thou hidden love of God, whose height,"

is a translation by the pen of John Wesley from the German of Gerhard Tersteegan. In his "*Plain Account of Perfection,*" Mr. Wesley tells us he wrote this hymn at Savannah, Georgia, in 1736, and quotes the following lines to show what his religious feelings then were:—

> "Is there a thing beneath the sun
> That strives with thee my heart to share?
> Ah, tear it thence, and reign alone,
> The Lord of every motion there!"

Dr. Southey, in his Life of Wesley, connects these lines with the love-affair with which Mr. Wesley was connected in this country, and which ended in disappointment, and thinks they were written on that occasion; nor are we aware of any objection to this theory of the matter.

The hymn,—

> "How happy is the pilgrim's lot!"

was the production of Mr. John Wesley, and, as Mr. Creamer has very justly said, has attracted as much attention as any other in the Methodist hymn-book. We cannot speak of this hymn better than in the words of the gentleman to whom we have referred:—"This hymn has been admired by thousands not known by the name of Methodists, with whom it has always been a great favorite, as well on account of the remarkable character of its sentiments as the elegant simplicity of its diction. Throughout the composition the author has made personal reference to himself. His opinions upon the subject of matrimony at one time of life are well known to all acquainted with his history; and this hymn was published about five years before his unhappy union with his wife, at a period when he had probably no intention of ever entering the marriage-state, and breathes only the language of one who had devoted to God, as he had done, his ease, his time, his life, his reputation. There are traits about it which cannot be mistaken; see, for instance, verses four, five, and six: but there is another verse, which has been omitted from our [the Methodist] hymn-book, that is still more characteristic of the author's sentiments at the time of life when it was written. It runs thus:—

'I have no sharer of my heart,
To rob my Saviour of a part
And desecrate the whole:
Only betrothed to Christ am I,
And wait his coming from the sky,
To wed my happy soul.' "

"Some of the expressions in this stanza," Mr. Creamer adds, "are very similar to many found in Moravian hymns, and may have resulted from his intimate intercourse with those people in the early part of his ministry."

"Behold the Saviour of mankind"

was written by the Rev. Samuel Wesley, the father of the Rev. Messrs. John and Charles Wesley, and is said to have been preserved in a very singular manner when its author's parsonage was consumed by fire, the second time, August 24, 1709, when John, his son, was saved from death almost by miracle. "Among other mementos of this calamity," says the editor of "*Dr. Adam Clarke's Wesley Family*," "four leaves of music may be noticed, the edges of which bear the marks of the fire and may be handed down to posterity as a curiosity. Charles Wesley, Jr., has written on one of the leaves, 'The words by my grandfather, the Rev. Samuel Wesley. Probably the music was adapted by Henry Purcell, or Dr. Blow.'" These remarks are followed by "A Hymn on the Passion: the words by the Rev. Mr. Samuel Wesley, Rector of Epworth, in the diocese of Lincoln."

That hymn, however, contains two verses which are now generally omitted. They were the second and sixth:—

"Though far unequal our low praise
To thy vast sufferings prove,
O Lamb of God, thus all our days,
Thus will we grieve and love!

"Thy loss our ruin did repair;
Death by thy death is slain:
Thou wilt at length exalt us where
Thou dost in glory reign."

Samuel Wesley, Jr., was the elder brother of John and Charles Wesley: he manifested a poetical taste even in childhood, and produced a few of the finest hymns in Methodist psalmody, including,—

"The Lord of Sabaoth let us praise,"

"Hail, Father, whose creating call,"

"Hail, God the Son, in glory crowned,"

and

"The morning flowers display their sweets."

The last-named hymn was written on the death of a

young lady, and is founded on Isaiah xl. 6, 8.:—"All flesh is grass, and all the goodliness thereof as the flower of the field. . . . The grass withereth, the flower fadeth; but the word of our God endureth forever." Mr. Creamer very truly says, "The author has completed his task in a most interesting and pleasing manner. The imagery is touching; and, although the subject is of a melancholy character, he has thrown light among the shadows and intermingled beauty with the gloom. The hymn cannot be read without emotion."

HENRY KIRKE WHITE.

THIS lovely youth, who died of excessive study at the age of twenty-one, has furnished several compositions to our hymnology, including the beautiful hymn,—

"When marshalled on the nightly plain."

He was the son of a butcher, and was born at Nottingham, England, in 1785. On account of the delicacy of his constitution, he was taught the trade of a stocking-weaver; but his attachment to learning became so well known that he was soon taken into the office of an attorney, where his marvellous love of Latin and Greek, in connection with his piety and his ambition for the clerical office, induced Messrs. Wilberforce and Simeon to send him to the University at Cambridge. At eighteen he published a poem; and after his death his "*Poems*,"

"*Letters and Fragments*" were edited by Dr. Southey in two octavo volumes. He lived greatly beloved and died much lamented. He was buried in the chancel of All-Saints' Church, Cambridge, where a few years afterward an American gentleman named Boott erected a handsome tablet to his memory, executed in bas-relief by Chantrey, on which are engraved the following beautiful lines from the pen of Professor Smyth:—

"Warm with fond hope and learning's sacred flame,
To Granta's bowers the youthful poet came:
Unconquered powers the immortal mind displayed,
But, worn with anxious thought, the frame decayed.
Pale o'er his lamp, and in his cell retired,
The martyr-student faded and expired.
Oh, genius, taste, and piety sincere,
Too early lost 'midst studies too severe!
Foremost to mourn was generous Southey seen:
He told the tale, and showed what White had been,
Nor told in vain; for o'er the Atlantic wave
A wanderer came, and sought the poet's grave;
On yon low stone he saw his lonely name,
And raised this fond memorial to his fame."

JOHN G. WHITTIER.

How this Quaker poet—nay, even this hymn-writer—would have fared among his own people some two centuries ago, it is now difficult to say; for assuredly they would have utterly opposed such doings, and would probably have "put him out of meeting." We, however, cordially thank him for the pleasure which his hymns have afforded us. Mr. Whittier was born in 1808, and has devoted the greater portion of his life to literature.

And yet, after all, while we think Mr. Whittier a poet,—the poet of humanity,—the Ebenezer Elliott of the United States,—we have no expectation that any of the hymns he has written will be sung in the worshipping assemblies of coming generations. They want the glowing ardor and the evangelical unction which only can make hymns popular with Christian masses. We should delight to see the honest Quaker possessing the piety of our old *Friend* Joseph John Gurney: he might then write hymns on "Christ and his Cross" which might live till the death of time.

REV. WILLIAM WILLIAMS.

THIS distinguished Welsh poet was born in 1717, in Caermarthenshire, and was originally educated for the medical profession. His biographer tells us that "his religious feelings were at first painful. His convictions of sin were deep and alarming, but his subsequent joy proportionably high." He was ordained a curate in the English Church, but, after thus laboring for three years, was encouraged by Whitefield and the Countess of Huntingdon to become an itinerant minister among the Calvinistic Methodists. His labors were incessant and greatly blessed. He is said to have travelled on an average two thousand two hundred and thirty miles a year for forty-three years, when there were no railroads and but few stage-coaches. His last illness was occasioned by intense study in writing a book called "*A View of the Kingdom of Christ*," and in his last hours his speech failed him; but he was evidently very happy. He died in 1791. He published several hymn-books in his own language, which are still much used, such as "*The Sea of Glass*," "*Hosanna to the Son of David*," etc.

His hymns,—

"O'er the gloomy hills of darkness,"

"Guide me, O thou Great Jehovah,"

and several others, are equally known and esteemed. His Memoir was published by a brother Welshman a few years ago.

NATHANIEL P. WILLIS.

THE beautiful hymn so often sung at the dedication of churches, and which has already appeared in several of our hymn-books, was written by its author for the dedication of a Unitarian house of worship in the city of New York in 1845.

Mr. Willis was born at Portland, in Maine, in 1807, and at fifteen entered Yale College. His first work, we believe, was "*Scripture Sketches*," which drew him into the literary circle, since which he has written little of a religious character. He has been the poet of society, but not of the sanctuary. His writings are distinguished for finish and melody. Would that they were fine gold which would pass current with heaven!

Perhaps the sweetest thought which Mr. Willis ever penned grew out of a reverence of his pious mother's prayers for him. Tossed by the waves in a vessel which was bearing him homeward, he wrote,—

> "Sleep safe, O wave-worn mariner,
>   Nor fear to-night nor storm nor sea:
> The ear of Heaven bends low to her:
>   He comes to shore who sails with me."

WILLIAM WORDSWORTH.

The late poet-laureate of England has contributed one or two hymns to the service of the Christian sanctuary, and therefore we contribute a few lines to him. He was born in 1770, and educated for the Church of England at the University of Cambridge. Throughout life he employed his leisure hours in writing poetry,—though he never rose very high in the estimation of the public till he attained gray hairs, when, on the death of Southey, he was appointed poet-laureate. He died in 1850, in his eighty-first year. None of his hymns will be valued by posterity.

The following extract of a letter written by Wordsworth to one of his correspondents in this country will be read with interest by at least some of our friends:—

"I took the journey to London solely to pay my respects to the queen on my appointment to the laureateship on the decease of my friend Mr. Southey. The weather was very cold, and I caught an inflammation in one of my eyes, which rendered my stay in the South very uncomfortable. I nevertheless did, in respect to the object of my journey, all that was required. The reception given me by the queen at her ball was most gracious. Mrs. Everett, the wife of your minister, among many others, was a witness to it, without knowing who I was. It moved her to the shedding of tears. This effect was in part produced, I suppose, by American habits of feeling, as pertaining to a republican government. To see a gray-haired man of seventy-five years of age kneeling down in a large assembly to kiss the hand of a young woman, is a sight for which institutions essentially democratic do not prepare a spectator of either sex, and must naturally place the opinions upon which a republic is founded, and the sentiments which support it, in strong contrast with a government based and upheld as ours is. I am not, therefore, surprised that Mrs. Everett was moved, as she herself described to persons of my acquaintance,—among others, to Mr. Rogers the poet."

FRANCIS XAVIER.

One, at least, of our popular hymn-books contains the hymn of this extraordinary Roman Catholic missionary,—

> "Thou, O my Jesus, thou didst me
> Upon the Cross embrace."

This "apostle of the Indies" was born at Navarre in 1506, and died, when about to land in China, in 1552. Of this distinguished missionary it has been well said that, weak and frail as he was, from the days of Paul of Tarsus to our own, the annals of mankind exhibit no other example of a soul borne upward so triumphantly through distress and danger in all their most appalling aspects. He battled with hunger, and thirst, and nakedness, and assassination, and pursued his message of love with ever-increasing ardor amidst the wildest war of the contending elements. When, on one occasion, reminded of the perils to which he was about to expose himself by a mission to the barbarous islands of the Eastern Archipelago, he replied, "If these lands had scented woods and mines of gold, Christians would find courage to go there; nor would all the perils of the world prevent them. They are dastardly and alarmed because there is nothing to be gained but the souls of men; and shall love be less hardy and less generous than avarice? They will destroy me, you say, by poison. It is an honor to which such a sinner as I am may not aspire; but this I dare to say that, whatever form of torture or of death awaits me, I am ready to suffer it ten thousand times for the salvation of a single soul." Well has John Angell James said, "This is a sublime heroism. Wondrous Xavier! whatever were thy errors, it would be the dregs of bigotry not to admire thy martyr-zeal."

ILLUSTRATIONS

OF THE

INFLUENCE OF HYMNS

ON

PERSONAL AND SOCIAL HAPPINESS.

INFLUENCE OF HYMNS

ON

PERSONAL AND SOCIAL HAPPINESS.

A UNIVERSITY STUDENT.—A highly-intelligent young man standing at his father's door was offered by a gentleman a slip of paper on which was printed the hymn written by John Newton,—

"Stop, poor sinner, stop and think."

This hymn he read, was much affected by it, and carefully committed it to memory. Five years afterward, while studying at Brown University, a spirit of unusual attention to religion was awakened in that institution, and this same young man entered a meeting for devotional exercises just as they were commencing the hymn,—

"Stop, poor sinner, stop and think."

His early impressions were instantly revived: he saw himself ruined by sin, that eternal woe was before him, and that peace of conscience and with God could only be obtained by the blood of the cross of Christ. The Holy Spirit enabled him to rest his soul on the atoning sacrifice of Christ; and this young man became an eminently pious and active physician.

An English Actress.—The fact we are about to relate has been told in several ways; but we are inclined to think that the version given in the "*Sunday-School Journal*" is the correct one. The hymn referred to was from the pen of Charles Wesley.

An actress in one of the English provincial or country theatres was one day passing through the streets of the town in which she resided, when her attention was attracted by the sound of voices in a poor cottage before her. Curiosity prompted her to look in at the open door,—when she saw a few poor people sitting together, one of whom, at the moment of her observation, was giving out the hymn, which the others joined in singing:—

"Depth of mercy! can there be
Mercy still reserved for me?"

The tune was sweet and simple; but she heeded it not. The words had riveted her attention, and she stood motionless, until she was invited to enter by the woman of the house, who had observed her standing at the door. She remained during a prayer which was offered up by one of the little company; and, uncouth as the expressions sounded, perhaps, to her ears, they carried with them a conviction of sincerity on the part of the person engaged. She quitted the cottage; but the words of the hymn followed her, and at last she resolved to procure the book which contained it. She did so; and the more she read it, the more decided her serious impressions became. She attended the ministry of the gospel, read her hitherto neglected and despised Bible, and bowed herself in humility and contrition of heart before Him whose mercy she now felt she needed, whose sacrifices are those of a broken heart and a contrite spirit, and who has declared that with such sacrifices he is well pleased.

Her profession she determined at once to renounce, and for some time excused herself from appearing on the stage, without, however, making known her resolution finally to leave it.

The manager of the theatre called upon her one morning and requested her to sustain the principal character in a new play which was to be performed the next week. She had frequently performed this character to general admiration; but she now, however, told him her resolution never to appear as an actress again, at the same time giving her reasons. At first he attempted to overcome her scruples by ridicule; but this was unavailing: he then represented the loss he would incur by her refusal, and concluded by promising that if, to oblige him, she would act on this occasion, it would be the last request of the kind he would ever make. Unable to resist his solicitations, she promised to appear, and on the appointed evening went to the theatre. The character which she assumed required her, on her first entrance, to sing a song; and, when the curtain drew up, the orchestra immediately began the accompaniment. But she stood as if lost in thought, and as one forgetting all around her and her own situation. The music ceased, but she did not sing; and, supposing her to be overcome by embarrassment, the band again commenced. A second time they paused for her to begin; and still she did not open her lips. A third time the air was played; and then, with clasped hands and eyes suffused with tears, she sang,—not the words of the song, but,—

"Depth of mercy! can there be
Mercy still reserved for me?"

It is almost needless to add that the performance was suddenly ended. Many ridiculed, though some were induced from that memorable night to "consider their ways," and to reflect on the wonderful power of the religion which could influence the heart and change the life of one hitherto so vain and so evidently pursuing the road which leadeth to destruction.

It will be satisfactory to the reader to know that the change in Miss —— was as permanent as it was singular: she walked consistently with her profession of religion for many years, and at length became the wife of a minister of the gospel of our Lord Jesus Christ.

An Irish Persecutor.—The singing of the Wesleyan Methodists has often been shown to possess great influence especially in the early history of that body. Charles

Wesley's hymns, with simple but effective tunes, spread everywhere among the societies; and hundreds of hearers who cared not for the preaching were attracted to their assemblies by the singing. Especially among the Irish did it secure them much success. At Wexford the society was persecuted by the Catholics, and met therefore in a closed barn. One violent opposer agreed to conceal himself in the barn before the worship began, that at a suitable time he might open the door to his comrades; and for that purpose he crept into a sack near the door. When the singing commenced, the Hibernian was so impressed with the music that he thought he would hear it through before he began the disturbance. The singing so much gratified him that he thought he would also hear the prayer; and such was the effect of the prayer that he was seized with remorse and trembling, so that he roared with fright,—which led the people to remove the sack, whereupon the Irishman was disclosed, praying with all his might as a penitent. Southey says, "This is the most comical case of instantaneous conversion that ever was recorded; and yet the man is said to have been thoroughly converted."

A Young Man.—The narrative we now give is from the pen of the Rev. J. Parker.

In the village of —— was a boarding-house kept by Mrs. F——, at whose house I was a lodger. Of the fifteen or twenty guests about the table was a young gentleman of about twenty-four years of age. He was full of animation, and his vivacity created the impression that, whoever else might be affected by the solemnities of the time, he was not.

On a Sunday morning the late Rev. Dr. Perrine preached a peculiarly effective sermon on the consequences of a life of sin. There was a singular unction and tenderness in the discourse, and its vivid pictures of hell's torments produced a most solemn and subduing effect.

As we were sitting at the dinner-table, and remarks were passing freely in regard to the morning service, the young man above mentioned expressed in strong terms his disapprobation of the sermon, and added, "Such preaching only hardens me and makes me worse." I replied, "It is possible that you think it makes you worse, when it only makes you conscious of sin that was before slumbering in your heart." "No," said he: "it hardens me. I am at this moment less susceptible to any thing like conviction for hearing that discourse. I feel more inclined to resist every thing like good impressions than usual." "Yet," I rejoined, "*good impressions* are those which are best adapted to secure the desired end; and I am greatly mistaken if an increase of the effect which you feel would not be greatly useful to you. If, for instance, you should read now Watts's version of the Fifty-First Psalm, beginning,—

'Show pity, Lord; O Lord, forgive,'

it would take a deep hold on your heart."

"Not the least," said he: "I could read it without moving a muscle. I wish I had the book: I would read it to you."

"We have one," said Mrs. F——, who was fully aware of the excitement under which he was laboring; and the book was handed him, opened at the place. He commenced to read, with compressed lips and a firm voice:—

"Show pity, Lord; O Lord, forgive;
Let a repenting sinner live:
Are not thy mercies large and free?
May not a sinner trust in thee?"

Toward the last part of the stanza a little tremulousness of voice was plainly discernible. He rallied again, however, and commenced the second verse with more firmness:—

"Oh, wash my soul from every sin,
And make my guilty conscience clean:
Here on my heart the burden lies,
And past offences pain mine eyes."

At the last part of this stanza his voice faltered more manifestly. He commenced upon the third with great energy, and read in a loud, sonorous voice,—the whole company looking on in breathless silence:—

"My lips with shame my sins confess."

As he read the second line,—

"Against thy law, against thy grace,"

his lips quivered, and his utterance became difficult. He

paused a little, and entered upon the third line with an apparently new determination:—

> "Lord, should thy judgment grow severe."

Yet before he came to the end his voice was almost totally choked; and when he began upon the fourth line,—

> "I am condemned, but thou art clear,"

an aspect of utter discouragement marked his countenance, and he could only bring out, in broken sobs, "I am condemned,"—when his utterance changed to such a heart-broken cry of grief, rising at the same time and rushing from the room, as I had never witnessed in a convicted sinner.

The dinner was interrupted; but that was the beginning of a change, leading on to a new life, in Mr. H.; and probably every person in that room retained the impression that a view of the awful justice of God, in connection with the grace that saves from it, is often effective in subduing those who say, "Prophesy unto us smooth things," and that sinners are not always good judges in respect to what produces the best effect upon themselves.

AN UNHAPPY MOTHER.—We have known very many instances of good resulting from the knowledge of hymns in early youth. They fasten themselves on the memory and remain there through life. A poor, wretched female, religiously educated, but afterward abandoned to sin and misery, was struck with horror at hearing her own child repeat, as soon as she could well speak, some of the profane language which she had learned from herself. She trembled at the thought that she was not only herself travelling to eternal perdition, but was also leading her child there. She instantly resolved that with the first sixpence she could procure she would obtain a copy of Dr. Watts's "*Divine Songs for Children*," of which she had some recollection from the days when she visited the Sunday-school, and would teach them to her infant daughter. She soon bought them; and on opening the book her eye caught the striking verse,—

"Just as the tree cut down, that fell
To north or southward, there it lies,
So man departs to heaven or hell,
Fixed in the state wherein he lies."

She read on: the Spirit of God impressed the words on her heart; the event led to her entire conversion, and she lived and died a consistent professor of the religion of Christ.

An English Nobleman.—One of the most interesting anecdotes illustrating the power of hymns in the family-circle we have ever met with was related in a social circle in England a few years ago by a clergyman well acquainted with the facts.

Lord ——, a nobleman of great wealth, was a man

of the world: his pleasures were drawn from his riches, his honors, and his friends. His daughter was the idol of his heart. Much had been expended in her education; and well did she repay, in her intellectual endowments, the solicitude of her parents. She was highly accomplished, amiable in her disposition, and winning in her manners; but, alas! the whole family were strangers to God. By a series of remarkable circumstances, the Hon. Miss. —— was led within the walls of a Methodist church in London and converted to the Lord Jesus. Henceforth she delighted in the service of the sanctuary and in social religious meetings. To her the charms of Christianity were overpowering, and the society of those who loved Jesus Christ a heaven upon earth.

The change was seen by her devoted father with deep solicitude. To see his lovely daughter thus infatuated was to him the occasion of intense grief; and he resolved to correct her erroneous views on the real pleasures and pursuits of life. He placed at her disposal large sums of money, hoping she would be induced to pursue the fashions and extravagance of others in her own rank of life, and to forsake the Methodist meetings; but she maintained her integrity. He took her on frequent and long journeys, hoping thus to divert her mind from religion; but she still delighted in the Saviour. After failing in all his other projects, he determined to introduce her into company under circumstances that would compel her to join in the amusements of the party or give high offence. It was arranged that on a festive occasion several young ladies should each accompany a performance on the piano-forte with a song. The hour arrived; the party assembled; several had delighted all with their performances; and all were in high spirits. The Hon. Miss —— was called on for her song; and many hearts beat high in hope of victory. The crisis was come. Should she decline, she would be disgraced as insulting her friends; and should she comply, their triumph would be complete. With entire self-possession, she took her seat at the instrument, ran her fingers over its keys, and commenced playing, singing in a sweet air the words of Charles Wesley,—

"No room for mirth or trifling here,
For worldly hope or worldly fear,
If life so soon is gone,—
If now the Judge is at the door,
And all mankind must stand before
The inexorable throne.

"No matter which my thoughts employ,
A moment's misery or joy;
But, oh! when both shall end,
Where shall I find my destined place?
Shall I my everlasting days
With fiends or angels spend?"

She rose from her seat. The whole party were subdued. Not a word was spoken. Her father wept aloud. One by one the visitors left the house. Lord —— never rested till he became a Christian. He lived and died consistently with his profession as a servant of Christ, having, during his union with the people of God, contributed to the cause of benevolence half a million of dollars.

Since writing the above, we have met with a very similar narrative of facts in connection with a young lady of this country, converted in the early days of Methodism, under the labors of the excellent Bishop Asbury.

An Irish Sunday-Scholar.—We have not unfrequently heard singers eminent for "science," "taste," and words of similar import, ridicule a certain class of hymns and tunes, altogether forgetting that these very compositions may exert on other minds a holy and happy influence. Let us illustrate what we mean by a condensed narrative from the pen of a living clergyman. He says, "One day, as I was busily engaged in my study, a man about half drunk very unceremoniously entered and handed me a note from the teacher of the infant class of our Sabbath-school, informing me that the bearer was the father of one of her scholars, that the child had met with an accident, and that they lived in such a place: she could not visit them, and she wished me to see to it.

"I looked at the man: he was Irish, very repulsive in his appearance, and he answered my questions with a rough brogue.

"'What is your name, sir, and where do you live?'

"'My name is Pater M——: I live on an ould canal-boat at the fut of Harrison Street. I wint there whin I was burnt out; and nobody at all at all has driv me out of it.'

"'And what is the matter with your child?'

"'Och! and is it Kitty, my own little darling Kitty, the only child I've lift of the six that has been born til me? Och! Kitty! she was playing about on a ship where I was til wark, and she fell down the hatchway and broke her leg, (saving your prisence,) and poor Kitty's leg is not set right, your riverence, for I have no money til pay a docther. Och! poor Kitty! and I've nothing to give her to ate, your riverence.'

"'Well, Peter, I will come down and see your Kitty, and see what can be done for you.'

"I did so, and found a wretched state of things. The poor little suffering child was overjoyed to see me. I remembered her countenance,—a sweet, mild little girl, not yet five years of age. She lay upon the 'locker' or side-seat of an old canal-boat which had been laid up for the winter. There was no fire, though it was a bitter-cold day,—no chair, no bed, no food, scarcely an article of furniture or any comfort whatever. I did what I could to relieve the wants of the little sufferer. Nothing could be done for the parents: they were both confirmed inebriates; and I found they had both been drunk the night previous, and in a quarrel had unintentionally knocked the child off the seat and broken the limb again after it had been set. I obtained the services of a surgeon and had the limb set again, and then sat down on the locker to talk to little Kitty, and fed her with some nourishing food which I had brought. I asked her if she could read. No, she could not read a word; 'but I can sing,' said she. 'What can you sing?' 'Something I learned at Sabbath-school.' 'Well, what is it you can sing, Kitty?' In a moment her sweet little voice broke out,—

'There is a happy land,
Far, far away,
Where saints in glory stand,
Bright, bright as day.'

"'Well, Kitty, that is sweet. Where do you think the land of Canaan is, Kitty?' 'Oh, I suppose it is up in the sky, where God lives and where the angels live.' 'Do you think you will ever go there, Kitty?' 'If I'm good and love God, I think I shall.'

"'Now, Kitty, is there any thing else you can sing for me before I go?' 'Oh, yes, sir: I can sing a little piece of another.' 'Well, what is that?'

'All who love the Lord below
When they die, to heaven will go,
And sing with saints above.
Oh! that will be joyful!
Joyful, joyful!
Oh! that will be joyful,
When we meet to part no more!'

"Poor Kitty could not read, nor could either of her parents read. She knew nothing about heaven and divine things except what she had been taught at the Sabbath-school; and most of what she remembered was associated with such despised words and sentiments as we have quoted. Eternity alone will unfold the power of such simple truth, and simple yet sweet tunes, upon infant minds."

Governor Hill.—We confess to a love of hymn-singing under almost all circumstances. The family, the social circle, nay, in many instances the sick-bed itself, may profit by it. But we have a beautiful illustration now before us of the advantages of singing in apparent solitude. In Governor Hill's account of his stage-ride over the Alleghany Mountains, in a dark night, shut up with strangers, he tells us that, to get rid of the fear of robbers, he began to sing one of Dr. Watts's hymns, certainly supposing that as a Christian he was alone. To his great delight, however, another pious New Englander responded in another hymn; and he was followed by another, who broke out in a popular camp-meeting air. The Governor was delighted to ascertain that three of the travellers out of the six proved to be New England Puritans. He threw his fears to the winds, and the morning found them safe beyond the dreaded haunts of the highway-robbers.

Campbell the Poet.—The influence which devotional singing sometimes produces on others may be inferred from a reminiscence of James Grahame, author of "*The Sabbath*," written by the poet Thomas Campbell, with whom he was intimate when both as young men resided in Edinburgh :—"One of the most endearing circumstances which I remember of Grahame was his singing. I shall never forget one summer evening that we agreed to sit up all night and go together to Arthur's Seat to see the sun rise. We sat accordingly all night in his delightful parlor,—the seat of so many happy remembrances. We then went and saw a beautiful sunrise. I returned home with him, for I was living in his house at the time. He was unreserved in all his devoutest feelings before me; and, from the beauty of the morning scenery and the recent death of his sister, our conversation took a serious turn on the proofs of infinite benevolence in the creation and the goodness of God. As I retired to my own bed, I overheard his devotions,—not his prayer, but a hymn which he sung, and with a power and inspiration beyond himself and beyond any thing else. At that time he was a strong-voiced and commanding-looking man. The remembrance of his large, expressive features when he climbed the hill, and of his organ-like voice in praising God, is yet fresh and ever pleasing in my mind."

A Taunting Lover.—A young gentleman, tenderly attached to a young lady, was obliged to take a journey. During his absence she became a follower of Jesus. He heard of the change, and wrote her a letter full of invectives against religion and its gloomy professors. Having a good voice, and playing well on the pianoforte, she had been accustomed to entertain him with her music, especially in performing one song, of which he was very fond, the burden of which was, "Ah, never! ah, no!" At their first interview after his return, he tauntingly said, "I suppose you cannot sing me a song now?" "Oh, yes," was her reply, "but I will;" and, proceeding to her piano, she sung a hymn she had composed to his favorite tune:—

"As I glad bid adieu to the world's fancied pleasure,
You pity my weakness: alas! did you know
The joys of religion, that best hidden treasure,
Would you bid me resign them? Ah, never! ah, no!

"You will surely rejoice when I say I've received
The only *true* pleasure attained below.
I know by experience in whom I've believed:
Shall I give up this treasure? Ah, never! ah, no!

"In the gay scenes of life I was happiness wooing;
But ah! in her stead I encountered a woe,
And found I was only a phantom pursuing:
Never once did I find her. Ah, never! ah, no!

"But in these bright paths which you call melancholy
I've found those delights which the world does not know.
Oh, did you partake them, you'd then see your folly,
Nor again bid me fly them! Ah, never! ah, no!"

It pleased God that by hearing these lines sung his prejudices were shaken, and within a short time he embraced the Christian principles he had hitherto so strongly opposed, and they became, as the reader has perhaps anticipated, a truly-happy pair.

A Dying Jewess.—A colporteur employed not long since by a Bible Society in London was offering Bibles for sale in that metropolis, when he was told that if any of the Jews should purchase his books, and become

Christians, they would certainly return to their former belief, "for," said the woman, "they must die in the faith of Abraham."

To this he replied, "It certainly is not always so; for I myself have seen a Jewess die who did not forsake her faith in the Redeemer. I was at that time a city missionary, and was desired to call upon her by those who well knew her previous history. This visit happened to take place on the day of her death.

"She had been brought from affluence to abject poverty for the faith of Christ. She had at one time kept her own carriage. One day she cast her eye on the leaf of a hymn-book which had come into the house covering some butter, and she read upon it these words:—

'Not all the blood of beasts
On Jewish altars slain
Could give the guilty conscience peace
Or wash away the stain.'

"The verse haunted her. She could not dismiss it nor forget it; and after a time she went to a box where she remembered she had a Bible, and, induced by that verse, began to read, and read on till she found Christ Jesus, 'the Lamb slain from the foundation of the world.'

"She became openly a convert to Christianity. This caused her husband to divorce her. He went to India, where he married again and died. She lived in much poverty with two of her nation, Jewish sisters, who had also become Christians. All this I knew; and it is now four years since I stood by the side of that death-bed. She did not renounce her faith in the crucified Lord, but died triumphing in him as her Rock, her Shield, and her exceeding great Reward, quoting and applying to him the Psalms of David, and passing with him, without a fear, through the dark valley, numbered among the Jews who, as we are told by the Apostle John, 'went away, and believed on Jesus.'"

A Chimney-Sweep.—The late Rev. Joseph Slatterie, of Chatham, in England, whom we knew many years ago, was once walking in that town, when his attention was arrested by a youthful voice singing,—

"The sorrows of the mind
Be banished from this place:
Religion never was designed
To make our pleasures less."

Pleased alike with the sweetness of the voice and the cheerful tones in which the verse was sung, our friend looked around to see whence the singing proceeded; but for some time he looked in vain. At length he saw a little sweep with his head popping out of a chimney and waving with a sort of triumph his brush over his head. "Oh," said the venerable minister to us, "it made me weep in gratitude to think how singing the praises of God contributes to make even a poor chimney-sweep happy."

A Suffering Mother.—Hymns have often administered comfort in the severest trials. A lady who was called to endure much anxious suffering became greatly perplexed as to the duty which devolved upon her, and retired to her room to consider the matters which caused her agitation. Being sorely grieved in spirit, she laid her head on the table and wept bitterly. So intense was her grief that she scarcely perceived her little daughter, who quietly sat in a corner of the room. Unable longer to bear the sight of her mother's distress, this sweet girl stole softly to her side, and, taking her hand in both of her own, she said, "Mamma, you once taught me a pretty hymn:—

'If e'er you meet with trials
Or troubles on the way,
Then cast your care on Jesus,
And don't forget to pray.'"

The counsel of the little monitor was taken, and relief came. The mother was repaid for rightly training her child by receiving from her in happy season the lesson she had herself given.

Robert Hall.—The distinguished Robert Hall, who was remarkable for his attachment to congregational singing, gives us an anecdote which the reader will be glad to see in his own words:—"I once heard a blundering, roaring preacher at Margate, who had all the roughness of the wind without any of its power; and, after being tortured for a whole hour, I was fully compensated by the delight I enjoyed at the close of the sermon. An old man, whose gray locks were hanging profusely on his shoulders, and whose countenance expressed much simplicity and piety, gave out with great feeling, in the recitative style,—

'Let the old heathen tune their song
Of great Diana and of Jove;
But the sweet theme that moves my song
Is my Redeemer and his love.'

"This so charmed me that I could at any time endure to hear such a preacher if I were sure it would be followed with such a delightful after-piece."

A Vermont Clergyman.—Mr. Gould mentions the influence of singing on the mind of a minister in Vermont. He was a stranger called to officiate for a Sabbath in a cold and dreary church. When he entered it, the wind howled, and loose clapboards and windows clattered. The pulpit stood high above the first floor: there was no stove, but a few persons in the church, and those few beating their hands and feet to keep them from freezing. He asked himself, "Can I preach? Of what use can it be? What shall I do? Can these two or three singers in the gallery sing the words if I read a hymn? I concluded to make a trial, and read,—

'Jesus, lover of my soul.'

"They commenced; and the sound of a single female voice has followed me with an indescribable pleasing sensation ever since, and probably will while I live. The voice, intonation, articulation, and expression seemed to me perfect. I was warmed inside and out, and for the time was lost in rapture. I had heard of the individual and voice before; but hearing it in this dreary situation made it doubly grateful. Never did I preach with more satisfaction to myself. And from this incident I learned a lesson,—never to be discouraged from unfavorable appearances, but, where duty calls, go to work cheerfully, without wavering."

A Sick Child.—Why cannot the whole of our families imitate the members of the Moravian Church, who *all* sing? We are sure that when religion flourishes as it should do this will be the case. Nor have we any special objection that singing, especially in the social circle, should be accompanied with an instrument. We have long thought that a sufficient knowledge of music for family devotion should form a part of every child's education,—whether boy or girl. Half the time and labor often spent in teaching a girl to play a number of tunes with only tolerable skill on the piano would teach her to perform a smaller number exceedingly well on the *melodeon,* and add much refinement and delight to her family and friends. All this will at once appear evident to a mind disposed to reflect on the subject.

We have before us an interesting account of a little girl, seven years old, who was recovering from sickness; and as her strength increased she inquired, "Father, won't you attend family worship up here?" The request could not be denied. "Won't you sing,—

'Yes, my native land, I love thee'?"

It was indeed beautiful to see the feeble child, as she sat in her bed supported by pillows, with her little hymn-book before her, exerting her almost exhausted powers in singing all the verses of a hymn which implies entire consecration to the missionary work.

AN AGED LADY.—An old lady of nearly fourscore years writes in reference to "Dr. Watts's *Divine and Moral Songs for Children*" as follows; and we can endorse almost every word of her testimony from our own experience:—

"Now, when arrived to the age of seventy-nine years, I may with truth say that I would not relinquish for any pecuniary consideration the usefulness and comfort of my recollection of '*Watts's Divine Songs*.' When I cannot sleep in the night, I often repeat all I can recollect at the time,—not orally, but in my thoughts. If every mother in our land would teach her children these beautiful hymns, we should see a train of blessings on the Church and our country. My excellent mother taught them to me when a child; and I taught them to my children. And I have the comfort of seeing my children teaching them to their children."

A YOUNG MAN IN VIRGINIA.—A fine, intelligent Virginian young man, while residing in the West, became an infidel and a blasphemer of the name of God. From this state he was delivered by reading the work of Soame Jenyns; but, while he acquiesced in the truth of revelation, he yet did not feel its power. He was attacked by a lingering and fatal disease, which led him to reflection and prayer but often made it difficult for him to converse. Three Christian friends sometimes visited him, to beguile the tedious hours by singing. They one day entered his room, and, almost without any previous remarks, began the hymn,—

"There is a fountain, filled with blood,"

and then,—

"The voice of free grace cries, Escape to the mountain."

He then said to them, "There is nothing I so much delight to hear as the first hymn you ever sung to me:—

'Jesus, lover of my soul.'"

We began to sing it to the tune *Martyn*, and found the solemnity which had reigned in the little circle while singing the two former hymns began to be changed to weeping. We struck the touching strains of the second stanza, and the weeping became loud: the heart of him who had reviled Christ broke; and we feared that to sing the remaining stanza would be more than he could bear. When singing in his room a few days after this, he said, "I don't think I shall ever hear 'Jesus, lover of my soul' sung again: it so excites me that my poor body cannot bear it."

A Dying Pastor.—How delightfully useful very often are hymns on a dying bed! Once, visiting a dying pastor, he said to us, "I have often wondered why when I visited many of my people in their last hours I found them so constantly using hymns as expressing their feelings, and sometimes half smiled that so many of them used the very same hymns; but I understand it all now. The people of Jesus think and feel alike as they get near to his throne; and the smoothness of a hymn conveys the idea they need without the effort of thinking. How sweet to me now is the ten-thousandth-time-repeated verse,—

> 'Jesus can make a dying bed
> Feel soft as downy pillows are,
> While on his breast I lean my head
> And breathe my life out sweetly there'!"

Mr. Pearson has very truly said that as the mental powers grow feeble there would seem to be a soothing and consoling influence in devotional poetry which speaks peace to the soul of the departing Christian. How often do we find the learned scholar, the profound theologian, or the keen controversialist, seeking spiritual comforts in his last hours from simple hymns! Such was Prudentius, the advocate, soldier, and courtier of the fourth century, who, as Izaak Walton relates, "not many days before his death charged his soul to present to his God each morning and evening a new and spiritual song." Such were the accomplished Walter Raleigh, the scholar and diplomatist Wootton, Dr. Donne, George Herbert, and the erratic but pious Edward

Irving, who died while singing the Hebrew of the Twenty-Third Psalm. Southey has truly said of the hymns of the Wesleys, "Perhaps no poems have ever been so devoutly committed to memory, or quoted so often on a death-bed."

A Military Officer.—A few years ago an interesting incident occurred at the funeral of a pious military officer at Montreal. Several officers and other Christian friends were sitting round a fire singing to an old minor tune the hymn,—

"Not all the blood of beasts,"

when Captain L—— said to his friend Captain Hammond, "I have a curious fancy concerning that hymn. I should like it sung by six young men as they lower me into the grave." But a short time elapsed before Captain L—— was removed from earth; and his request was carried into execution. We can scarcely imagine any thing more impressive than such a scene in the presence of his military friends at such a time and under such circumstances. A short time afterwards Captain Hammond followed his friend to the world of spirits.

The Blind Psalmist.—We do not dread giving offence to our readers by here quoting some beautiful lines from the pen of Mrs. E. C. Kinney, written on hearing a blind clergyman, aged eighty-six, sing hymns, accompanying himself on the bass-viol:—

"He sang the airs of olden times
In soft, low tones, to sacred rhymes,
Devotional but quaint;
His fingers touched the viol's strings,
And, at their gentle vibratings,
The glory of an angel's wings
Hung o'er that aged saint.

"His thin, white locks, like silver threads
On which the sun its radiance sheds,—
Or like the moonlit snow,—
Seemed with a lustre half divine
Around his saintly brow to shine,
Till every scar or time-worn line
Was gilded with its glow.

"His sightless eyes to heaven upraised,
As through the spirit's lens he gazed
On things invisible,
Reflecting some celestial light,
Were like a tranquil lake at night
On which two mirrored planets bright
The concave's glory tell.

"Thus, while the patriarchal saint
Devoutly sang to music quaint,
I saw old HOMER rise,
With buried centuries, from the dead,
The laurel green upon his head,
As when the choir of bards he led
With rapt, but *blinded*, eyes.

"And Scio's isle again looked green
As when the poet there was seen
And Greece was in her prime;
While Poesy with epic fire
Did once again the bard inspire,
As when he swept his mighty lyre
To vibrate through all time.

"The vision changed to Albion's shore:
I saw a sightless bard once more

From dust of ages rise:
I heard the harp and deathless song
Of glorious MILTON float along,
Like warblings from the birds that throng
His muse's paradise.

"And is it thus when *blindness* brings
A veil before all outer things,
That visual spirits see
A world within, than this more bright,
Peopled with living forms of light,
And strewed with gems, as stars of night
Strew diamonds o'er the sea?

"Then, reverend saint, though old and blind,
Thou with the quenchless orbs of mind
Canst natural sight o'erreach,—
Upborne on Faith's triumphant wings,
Canst see unutterable things,
Which only through thy viol's strings
And in thy songs find speech."

TWO SISTERS IN NEW YORK STATE.—To the comparatively few persons among our readers who knew the truly-excellent Rev. Dr. Nettleton, it will be pleasant to be reminded of him. During one of his tours which were so remarkably blessed to the salvation of men, he stopped at a house in the region of the Catskill Mountains. While conversing with the older members of the family, he heard two young, sweet, and clear voices in a room above warbling the exquisitely-beautiful air of "*Bonnie Doon.*" "Ask them," said he to their parents, "to come down and sing it to me; for I am ardently devoted to music." The request was complied with, and he listened with delighted attention till the close of the song, when, kindly turning to the young ladies, he said, "I think I can teach you some far better words to that tune," and then sang to them that almost matchless hymn,—

"When marshalled on the mighty plain,"

and proceeded so touchingly and tenderly to call their attention to the beauty of its sentiments, that tears soon flowed from their eyes; and these two young girls were among the first subjects of a revival which was the blessed fruit of his labors.

THE YOUNG CAPTIVE AND HER MOTHER.—The following narrative of facts, which will show how a hymn may be useful in a very unexpected manner, was written by Pastor Rone, formerly of Elsinore:—

Many years ago, several German families came over and settled in this country, among whom was a man from Wurtemberg, who with his wife and a large family established himself in Pennsylvania. There were no churches or schools in the neighborhood, and he was compelled to keep the Sabbath at home with his family, instructing them himself to read the Bible, and praying to God. He used very often to read the Scriptures to them, and always used first to say, "Now, my children, be still, and listen to what I am going to read; for it is God who speaks to us in this book."

In the year 1754 a dreadful war broke out in Canada between the French and the English. The Indians took part with the French, and made excursions as far as Pennsylvania, where they plundered and burned the houses they came to and murdered the people. In 1755 they reached the dwelling of the poor family from Wurtemberg, while the wife and one of the sons were gone to a mill four miles distant to get some corn ground. The husband, eldest son, and two little girls, uamed Barbara and Regina, were at home. The father and his son were instantly killed by the savages; but they carried the two little girls away into captivity, with a great many other children who had been taken in the same manner. They were led many miles through woods and thorny bushes, that nobody might follow them. In this condition they were brought to the habitations of the Indians, who divided among themselves all the children whom they had taken captive.

Barbara was at this time ten years old and Regina nine. It was never known what became of Barbara; but Regina and a little girl two years old, whom she had never seen before, were given to an old widow, who treated them very cruelly. Her only son lived with her and maintained her; but he was sometimes from home for weeks together, and then these poor children were forced to go into the forest to gather roots and other provisions for the old woman; and when they did not bring her enough to eat she would beat them in so cruel a manner that they were nearly killed. The little girl always kept close to Regina; and, when she knelt down under a tree and repeated the prayers to the Lord

Jesus and the hymns which her father had taught her, the little girl prayed with her and learned the hymns and prayers by heart. In this melancholy state these children remained nine long years, till Regina reached the age of nineteen and her little companion was eleven years old. While captives, their hearts seem to have been drawn toward what was good. Regina continually repeated the verses from the Bible and the hymns which she had learned at home, and taught them to the little girl. They often cheered each other with one hymn from the hymn-book used at Halle, in Germany:—

> "Alone, yet not alone, am I,
> Though in this solitude so drear."

They constantly hoped that the Lord Jesus would some time bring them back to their Christian friends.

In 1764 the hope of these children was realized. The merciful providence of God brought the English Colonel Boquet to the place where they were in captivity. He conquered the Indians and forced them to ask for peace. The first condition he made was that they should restore all the prisoners they had taken. Thus the two poor girls were released. More than four hundred captives were brought to Colonel Boquet. It was an affecting sight to see so many young people wretched and distressed. The colonel and his soldiers gave them food and clothing, took them to Carlisle, and published in the newspapers that all parents who had lost their children might come and seek them, and they should be restored.

Among other bereaved parents, poor Regina's mother came; but, alas! her child had become a stranger to her. Regina had acquired the appearance and manners of the natives, and by no means could the mother discover her daughter. Seeing her weep in bitter disappointment, the colonel asked her if she could recollect nothing by which her poor girl could be known. She at length thought of, and began to sing, the hymn,—

"Alone, yet not alone, am I,
Though in this solitude so drear:
I feel my Saviour always nigh,—
He comes the weary hours to cheer.
I am with him, and he with me;
Even here alone I cannot be."

Scarcely had the mother sung two lines of it when Regina rushed from the crowd, began to sing it also, and threw herself into her mother's arms. They both wept for joy; and with her young companion, whose friends had not sought her, she went to her mother's house. Happily for herself, though Regina had not seen a book for nine years, she at once remembered how to read the Bible.

A Family in Louisiana.—The late Rev. James Haxley, about the year 1806, was sent by a Methodist Conference to itinerate as a missionary in Louisiana, then chiefly inhabited by French Catholics. Jimmy, as he was familiarly called, had small expectation of comfort without payment; and he seldom possessed any money. He was one evening reduced to the very verge of starvation: he had spent the preceding night in a swamp, and had taken no food for thirty-six hours,—when he reached a plantation. He entered the house and asked for food and lodging. The mistress of the house, a widow, with several daughters, and several negro children playing about, recognised his calling, and insultingly refused his request. He obtained, however, permission to warm himself for a few minutes before the fire. As he sat thus, he felt the demands of hunger and sleep, and looked forward to another night in the swamp. Feeling this might prove his last night on earth, he thought sweetly of the celestial city to which he felt he was travelling; his heart swelled with gladness, and he cheerfully sung one of his favorite hymns:—

"Peace, my soul! thou needst not fear:
The Great Provider still is near."

He sang the whole hymn; and when he looked around him the mother, daughters, and negroes were all in tears. "Here, Sally," said the mother; "get the preacher a good supper. Peter, put up his horse: he shall stay a week, if he pleases." Has hymn-singing no influence?

THE BROTHERS AND SISTER.—More than thirty years ago, a pious young lady in ill health was resting on her couch, and by her side sat a beloved brother, himself scarcely well, and utterly without a feeling of love to God His sister, as descriptive of the emotions of her soul, repeated to him, with remarkable emphasis, the lines,—

"Oh, what hath Jesus bought for me!
Before my ravished eyes
Rivers of life divine I see
And trees of paradise!
I see a world of spirits bright,
Who taste the pleasures there:
They are all robed in spotless white,
And conquering palms they bear."

Scarcely had she uttered these words before he began to think seriously on the state of his soul, and asked himself, "Has he bought nothing for me?" His dear sister had soon the happiness of having him as a companion in her Christian course; and both brother and sister, with another brother, not long after departed for missionary fields in the island of Ceylon.

TWO YOUNG WOMEN.—When the late Rev. Sylvester Hutchinson was stationed on Salem Circuit, New Jersey, his first station, and while he was yet a boy, he was sitting in his temporary boarding-house waiting for the hour of preaching, when two young women came in to have some sport with the boy-preacher. They began to ridicule his size and his insignificant appearance, when, suddenly lifting up his head from a reclining posture, he repeated, in slow and solemn tones,—

"My thoughts on awful subjects roll,—
Damnation and the dead.
What horrors seize the guilty soul
Upon a dying bed!"

His voice, his countenance, his manner, were all adapted to make them feel that

> "'Tis not the whole of life to live,
> Nor all of death to die."

The words of the preacher were "like nails fastened in a sure place by the Master of assemblies." Tears rolled down their cheeks: they left the room, and rested not till they found a refuge in the Son of God. Not long after, they each said to the Church, "Thy people shall be my people, and thy God my God."

QUARRELSOME NEIGHBORS.—Three men became hopefully pious about the same time. They were neighbors, heads of families, and singers. For a season they lived in love and exhibited in their lives the graces of the Holy Spirit. During this period they often united in sweetly singing the praises of God. But, as one of them was once passing the house of another, he heard loud words and found his friends in angry dispute. He went into the house, and began by saying, "Come, neighbors, let us sing one of our favorite hymns:—

> 'How pleasant 'tis to see
> Kindred and friends agree!'"

They became silent, looked first at him and then at each other, and then *one* joined the singing. The other very soon followed his example, and the three neighbors sang harmoniously together as usual, till all their angry passions were lulled to sleep. They parted in peace, and ever afterward lived in harmony. In this instance, at least, a hymn was better than an exhortation.

KLOPSTOCK AND HIS WIFE.—Frederick Klopstock, who died at the age of eighty, at Hamburg, in 1803, in the presence of fifty thousand people, and who is still remembered as "the Milton of Germany," was a poet before he had ever seen a verse written, and commenced his "*Messiah*" knowing nothing of his subject or of the style in which it was written but what he learned from a large collection of Bibles in his father's library, but which contained "not a single production of any muse." Beautifully did he write, "How happy shall I be if by the completion of the '*Messiah*' I may contribute somewhat to the glory of our great and divine religion! How sweet and transporting is this idea to my mind! That is my great reward."

In early life Klopstock knew a lady worthy of himself. They loved and breathed poetry together. At the end of four years she wrote concerning him, "If you knew his poem, I could describe him very briefly in saying he is in all respects what he is as a poet." But, alas! soon after this he wrote thus to a friend, seven days after her removal from earth:—"I supported first myself, and then her, by repeating that without our Father's will not a hair in her head could fall; and more than once I repeated to her the following lines from my last Ode. Once I was so much affected as to be compelled to stop at every line:—

'Though unseen by human eye,
My Redeemer's hand is nigh:
He has poured salvation's light
Far within the vale of night;
There will God my steps control,
There his presence bless my soul.
Lord, whate'er my sorrows be,
Teach me to look up to thee.' "

This truly-great man was buried under a weeping-willow, with a single line on his tomb:—

"SEED SOWN BY GOD TO RIPEN FOR HARVEST."

REV. SAMUEL BRADBURN.—Few things are of more importance than a good enunciation of hymns; yet perhaps in nothing more than in this do our clergymen fail. Let us illustrate its importance.

William Dawson,—a late very eminent local preacher in England,—before he began to preach, having heard of the fame of the Rev. Samuel Bradburn as an orator, went to Leeds, in the year 1793, to hear him in the Rev. Edward Parsons's church. His commanding figure, powdered hair, and advanced age fixed Dawson's eye and attracted his admiration. The subject of his sermon was the kingly office of Christ: it was a masterly performance; and Dawson was filled with admiration.

On reading the last hymn, Mr. Bradburn inclined his person over the front of the pulpit, and, looking to the precentor, or clerk, as though somewhat displeased with him,—or rather preferring, like his Methodist brethren in general, to read the hymns to be sung,—he said, "I will give out the last two verses myself:"—

"The government of earth and seas
Upon his shoulders shall be laid,
His wide dominion shall increase,
And honors to his name be paid.

"Jesus, the holy child, shall sit
High on his father David's throne,
Shall crush his foes beneath his feet,
And reign to ages yet unknown."

Mr. Dawson had never heard these words before; but Bradburn's manner of repeating them was such that he ever after remembered them.

Rev. Dr. E. D. Griffin.—Of the late Rev. Dr. E. Griffin it has been said that, while in reading the Scriptures he seemed to evolve a meaning and richness never thought of before, in reading hymns he gave more force of expression, and often more impressiveness to their sentiments, than could be given by the singing of even a good choir. Indeed, the great masters of sacred music are not more careful to bring the force of their art to bear on each note than was the excellent doctor to bring the resources of eloquence to bear upon every syllable of the hymn which he read. He read slowly, and gave himself time to throw the right and full expression and inflection on each word. Moreover, he infused his whole pathos into the reading, as much as if the lines were a fresh and original utterance of his own feelings. It has been often said that by the simple reading of the hymn,—

> "Mighty God, while angels bless thee,
> May an infant bless thy name,"

he would produce as much impression upon an audience as would ordinarily be effected by an eloquent sermon.

The late extraordinary man, Robert Hall, of England, eminently excelled in reading hymns. No one who ever heard him at his social prayer-meeting can forget the intense dignity and feeling with which he would enunciate the words of Dr. Doddridge,—

> "The splendid crown which Moses sought
> Still beams around his brow,
> Though soon great Pharaoh's sceptred pride
> Was taught by death to bow."

REV. DR. STILLMAN.—Few men could read a hymn with more effect than the Rev. Dr. Samuel Stillman, of Boston, who died in 1807. None who ever heard him will forget the verse of Watts, as it was enunciated by him from the pulpit:—

> "Well, the Redeemer's gone,
> To appear before our God,—
> To sprinkle o'er the flaming throne
> With his atoning blood."

Some cold-blooded critic, who probably never read Numbers xxv. 2, has censured this verse; but I think he would have been disarmed had he heard Dr. Stillman read it. His voice had a beautiful circumflex to it:

he threw his emphasis on the word "well," then a pause, —and the rest of the verse was pronounced in that cheerful and animating tone which seemed to rend the veil and transport the hearer into the unseen world. The most skilful actor never made a more sudden and happy transition. There was no apparent art in his style or delivery. It was all earnest simplicity.

Rev. Dr. Broaddus.—The Rev. Dr. J. L. Dagg gives an interesting account of the manner in which the late Rev. Dr. A. Broaddus, a Southern Baptist minister, conducted public worship. The manner in which he read his hymns may furnish an important hint to ministers. Dr. D—— says, "He read the hymn of Dr. Watts, which begins,—

'Lord, we are blind, we mortals blind;
We can't behold thy bright abode:
Oh, 'tis beyond a creature mind
To glance a thought half-way to God.'

His manner of reading was to me new and attractive; and before he had finished this first stanza my attention was riveted. He read through the hymn; and the impression produced on my mind forty years have not erased. From that time I have regarded this hymn—perhaps on account of the impression then made—as one of the most beautiful that Dr. Watts ever composed."

Thoughtless Clergymen.—We really do wish that our ministers were always careful in the selection ot their hymns, that they may be appropriate and seasonable. We have heard a hymn written to describe winter and to draw from it appropriate lessons read to be sung in the sultry heats of July or August; and some time ago a somewhat aged minister, in a large, intelligent, and pious congregation, announced, on a bright Sabbath morning, the beautiful evening hymn written by Edmeston,—

"Saviour, breathe an *evening* blessing,
Ere repose our spirits seal."

What a lamentable indication of bad taste!

A still more ludicrous scene, arising from a similar cause, has been described to us by a Methodist clergyman, in one of the papers of that body of Christians. He says:—

"I had preached my last sermon at a favorite appointment on my first circuit. The people had been kind and generous, and I loved them dearly. The house was full; it was my final appeal to the flock beloved; and, though almost overcome with emotion, I had got through, somehow, with the 'farewell sermon,'—my first and last. I knew that, either from sympathy or sorrow, the congregation was sharing largely in my feelings,—that I was not alone 'in the melting mood.' As I sat down, overwhelmed with grief at the sore parting, a local preacher, whom I had invited to close the service, rose, and, opening the book at random, read, in solemn tones, the hymn commencing,—

'Jesus, we lift our souls to thee:
Thy Holy Spirit breathe,
And let this little infant be
Baptized into thy death.'

The effect of this *malapropos* selection you may possibly imagine, but I cannot describe."

Another illustration of inappropriate hymns arises from the custom, allowed by some ministers, of permitting the choirs to sing voluntaries at all times and under all circumstances. We have heard a doctrinal sermon directly opposed by the "voluntary" sung after it; and we have just read of the choir of a very large congregation in Massachusetts, who sang at the funeral of a man of distinction, with great unction,—

"Believing we rejoice
To see the curse remove."

A Tory Minister.—It is of no small importance that the clergy should be acquainted with hymns and psalms before they read them with a view to their being sung by congregations. Some years ago, a somewhat idle Tory Congregational minister in England announced Dr. Watts's version of the Seventy-Fifth Psalm, "To thee, most holy and most high," etc. When he had reached the second verse, "Britain was doomed to be a slave," etc., he became alarmed, and fled to the sixth verse, which, to his sad amazement, flatly denied the divine right of kings:—

"No vain pretence to royal birth
Shall fix a tyrant on the throne:
God, the great Sovereign of the earth,
Will rise and make his justice known."

His confusion became apparent; but, happily for him, the people supposed he might have a reference to the King of Hanover, then very unpopular among the British people, but who, on the first accession of Queen Victoria, and before she had a family, was heir-presumptive to the throne.

Doctor Mason.—Doctor Lowell Mason has given us a very striking narrative illustrating the importance of carefully examining a hymn before even abridging it. Some years ago, when that gentleman was organist and the conductor of the singing at the Bowdoin Street Church, Boston, a visiting clergyman conducted the service. Dr. Mason says, "The whole hymn was first read by the minister, and then, just before the singing-exercise commenced, the direction was given, 'Omit the second stanza.' The following are the first three stanzas, and the connection between the first and third stanzas will be seen at a glance:—

'When thou, my righteous Judge, shalt come
To take thy ransomed people home,
Shall I among them stand?
Shall such a worthless worm as I,
Who sometimes am afraid to die,
Be found at thy right hand?

'I love to meet thy people now,
Before thy feet with them to bow,

Though vilest of them all;
But—can I bear the piercing thought—
What if my name should be left out
When thou for them shalt call?

'O Lord, prevent it by thy grace:
Be thou my only hiding-place
In this the accepted day;
Thy pardoning voice, oh, let me hear,
To still my unbelieving fear,
Nor let me fall, I pray.'

"The organist did not perceive the fearful connection between the first and third stanzas until a moment before it was time to commence the latter, when, startled and terrified, he cried out, 'Sing the second stanza!' just in time to avoid the utterance of the frightful petition."

Dr. Mason properly adds, "It is unquestionably the duty of the choir to follow implicitly the directions of the minister in all that appertains to the singing in public worship; and the habit which prevails in some places of inattention to the directions given from the pulpit in relation to the abridgment of the hymn is wholly unjustifiable; but there seem to be exceptions to almost all rules, and here was an occasion when disobedience to the oral rubric seemed to be positively required: indeed, it was a case of life or death, and it was impossible to follow it. Warm were the thanks expressed by members of the congregation after the service for their deliverance from the terrible moral collision with which they were threatened."

MR. DAWSON.—We have sometimes, when conducting the worship of God, felt strongly disposed to interrupt the choir for the sake of a striking remark on what is too often thoughtlessly sung. We have before us an instance in which the monotony was broken with good effect. Mr. Dawson, an eminent English Wesleyan local preacher, had once preached a very impressive sermon, and at its close read Charles Wesley's beautiful hymn,—

"O love divine, how sweet thou art!"

When the choir were singing the third verse,—

"God only knows the love of God,"

he stopped them and said, "Stop, friends! If angels, the first-born sons of light, cannot understand the height, the breadth, the depth, the length, of the love of God, *how can we expect to fathom it while here below?*" He then repeated, with profound feeling, thrilling his large anditory,—

"'God only knows the love of God.'

Let us sing it again, friends; for we shall have to sing it in heaven:—

'God only knows the love of God.'"

FAULT FOUND.—It is usually true that the members of every denomination praise their poets and their hymns; but we have before us a remarkable fact of an opposite character. The Rev. Samuel Bradburn, a man of fine talents, and of wit as well as piety, and an eminent preacher among the English Wesleyan Methodists, was once engaged to preach, and read the hymn written by Charles Wesley contains this verse:—

"Ah, lovely appearance of death!
What sight upon earth is so fair?
Not all the gay pageants that breathe
Can with a dead body compare."

He broke out:—"What business has this hymn in our book, containing as it does a sentiment so false,—'Ah, lovely appearance of death!'—when there is nothing lovely about it. Why did Abraham's beloved and beautiful Sarah, when she died, become so unlovely that he expressed his wish, 'Bury my dead out of my sight'?"

It is right to say that the Methodists of this country have omitted this hymn from their book.

A Clergyman in Georgia.—A few years ago, an aged minister was officiating for the first time in a Methodist church in Georgia, where they keep up the old custom of having the hymns "lined," that the whole congregation may, according to the wise discipline of that Church, join in the singing, whether they have hymn-books or not. The venerable man could not see distinctly, and intended to omit singing during that service. To announce his purpose, he arose and said,—

"My eyes are dim: I cannot see" ——

and immediately the chorister commenced singing it to the tune of "*Old Hundred.*" Surprise and mortification made the clergyman almost speechless; but he stammered out,—

"I meant but an apology."

This line was immediately sung by the congregation, and the minister, now quite excited, exclaimed,—

"Forbear, I pray: my sight is dim" ——

but the singing proceeded, and the couplet was finished by his troubled and beseeching explanation,—

"I do not mean to read a hymn."

Strange as it may seem, this was also sung with much energy, while the worthy old gentleman sat down in actual despair of accomplishing his purpose to do without singing.

A Deacon in a Difficulty.—Deacons, as well as ministers, have sometimes been placed in an awkward predicament. On one occasion, in New England, a gentleman of this order had been called on to *deacon* the hymns,—that is, to read them line by line. He looked at his book for some time, endeavoring to spell out the words; but, having unfortunately left his spectacles at home, he was compelled to make known his difficulty, and said,—

"My eyes, indeed, are very blind."

The choir, who had been impatiently waiting for a line, supposing this to be the first of a common-metre hymn, immediately sang it. The good deacon exclaimed, with emphasis,—

"I cannot see at all."

This, of course, they also sung, when the astonished pillar of the church cried out,—

"I really think you are bewitched!"

which the choir at once repeated in full tone; and the deacon added,—

"The mischief's in you all;"

when the choir finished the verse by echoing the last line, and the deacon sat down in despair.

Regulations of Singing.—The History of the Presbyterian Church at Rockaway, New Jersey, tells us, "That part of divine service pertaining to the singing of psalms, and what version of psalms should be used in worship, having made great uneasiness and inquietude, in April, 1780, it was voted to appoint four choristers to set the tunes; that Benjamin Jackson, Francis M'Carty, and Jacob Lyon be appointed choristers; that they sing in the afternoon without reading the psalm *line by line;* and David Beeman to sing the forepart of the day, unless otherwise agreed on by Mr. Beeman and the other choristers; and that they sing any tunes that are sung by the neighboring churches, as they shall judge proper." . . . April, 1789, some further difficulty having arisen respecting the singing in the church, "It was voted at a parish meeting to have the psalms read *line by line*, or by *two lines*, in singing, in future, except on particular occasions." . . . At a parish meeting May 14, 1792, "The mode of *singing* was *again adjusted* by the appointment of Benjamin Johnson, Russel Davis, and Daniel Hurd as choristers, and that they act discretionary when to sing *without reading the lines*."

IMPORTANCE OF RIGHT FEELINGS.—In "*Hood's History of Music in New England*," it is said that when, in 1646, the unhappy Charles I. fled from Oxford, he threw himself upon the army of his countrymen, then encamped before Newark. Here, instead of being befriended, he was reproached and insulted to his face. Upon one occasion during public service, one of the chaplains, after having used harsh language, directed the Fifty-Second Psalm to be sung, beginning,—

> "Why dost thou, tyrant, boast thyself
> Thy wicked deeds to praise?"

As soon as they had sung it, the king rose and requested the soldiers to sing the Psalm,—

> "Have mercy on me, Lord, I pray;
> For men would me devour."

This was accordingly sung in compassion for his distress, which saw no relief till he reached the scaffold ordered by the High Court of Justice.

The history of our country relates a not dissimilar anecdote of the visit in 1686 of Sir Edmund Andross to

New Haven in search of Goffe, one of the regicides, who really was present at the church when Sir Edmund was there. The clerk felt it his duty to select a psalm not incapable of a double application, and which accordingly hit Sir Edmund in a tender part:—

"Why dost thou, tyrant, boast thyself,
Thy wicked deeds to praise?"

All his attempts to discover "his man" utterly failed.

A *complete* history of hymns would develop facts both pleasing and painful as to the state of religion in different places and at different periods. The Rev. John Adams, of Durham, New Hampshire, graduated at Harvard College in 1745, and was ordained in 1748. After thirty years' residence at Durham, difficulties arose with his people, and he was dismissed. We fear that Christian feeling did not abound even in his heart; for at the close of his farewell sermon he requested his people to "sing to the praise and glory of God, and to their own edification," the first three verses of the One Hundredth and Twentieth Psalm of Dr. Watts,—

"Thou God of love, thou ever blest,
Pity my suffering state:
When wilt thou set my soul at rest
From lips which love deceit?

"Hard lot of mine! my days are cast
Among the sons of strife,
Whose never-ceasing brawlings waste
My golden hours of life.

"Oh, might I fly to change my place,
How would I choose to dwell
In some wild, lonesome wilderness,
And leave these gates of hell!"

An Old Parody.—

"Come, thou Almighty King,"

is a parody on the old English national anthem, "*God save the King*," and first appeared in that country some nineteen years after "God save the King" had been first printed in the "*Gentleman's Magazine*," which was in 1745, where it was simply called "*A song for two voices.*" It is now common among us under the disguise of "*America.*" The first appearance of the hymn was in 1764, in a collection of Psalms and Hymns, extracted from various authors, by the Rev. Spencer Madan. From this fact it is often attributed to Madan's own pen; but of this there is no evidence: all believe the real author to be as much unknown as that of which it is a parody. It has ever since retained its place in most of our collections, with remarkable integrity and freedom from "emendations," and will probably do so till the Church loses its militant character.

Singular Music.—One of the most singular curiosities of musical literature with which we are acquainted relates to a fugue tune to which is sung a version of the One Hundred and Thirty-Third Psalm, in the prodigious effort of the performance of which the ear-splitting combination of the several voices scarcely bears a resemblance to that oily current poured on Aaron's head, which

"Ran down his beard and o'er his head—
Ran down his beard——
—— —— —— his robes
And o'er his robes ——
Ran down his beard —— ran down his ——
—— —— —— o'er his robes
His robes, his robes, ran down his beard
Ran down his ——
—— —— —— o'er his robes
Ran down his beard
—— —— —— h-i-s b-e-ard
Its costly moist ——
Ran down his beard ——
—— ure — beard — his — beard — his — shed
— ran down his beard — his — down
his robes — its costly moist — his beard
ure shed — his — cost — his robes — robes — ure shed
I-t-s c-o-s-t-l-ie moist—ure——————s-h-e-d."

Bishop Seabury, on one of his visitations, was asked his opinion of this composition; and his reply was that he had paid no attention to the music, but that his sympathies were so much excited for poor Aaron that he was afraid he would not have a hair left.

Hymns of the Old Style.—It may be of some interest to the reader to have before him two or three verses of the hymns in use before the days of Dr. Watts, which gradually gave way, as the taste for harmony and beauty increased in our churches, to the hymns now in use. To understand the true character of these verses, they should be "deaconed off," and sung one line at a time.

"'Tis like the precious ointment
Down Aaron's beard did go;
Down Aaron's beard it downward went,
His garment-skirts unto."

Here is another specimen; and though our readers may smile at it, their fathers did not:—

"Ye monsters of the bubbling deep,
Your Maker's praises spout;
Up from the sands, ye codlings, peep,
And wag your tails about."

The following specimen, and our last, contains *truth*, whatever may be said of its poetry:—

"The race is not forever got
By him who fastest runs;
Nor the battle by those people
Who shoot the longest guns."

SINGING AT BANGOR.—It is both interesting and profitable to understand the manner in which our fathers conducted their worship. A concert by the Billings and Holden Society of Bangor, Maine, composed of elderly ladies and gentlemen, was held in that city in 1848. They were "singers of the olden time," veritable antiquarian musicians, worshippers of the majestic melodies of Luther, Pleyel, Tansur, Holyoke, and the rich *fugucs* of Billings, Holden, Edson, and Read, of by-gone days. The enraptured writer of the description of this meeting exclaims, "Oh, could you have been there! It was a glorious *sight* as well as sound. Those old gentlemen took us back again to thirty or forty years ago! But let me give you a description of them.

"The number of singers, I should judge, was nearly a hundred: at any rate, they filled the singing-gallery and part of the side galleries of the First Baptist Church. Among them were at least four deacons, four colonels, several captains, judges, doctors, lawyers, esquires of the old school, and, last, though not least, the chief members of the Bangor Antiquarian Society. All classes were represented. An ancient colonel led off the singing, with a white wand and blue ribbon. He is a stout man, between fifty and sixty years of age, with gray hair, of considerable vigor, with a voice commanding and precisely adapted to the music sung that evening. On his right was an elderly tenor deacon, who at times was evidently as near heaven as he could be and still be on earth. He is a tall man; and not unfrequently, during the performance of some unique passage, you might have heard the whisper, 'See him go up!' as, while beating time, he would draw up his tall form to its full height and elevate his face toward the ceiling. On the left of the leader was an ancient tenor judge, who prides himself on being able to sing all the 'old tunes' without looking at a note. He stood erect, looking straight forward, preserving an astonishing equanimity during the whole evening, although he beat time—as did all the other singers—quite emphatically. At the extreme right of the choir were the ladies,—matronly personages in caps, with strong voices and peculiar intonations. Indeed, the style of singing was quite different from that of the present day throughout; and I was happy to find that the rich nasal sound of forty years ago is not yet forgotten, and that the practice of beating time with the hand still exists.

"The number of tunes sung was about thirty. Some were repeated. Among the tunes were Bridgewater, Element, Tilden, Bristol, Portland, Buckingham, Lynnfield, Montague, Rainbow, Sherborne, Victory, Ode on Science, Heavenly Vision, Calvary, Invitation, etc. Invitation was encored. It was sung in magnificent style. When the part beginning

'Fly like a youthful hart or roe'

was repeated, one could hardly help imagining himself among a flock of young deer, scampering

'Over the hills where spices grow,'

so swiftly did the chorister lead off and the singers follow.

"The singing commenced at seven, and continued without cessation, except during a recess of a few minutes to get breath, until nine o'clock. The audience were delighted not only with the music, but with the high enjoyment manifested by the venerable musicians."

Redstone Presbytery.—In the latter part of the eighteenth century considerable discussion took place in the Old Redstone Presbytery in reference to the introduction of Dr. Watts's Psalms and Hymns, most of the older people being in favor of the older version. In some places a compromise was adopted. They would begin with an old psalm and conclude with a psalm or hymn from Watts. Though Dr. Power used Watts in his own family, he yielded to the preferences of his people in the use of Rouse in public worship. The lines were "given out" by a precentor, or clerk, as he was called. Dr. Power's clerk used to give out one line at a time, and always, in doing so, sounded the last syllable on a dead level with the first note of that part of the tune, prolonging the sound a little, so as to slide gracefully and imperceptibly into the singing. To a stranger the effect was rather ludicrous; but he was considered a great master of his business, especially by the older people.

At Buffalo and Cross Creek, Watts's Psalms and Hymns were used at the prayer-meeting, though Mr. Porter scarcely approved of it. On one occasion, however, his people sang with great animation the lines,—

"Let those refuse to sing
Who never knew our God,"

when the old gentleman was constrained to join in the service, saying afterward, "If my conscience won't let me sing, I'll wring its neck."

BOSTON CONGREGATIONS.—A beautiful fact in connection with singing is told of the excellent George Whitefield. During the delivery of a sermon in Boston on the wonders of creation, providence, and redemption, a violent tempest of thunder and lightning came on, which so alarmed the congregation that they sat in breathless awe. The preacher closed his note-book, and, stepping into one of the wings of the desk, fell on his knees, and, with much feeling and fine taste, repeated from Dr. Watts,—

"Hark! THE ETERNAL rends the sky!
A mighty voice before him goes,—
A voice of music to his friends,
But threatening thunder to his foes.

"Come, children, to your Father's arms!
Hide in the chambers of my grace
Till the fierce storm be overblown
And my revenging fury cease!"

"Let us devoutly sing to the praise and glory of God this hymn:—Old Hundred."

The whole congregation instantly rose and poured forth the sacred song. By the time the hymn was finished, the storm was hushed, and the sun, bursting forth, showed the magnificent arch of peace. Resuming the desk, the preacher quoted, with admirable tact, "Look upon the rainbow: praise Him that made it. Very beautiful is it in the brightness thereof! It compasseth the heaven about with a glorious circle; and the hands of the Most High have bended it." The episode added intense interest to the service.

COINCIDENCE.—One of the Boston papers, a few years ago, related a very beautiful coincidence. During the morning service at Christ's Church, Salem Street, an incident occurred which would have been interpreted by some of the ancients as a signal of divine approbation. The Rev. Mr. Marcus, of Nantucket, the officiating minister, read, in order to be sung, the Eighty-Fourth Psalm, in which may be found the verse,—

"The birds, more happier far than I,
Around thy temple throng:
Securely there they build, and there
Securely hatch their young."

While he was reading this psalm, a dove flew in at one of the windows and alighted on the capital of one of the pilasters near the altar, and almost over the head of the reader. A note of the psalm and hymn to be sung had been previously given, as is customary, to the choir, or it might have been supposed that there was design in the selection; for the second hymn commenced,—

"Come, Holy Spirit, Heavenly Dove,
With all thy quickening powers!
Kindle a flame of sacred love
In these cold hearts of ours!"

The preacher was unconscious of the presence of the bird until the close of the services, when the innocent visitor was suffered to depart in peace.

"CHINA."—Say what we will, and whatever may be the taste of different persons as to tunes ancient and modern, it is certain that we all enjoy the occasional treat of an old tune. A congregation in Boston, a few years ago, who seldom heard old-fashioned music, were one day surprised and delighted when the choir sung the tune of "*China*," as set to the well-known words of Dr. Watts,—

"Why do we mourn departing friends,
Or shake at death's alarms?"

The incident led one of the hearers to express his feelings in some lines which may gratify the reader:—

"The preacher had his sermon preached,
And prayer befitting marked its course,
When, lingering yet where prayer was made,
The preacher and the people rose.
They sung a hymn: the hymn was old,
The lines were like familiar things;
But, bursting as from harps of gold,
The music swept a thousand strings,
While, with a low and reverend air,
The people bowed and worshipped there.

"The young man paused, and wondered why
He had not heard such strains before;
The old man wept, and seemed again
To live his very childhood o'er,
As quickly from the treasured past
Came visions of the olden time,
When his dear father worshipped God
While swaying to the music's charm,
And by his side they sat who shared
The sunshine of his early days:
What other could he do than weep
To hear once more those good old lays?

"Oh, art may charm, and newer strains
May better please the youthful breast;

But unto him whose locks are gray
  The oldest music is the best.
And so methought, as died away
  Those strains within that place of prayer,
That heaven to some will sweeter be
  If "*China*" is remembered there."

REV. DR. EMMONS.—The late distinguished Dr. Emmons was a great lover of sweet sounds,—that is, the sound of the human voice,—and religiously excluded from his meeting-house all instrumental music except a little mahogany-colored wooden pitch-pipe, about five inches by three. A member of his choir had learned to play the bass-viol, and, anxious to exhibit his skill, early one Sunday morning most unadvisedly introduced his big fiddle into the singing-gallery. After the first prayer was ended and the doctor began to handle his "*Watts*," the "bass-violer" lifted up his profanation, and, trying his strings, instantly attracted the doctor's attention. He paused, laid down his hymn-book, took his sermon from the cushion, and proceeded with his discourse as if singing was no part of public worship, and finally dismissed the congregation "without note or comment." The whole choir were indignant. They stayed after "meeting," and all the girls and young men resolved not to go into "the singing-seats" at all in the afternoon; and the elders who did go there bore the visages of men "whose minds were made up."

Services in the afternoon began as usual. The doctor took his psalm-book in his hand, looked over his spectacles at the gallery, and saw only a few there, but, nothing daunted, read a psalm and sat down. No sound followed; no one stirred; and the "leader" looked up in utter unconsciousness. After a long and most uneasy silence, the good man, his face somewhat over-flushed, his manner rather stern, read the psalm again, paused, then re-read the first verse, and, pushing up his spectacles, looked interrogatively into the gallery. The leader could bear it no longer, and, half rising, said, decidedly, "There won't be any singing here this afternoon."

Quick as thought the doctor replied, "Then there won't be any preaching;" and, taking his cocked hat from its peg, he marched down the pulpit-stairs, through the broad aisle, and out of the house, leaving his congregation utterly astounded. We need not inform our readers that "the big fiddle" did not appear in "the singing-seats" afterward.

English Clerks.—It is well known that in most of the congregations of England the hymns are "given out" by a clerk, who occupies a seat below the pulpit. These gentlemen are not always remarkable either for their intelligence or their humility; and if the minister leaves the choice of the hymns to them they will sometimes select such as may reprove him or some other persons for what they may consider errors or faults; or sometimes they will make alterations of even a ludicrous character in the hymns or psalms. We remember once to have heard an occasional sermon, which was a somewhat singular one, from a singular man. His text was, "Every man that hath this hope in him purifieth himself, even as he is pure," (1 John iii. 3,)—the common understanding of which is that the Christian aims to imitate the purity of Christ; but worthy Pastor Renals treated the text so as to make the Christian the source of his own purity. In this view of the matter, Brother Beal, as we think, properly differed from him,—though no one expected a public reproof administered by him to the minister. No one who was present will ever forget how the said clerk rose, with majestic mien and powerful voice, to "give out" the hymn Dr. Watts founded on the text, or with what emphasis he read the last two lines of the verse,—

"A hope so much divine
May trials well endure,—
May purge our souls from sense and sin,
As Christ the Lord is pure."

The clerk evidently exulted, the congregation smiled; but the poor preacher looked unutterable things, and, the hymn having been sung, he omitted the last prayer and pronounced the benediction. He could never be prevailed on to preach in that pulpit again.

In the days of our youth we remember to have preached a sermon which gave offence to one of these gentlemen,—he having, contrary to our own view of the matter, an insurmountable objection to unregenerated sinners being exhorted to pray or to do any other spiritual act. At the close of the sermon he led us to sing, with what of good feeling we might, the lines of Watts,—

"The men who fear thy word
*Grow wiser than their teachers are
And better know the Lord.*"

In a note in the fourth volume of his "*History of the Baptists*" Mr. Ivimey tells us that he one evening stepped into a meeting-house in London, where one of these hyper-Calvinistic gentlemen was "the clerk," and heard him perpetrate a somewhat remarkable change in some lines of Watts. The good doctor, speaking of the kindness of God to his people, wrote,—

"And fixed my standing more secure
Than 'twas before I fell."

The very *sound* clerk, however, changed it to,—

"And fixed my standing *most secure
In Christ before I fell.*"

Possibly some of the congregation regarded this change as an improvement; but Mr. Ivimey asks, with something like common sense, "If the good man was made so secure *before he fell*, how came he to fall at all?"

The late eminent Robert Hall used to tell an amusing anecdote of a clerk of his church in Leicester. It appears that an unpleasant feeling had for some time existed between the said clerk and the choir. The dispute was referred to Mr. Hall, and the clerk was dismissed. Such, however, was the grief of the worthy official on the loss of his dignity that he was soon after reinstated in office. On the following Sabbath morning the honest precentor extorted an almost general smile by commencing the service with Dr. Watts's version of the Twenty-Seventh Psalm, reading with much emphasis the lines,—

"Now shall my head be lifted high
Above my foes around,
And songs of joy and victory
Within thy temple sound."

Facts about Anthems.—While speaking of hymns, a few interesting facts relating to anthems will be perhaps acceptable. In the last century, the noble Count S——, of Hungary, had lost, under the most distressing circumstances, his only child, a beautiful girl, who was on the eve of marriage. Although two years had elapsed since this bereavement, the unhappy father remained in the most melancholy condition. From the hour when he had taken his last look at the dead body of his child, he had remained in the same room, shedding no tears and uttering no complaints, but remaining in a speechless state of despair. The most celebrated physicians had been consulted, and every means which could be thought of used to rouse the count from his lethargy of grief; but all in vain, and his physician became hopeless of his recovery.

Under these circumstances, a member of his family

remembered to have heard the distinguished Elizabeth Mara, for ten years the first singer at the Prussian court, sing some exquisitely beautiful sacred pieces, and became impressed with the thought that, if any sound on earth could reach the heart which was already buried in his daughter's grave, her voice, which seemed to be that of an angel rather than of a human being, would have that power. Arrangements were at length made for the trial; and, to give every possible effect to the powers of the singer, an ante-room, opening into that where the count sat, was prepared. Mara stood alone in the foreground, yet in such a position that she could not be seen in the next room, which was hung with black, and a faint, shadowy twilight only admitted, except a few golden rays from a small lamp which burned in a niche before a beautiful Madonna. Suddenly upon the solitude and silence of that sick-room there broke a wonderful harmony. Elizabeth had chosen Handel's "*Messiah*," and took her place, deeply moved by the singular circumstances under which she was called to exert her talents.

At first the music and that heavenly voice all seemed to be unheeded; but by degrees the desolate parent raised himself on his couch and glanced with earnest longing toward the spot whence those soul-moving sounds proceeded. At length, when Mara sung the words, "Look and see if there be any sorrow like to my sorrow," she appeared inspired by the sympathy she felt; and the relatives of the count, who listened with beating hearts, could not restrain their tears. Nor did these alone bear witness to the singer's power: heavy sighs escaped from the sufferer; large tears stood in those eyes which the very extremity of grief itself had long forbidden to weep. Crossing the room with feeble steps, he prostrated himself before the image of that Heavenly One who "bore all our griefs;" and, when the full choir joined in the Hallelujah Chorus, his voice of praise and thanksgiving mingled with those strains. The recovery was complete and lasting, and was the marvel of all Germany.

A lady had been in deep despondency for many months. Her sins appeared so numerous and aggravated that she dared not trust in the promises of the gospel. These promises seemed very precious for others, but could not avail for her. Conversations with her minister and with Christian friends added to her gloom, instead of dissipating it. She attended with great eagerness the means of grace, read her Bible almost incessantly at home, and withdrew herself from all gay companions, and even from the most innocent social enjoyments. Her health began to suffer from extreme depression of spirits, and her friends were apprehensive of an early death.

When she heard that Jenny Lind was to visit the city near which she resided, her curiosity was excited to hear her. She consulted her minister; and he advised her to go on the evening when "The Messiah" was to be sung. The rendering of those sublime passages, "I know that my Redeemer liveth," and "Come unto me, all ye that labor and are heavy laden," by the Swedish songstress, quite overwhelmed her. She was spell-bound. The words seemed clothed with a fulness of meaning she had never before discovered. The fitness of Jesus to save sinners, and his infinite condescension and pity, melted her heart. She wondered that she had ever distrusted him, and with a childlike faith threw herself on the promises, knowing that in her case they would not fail of fulfilment. From that hour her gloom vanished, and she went forward in the path of Christian duty with a joyous and obedient heart.

We transcribe another fact from a letter of Dr. Beattie to Dr. Laing, in 1780:—"When Handel's 'Messiah' was first performed, the audience were exceedingly struck and affected by the music in general; but when the chorus struck up, 'For the Lord God omnipotent reigneth,' they were so transported that they all, together with the king, [George III.,] who happened to be present, started up, and remained standing till the chorus ended; and hence it became the fashion in England for the audience to stand up while that part of the music is performing. Some days after the first exhibition of the same divine oratorio, Mr. Handel came to pay his respects to Lord Kinnoul, with whom he was particularly acquainted. His lordship, as was natural, paid him some compliments on the noble entertainment which he had lately given the town. 'My lord,' said Handel, 'I should be sorry if I only entertained them: I wished to make them better.'"

It is a somewhat curious fact that on the first performance of "*The Messiah*" in London, in 1741, it excited a very small degree of attention, but soon afterward in Dublin it called forth every proof of the highest admiration. This fact led to a powerful and pathetic passage in "Pope's *Dunciad*."

This will not be considered an inappropriate place to add a few lines on the feelings and habits of this, one of the greatest of human composers. Being once inquired of as to his ideas and emotions when writing the "*Hallelujah Chorus*," he replied, in the best English he could command, "I did think I did see heaven all before me, and the great God himself." It is said that a friend called upon him when he was setting to music the pathetic words, "He was despised and rejected of men," and found him actually sobbing. And Shield tells us that when Handel's servant used to bring him in his chocolate in the morning he often stood in silent astonishment to see his master's tears mingling with his ink as he wrote his masterly works. Indeed, it appears to have been usually the case that during his compositions his face would be bathed in tears.

Another statement has been given, which may properly suggest the importance of cultivating right feelings alike in the composition and the performance of sacred music. Handel was once asked by a friend why his church-music was always so cheerful. His admirable reply was, "I cannot make it otherwise: I write according to the thoughts I feel. When I think on God, my heart is so full of joy that the notes dance and leap, as it were, from my pen; and, since God has given me a cheerful heart, it will be pardoned me that I serve him with a cheerful and devout spirit."

Handel's habit of composition was exceedingly rapid; but still the motion of his pen could not keep up with the rapidity of his conceptions. The mechanical power of his hand was not sufficient for the volcanic torrent of the brain. Novello, his learned publisher, who seems to have well studied the manuscripts at the Fitzwilliam Museum, in London, seeing a page on which the sand is still upon the ink at the top as well as at the bottom of the page, left in the book the remark, "Observe the speed with which Handel wrote. The whole of this page is spotted with sand, and, consequently, must have been all wet at the same time."

Another fact or two on this subject will be permitted. A pious old deacon, who died at Bradford, in New Hampshire, in 1825, some years before his decease attended a meeting of the Musical Society of that State. A very large company were assembled to rehearse the anthem "O Lord God of Israel" when he entered the hall. The sudden opening of the door and the burst of sound that met his ear nearly paralyzed his whole frame; his whole man trembled, his limbs refused to act, and he appeared almost intoxicated. A gentleman, who had witnessed the powerful effect of good singing upon him many years before, obtained him a seat; and, when the venerable saint collected power to speak, he broke silence with the remark, "If I cannot bear the combined voices of a hundred singers here on earth, am I prepared, and can I bear the sound of an innumerable multitude of voices in heaven, where I soon hope to be?"

One fact more, and we will close. The late Rev. Roger Harrison, who died in Connecticut, in 1853, at the age of eighty-four, once spent a night at the house of the Rev. Dr. Cooley, of Granville, and at family worship sang the Judgment Anthem with such thrilling effect that one of the doctor's students sprang from his chair, rushed at the singer, and was entirely bewildered for several hours.

Congregational Singing.—It would be almost an act of injustice were we to omit a reference to the general excellence of the African ear for singing, which is so commonly shown in many of the ordinary occurrences of life as to be a frequent subject of remark in every part of our country. Indeed, it has been stated, apparently on sufficient grounds, that much of our popular music can be traced to negro origin.

But most of all do we love to hear the hymn-singing

of the African race, and entirely sympathize with the Rev. Mr. Kirkland, who writes, "You know how sweetly a congregation of plantation-negroes can sing the songs of Zion. Tell me not of city choirs. I would rather hear 'I am passing away,' or 'Give me Jesus,' sung as we sometimes hear them, out of full hearts, by hundreds of these poor people, than their best performances. It is spirit-stirring: there are life and soul in it."

Lady Mary W. Montague, in a letter to Dr. Beattie, thus gives her opinion of the influence of plain congregational singing on a worshipping assembly:—"I think psalms written with great and noble simplicity, and sung in the same manner, friendly to devotion; and it is almost an offence to call in the aid of insensible and inanimate things to praise the Giver of life and reason. A psalm decently sung by the congregation always excites my devotion more than the organ. I would employ musical instruments in a pagan temple, but only the voice of man in a Christian church."

We can easily imagine the scene presented at the Music Hall in Surrey Gardens, London, at one of the assemblies of from eight to ten thousand people worshipping under the guidance of the popular Charles H. Spurgeon, as described by one of our countrymen:—

"The prayer concluded, Mr. Spurgeon announced the well-known Psalm beginning,—

'Before Jehovah's awful throne.'

He read it through, having first announced that the

tune would be the '*Old Hundredth*,' and then read each verse separately before it was sung. It is scarcely possible to give any idea of the sublime effect produced by those ten thousand voices as they swelled the massive harmonies of that grand tune with a fulness of sound rarely heard. After singing the second verse, Mr. Spurgeon said, 'I will read the third verse, and you will sing the fourth; and let the uplifting of your voices be as the sound of many waters.' His auditory responded to his wish. The words were,—

'We'll crowd thy gates with thankful songs,
High as the heavens our voices raise,
And earth, with her ten thousand tongues,
Shall fill thy courts with sounding praise.'

Most magnificent was the shout of praise that now went up. Not a voice was mute, save where occasionally some one's nerves were overpowered by the massive rolling chorus that rose on every side. Never did we before so realize what congregational singing might become. It was an uplifting of voice and heart such as one can hope to hear only a few times in the course of a life. Much of this grand effect was no doubt owing to the majesty of the tune itself,—much to the fact that all the congregation knew it,—and perhaps not a little to the practice of reading each verse before it was sung, a practice we have always thought a very reasonable one, and commonly adopted in England, especially among the poor and those who cannot read."

Though this is a striking instance of the grandeur of *con-*

gregational singing, it was by no means singular. Gould very properly asks, "Who has ever attended a meeting of several churches, or some religious anniversary, where there were a multitude of professors of religion, a great proportion of whom are always found able to join in singing, when they rise and sing a hymn at the celebration of the Lord's Supper, and has not felt the power of sacred music sung with both the spirit and understanding? How many who have been spectators only at the time have felt its power and been led to decide that it was something to them who were passing by, and from that time realized that unless they repented they never could join the angelic host, either on earth or in heaven!"

Even on occasions less solemn than these have vast effects been produced by singing. Was it not an impressive scene when, at the collegiate dinner-table at Andover, in 1858, upon an unexpected communication being made of the successful laying of the telegraphic cable, a thousand gentlemen spontaneously rose and, in the majestic sounds of "*Old Hundred*," sang the fine words of Bishop Ken?—

"Praise God, from whom all blessings flow!"

And, on a smaller scale, intense must have been the feeling among a number of converted sailors on board the *North Carolina* in the revival of 1858–59. They were speaking of the different countries in which they were born; and it was found that they represented ten different nations, the last man having said that he was born in Greenland. Unable to contain themselves longer, one commenced, and the others followed, in the hymn,—

"From Greenland's icy mountains,"

which was sung with delightful earnestness.

CHURCHES IN SCOTLAND.—We have met with some beautiful incidents of singing in the Scottish churches. They use a metrical version of "*The Psalms of David*," adopted in 1650, and "*The Paraphrases*," which are free renderings of various parts of Scripture, adopted in the present form in 1781. The tunes in use are nearly all the old and familiar ones sung by the Reformers and the persecuted Covenanters, and associated in the Scottish mind with so much that is tender and solemn in the past. "So averse," says Dr. Jameson, "are the people generally to innovations in these melodies, that when, early in the present century, a few tunes were introduced in which one and another of the lines in a stanza were sung twice over, numbers of the old people refused to join in the praise, left the place of worship."

The Scottish children are taught to commit to memory many of the psalms and paraphrases. Every one can sing the Twenty-Third Psalm. On a dark Sabbath afternoon, more than twenty years ago, the service in the Rev. Dr. Gordon's church, in Edinburgh, was drawing to a close at near four o'clock, and the gas had been lighted; but, by some accident, the light had become very feeble. The minister could not see to read the hymn with which he had intended to close and simply said, "Let us sing the Twenty-Third Psalm." The whole congregation, old and young, a thousand voices, united, amid the flickering lights, in that beautiful composition.

An Impressive Scene.—It will scarcely be believed in coming generations that many Christians in the United States, in the middle of the nineteenth century, transferred much of the public singing of the praises of God in their houses of worship to choirs, while the members of churches sat quietly in their pews, or, as a good old man in Boston expressed it, thanking God that they could hear singing, though public opinion prohibited their joining in it. Some few congregations in large cities went even beyond this, and, at an expense which exceeded the combined average salary of four pastors, employed *four* persons in their singing-gallery—generally performers at the opera-houses—to praise God for them. We attended, in 1855, the dedication of a house of worship in one of our largest cities, when one of these "*Quartets*" entered on their so-called duties. A programme had been published, and the first hymn was duly "performed in fine style;" but, most unfortunately, the excellent preacher required that the second hymn should be laid aside and that an old favorite of his should be substituted, beginning,—

"There is a fountain filled with blood."

The "*Quartet*" got through the first verse very gracefully; but, when the second was begun,—

"The dying thief rejoiced to see
That fountain in his day,"

a voice was heard here and there in the congregation "spoiling the music" by joining in the singing; and, when the third line commenced, all bounds were broken, and, in a voice "like many waters," the vast mass of people, rising from their seats, burst forth,—

"Oh, may I there, though vile as he,
Wash all my sins away!"

No language can describe the scene or the feelings which it inspired. Some *scientific* gentlemen spoke of it as the grandest thing they had ever witnessed.

A Real Amendment.—The scene was a small prayer-meeting of a rural village church. Very few were present; for it was a time of much coldness and great apparent decline. But a few Christian hearts even there had deep feeling. Their strong emotions and prayers were unconfessed to each other, but the object of their worship had observed them all. The prayer-meeting was going on as usual, though the pastor was absent and his place was occupied by one of the deacons. This worthy man was plain in his manners, a true son of the soil, with a bronzed countenance, hard hands, and wearing his working-dress. But with all the earnestness of his soul he had for months past been mourning in secret over the desolation of the church. The hymn he selected with which to commence the service was the one often sung by our fathers:—

"Hear, gracious Sovereign, from thy throne,
And send thy various blessings down."

Two or three verses were sung to an old tune, till the good deacon came to the last, which thus reads. The reader will observe especially the last two lines :—

"In answer to our fervent cries,
Give us to see thy church arise;
Or, if that blessing seem too great,
Give us to mourn its low estate."

While reading this verse, the good man paused: it evidently did not exactly accord with the feelings of his soul: it was not the expression of *his* prayer. He indulged a moment's thought,—swift and excellent: an alteration suggested itself,—his eye sparkled with joy,—and out it came :—

"In answer to our fervent cries,
Give us to see thy church arise:
That blessing, Lord, is not too great,
Though now we mourn its low estate."

Every heart was arrested, and sudden emotion so overpowered all in the little assembly that they could scarcely sing the words; but each in silence gave to the sentiment his own earnest amen. They happily proved it to be true. From that evening a revival began: the church arose from its slumber to new faith and works; and very soon the windows of heaven were opened and a plenitude of blessings was showered down, which continued for several years.

Miscellaneous Facts.—An aged clergyman in Massachusetts was, some years since, preaching from the text, "I speak as to wise men: judge ye what I say," (1 Cor. x. 15,) when, having advanced as far as "thirdly," he observed that many of his hearers, overcome by the heat of the day, had fallen asleep. Stopping in his discourse and wiping the perspiration from his forehead, he exclaimed, "My friends, as the day is oppressively hot, I will stop a while and request the choir to sing the tune '*Coronation*' to the words,—

"My drowsy powers, why sleep ye so?'"

The effect was electrical, bringing the audience to their feet. They sang the hymn: sleep was entirely driven away, and the preacher resumed his discourse at "thirdly."

A very trivial affair led to the dismission of a clergyman. At one of the meetings of the congregation the pastor read the hymn,—

"I love to steal a while away,"

and the chorister commenced singing, but, forgetting the tune, could proceed no further than "I love to steal," which he did several times,—when the clergyman, somewhat smilingly, relieved him from the dilemma by saying, "It is very much to be regretted," and adding, "Let us pray."

It is said that in 1785 the vestry of Christ Church, Philadelphia, gravely determined "that the clerks be required to sing such tunes only as are plain and familiar to the congregation, and that the singing of other tunes, and the frequent changing of tunes, are deemed disagreeable and inconvenient."

It may at least excite a harmless smile to be told that a good old lady, a member of Dr. John Gill's church in London, once waited on her venerable pastor to complain about "the new-fangled notions" which had got among the congregation about singing. The good doctor was anxious, if possible, to calm her agitated spirit,—which he found was no easy matter. At length he asked her what tunes she would wish to have sung, and the venerable lady replied, with avidity, "I want David's tunes sung, sir." "So do I," said the worthy pastor, "but most unfortunately they have been lost; but I will give you my promise that, as soon as they can be found again, we will sing David's tunes and no others." The good lady, it is said, went away considerably relieved by her pastor's promise.

A Private Circle.—Charles Butler, in his very interesting letter on ancient and modern music, introduces the following anecdote, relating to Mara, an Italian vocalist:—

"Once, in a private society, in consequence of something that fell in conversation, she sang, without any accompaniment, the simple air, in Marcello's Psalms, 'In my distress I called upon Jehovah, and he did hear me,' with such exquisite taste and pathos that she entranced every hearer. To our infinite gratification, she repeated it half a dozen times, and every time more beautifully and impressively than before. A person, observing that there was a violoncello in the room, requested that she would permit the late Mr. Paxton, who was present, to accompany her. This was done. It was fine,—very fine; but the charm was lost. This little circumstance," says Butler, "may be thought to strengthen Rousseau's hypothesis,—'that harmony is unnatural, and rather weakens than increases the effect of simple melody.' Mara was particularly distinguished by the manner in which she sung, 'I know that my Redeemer liveth.' It was beyond singing: it was eloquence. She opened it with great solemnity; hope was discernible,—but it was only the dawn of hope. As she proceeded, it brightened and expanded; but when she came to the last repetition of the sentence, the firm and animated confidence with which she uttered the words 'I know,' and the jubilation of soul with which she pronounced the words 'and in my flesh I shall see God,' no language can adequately tell. The audience thought not of the air, or of the band, or even of the singer: they only felt the sentiment; and they felt it in all its sublimity."

A VAST CROWD.—Few events in English history will ever be invested with a more touching interest than the fact that at the inauguration of a beautiful park and public hall secured for the use of the working-classes of Birmingham, in the year 1858, *forty-seven thousand Sunday-school children* sang a hymn in the presence of her majesty Queen Victoria. The account given by a public reporter may be read with more than common pleasure. We give a short extract:—"Each section had its musical conductor, armed with a long white wand by way of baton, and assisted by a drummer and two cornets,—the first to give the little singers the signal to begin, and the latter to play over the simple music of this wonderful child-concert. As her majesty passed, they sang, in a low, gentle manner,—almost seraphic,—a hymn, which moved the royal lady and thousands of others even to tears."

ANNIVERSARY AT ANDOVER.—Perhaps one of the most interesting and touching incidents connected with the history of singing occurred, at the separation from each other of thirty students, at the Andover Theological Seminary in 1832. A question was proposed by a single finely-toned voice from the orchestra, and a response was made from the stage on which the graduated class stood,—first by the *Foreign Missionaries,* then by the *Domestic Missionaries,* and finally by the *Home Preachers:* then followed the chorus from *the whole.* The reader will be gratified to have the whole hymn before him:—

Question.—"And I heard the voice of the Lord, saying, Whom shall I send, and who will go for us?"—Isa. vi. 8.

Foreign Missionaries.

From dear New England's happy shore,
Where all our kindred dwell,
We go,—on pagans light to pour:
Our native land, farewell!

Question.—"And I heard the voice of the Lord, saying, Whom shall I send, and who will go for us?"

Domestic Missionaries.

We go where seldom on the ear
Salvation's tidings swell:
We go to dry the mourner's tear:
Our pleasant home, farewell.

Question.—"And I heard the voice of the Lord, saying, Whom shall I send, and who will go for us?"

Home Preachers.

Where all our earthly friendships blend,
Of Jesus' love we'll tell,
And in the work our lives will spend:
Brethren, a short farewell.

Chorus.

From all these cherished scenes we go,—
The home of praise and prayer,—
To meet earth's gladness or earth's woe,
And many a toil to bear.

Farewell, ye friends who shared our joy,
Ye in whose hearts we dwell:
A noble work shall now employ
Our energies. Farewell!

Brethren, we press the parting hand:
  Our songs of parting tell:
Then, till we reach heaven's holy land,
  A sweet but brief farewell!

The whole presented an extraordinary scene.

The audience felt that it was not a mere show,—not an exhibition of musical skill. The tones in which the hymn was sung were those of deep emotion; and many hearts were melted as these young servants of Christ poured forth their impassioned farewell,—some of them to the scene of their sacred studies, others to the pleasant hills and valleys and churches of New England, and others to all the endearments of their native land.

THE MISSIONARY'S LANDING.—Deeply do we sympathize with an honored missionary who writes a narrative now before us of his first arrival, with fifteen other missionaries and their wives, on a foreign shore, where the best years of his life were devoted to labors for the conversion of the heathen; and most heartily do we pity the reader who can suppose that singing such a hymn under such circumstances produced no happy or lasting effect, or who can even read the fact without emotion. Our friend says,—

"To prepare for landing was all our care. Soon we were delighted to see some of the 'Mission Family,' as we found the whole of the Baptist missionary brotherhood were termed. But our first tidings were sad. One dear brother had just been laid in his grave. To some of us how appropriate a memento was this! In little more than half a year *two* of our affectionate party were also in *their* graves.

"We landed, singing Addison's hymn,—

'How are thy servants blest, O Lord,'

every word of which went to our hearts and seemed from thence to arise to God. With many tears that hymn was sung; and *well* did the last verse bring us to the shore:—

'Our life, whilst thou preserv'st that life,
Thy sacrifice shall be,
And death, when death shall be our lot,
Shall join our souls to thee.'

"With most hearty greetings were we welcomed to that shore. Every one present seemed to vie with every other in expressing gladness and gratitude and praise to our God. What eagerness was there to get one grasp of the hand and to speak or to hear but one word with the '*new massas*' and the '*new* ladies'!"

Such is the account given by the Rev. P. H. Cornford, an English Baptist missionary, of the landing of himself and a missionary party on the island of Jamaica in January, 1841.

From another source we learn that the missionaries and their friends did not monopolize the whole of the singing. Mr. Hinton tells us, "As soon as their voices had ceased, their African brethren and sisters struck up a response, singing a few verses of affectionate welcome which had been written for the occasion."

OFFICERS OF THE BRITISH NAVY.—That singing the high praises of God has sometimes a salutary influence on unconverted men was clearly proved during the War of 1812, in the case of the late eminently worthy Deacon Epa Norris, who lived and died in the Northern Neck,—the peninsula formed by the Chesapeake Bay and the Rappahannock and Potomac Rivers in Virginia. During the war between the United States and Great Britain, this excellent man was taken prisoner, hurried on board, and required to give information as to the strength and position of the American forces. He told his inquirers that he did not read the papers and had very little knowledge of national affairs, but that if he had the knowledge they desired he would suffer death before he would communicate it to them. By degrees the officers became convinced that he was an honest and unsophisticated man, and admired his patriotism and heroic firmness. The commandant of the ship gave a dinner to the officers of the fleet, and did Mr. Norris the honor to select him from the American prisoners of war to be a guest. The deacon, in his homespun attire, took his seat at the table with the aristocracy of the British navy. The company sat long at the feast: they drank toasts, told stories, laughed and sang songs. At length Mr. Norris was called on for a song. He desired to excuse himself, but in vain: he must sing. He possessed a fine, strong, musical voice, which had been improved by singing simple and plain tunes. In an appropriate and beautiful air, he commenced singing the Ninety-Second Psalm of Watts:—

"Sweet is the work, my God, my King,
To praise thy name, give thanks, and sing."

Thoughts of home and of his lost religious privileges, and of his captivity, imparted an unusual pathos and power to his singing. One stanza of the excellent psalm must have seemed peculiarly pertinent to the occasion:—

"Fools never raise their thoughts so high:
Like brutes they live, like brutes they die;
Like grass they flourish, till thy breath
Blast them in everlasting death."

When the singing ceased, a solemn silence ensued. At length the commandant broke it by saying, "Mr. Norris, you are a good man, and shall return immediately to your family." The commodore kept his word; for in a few days Mr. Norris was sent ashore in a barge, with a handsome present of salt,—then more valuable in the country than gold.

New York Merchants.—Not long since, a newsboy in New York was heard crying, "'*Bank-Note Reporter*,' sir? Three more banks down!" The little fellow had not known half a score years, but his eyes were bright, his tongue fluent, and his manners attractive. Stepping into a counting-house, with his bundle of papers under his arm, he saw two gentlemen sitting in front of a fire, engaged in trifling conversation, and proposed to one of them his inquiry, "Bank-Note Reporter, sir?"

"No," replied one of the gentlemen: "we don't want any. But stop! if you will sing us a song we will buy one of your Reporters."

The boy agreed to the terms, and the gentlemen, with an air which showed that they anticipated sport, placed the little fellow on a high stool and told him to proceed to sing. They evidently expected to hear some jovial song, —when, to their astonishment, he began the beautiful hymn,—

> "I think, when I read that sweet story of old,
> When Jesus was here among men,
> How he called little children the lambs of his fold,
> I should like to have been with them then."

The effect upon his listeners was at once perceptible, and before he had sung through the four verses they were both in tears. When he had finished, one of the gentlemen inquired, "Where did you learn that hymn?" "At Sabbath-school," replied the boy.

The reader will, of course, expect to hear that the gentlemen purchased the "*Reporter*," and will not be sorry to learn that, in addition to this, they presented him with a sum of money, and after they had obtained his name and residence they allowed him to go on his way. Is there nothing to move and improve the heart even in the singing of a child?

Miscellaneous.—Two of our modern poets have made an admirable use of the story of Damocles, as told by Cicero. Damocles was one of the flatterers of Dionysius, the monarch of Sicily, who died three hundred and sixty-eight years before the Christian era. He admired the wealth and grandeur of that sovereign and pronounced him the happiest man on earth. Dionysius, wishing to correct his views, prevailed on him to undertake for a time the charge and the duties of royalty. Damocles consented; and, having ascended the throne, he gazed with delight on the splendor and luxury by which he was surrounded. But he soon perceived a sword suspended by a horse-hair directly over his head. This spoiled all his enjoyment; and he speedily begged permission to relinquish so dangerous a position.

The Rev. Joseph Stennett, in his paraphrase of Proverbs xiv. 9, thus alludes to the fact:—

> "Who laughs at sin laughs at his Maker's frowns,
> Laughs at *the sword of vengeance o'er his head.*"

And Charles Wesley, in one of his hymns, says,—

> "Show me the naked sword
> Impending o'er my head."

The celebrated William Byrd, the author of "*Non nobis Domine,*" gave the following very forcible reasons for learning to sing, in a scarce work published in 1598, entitled "*Psalms, Sonnets, and Songs of Sadness and Pietie.*

"First, It is a knowledge easilie taught and quickly learned, when there is a good master and an apt scholar.

"Secondly, The exercise of singing is delightful to nature and good to preserve the health of man.

"Thirdly, It doth strengthen all parts of the heart, and doth open the pipes.

"Fourthly, It is a singular good remedie for a stuttering and stammering in the speech.

"Fifthly, It is the best means to preserve a perfect pronunciation and to make a good orator.

"Sixthly, It is the only way to know when Nature hath bestowed a good voice,—which gift is so rare that there is not one amongst a thousand that hath it; and in many that excellent gift is lost because they want an art to express nature.

"Seventhly, There is not any music of instruments whatsoever comparable to that which is made of men's voices when the voices are good and the same well sorted and ordered.

"Eighthly, The better the voice is, the meeter it is to honor and serve God therewith; and the voice of man is chiefly to be employed to that end."

FIRST LINES OF HYMNS REFERRED TO IN THIS VOLUME.

INDEX.

THE END.

STEREOTYPED BY L. JOHNSON & CO.
PHILADELPHIA.

www.ingramcontent.com/pod-product-compliance
Lightning Source LLC
LaVergne TN
LVHW020059110826
845151LV00001B/23